D1590180

GLOVE AFFAIR

GLOVE AFFAIR

My Lifelong Journey in the World of Professional Boxing

Randy Gordon

ROWMAN & LITTLEFIELD
Lanham • Boulder • New York • London

Published by Rowman & Littlefield
An imprint of The Rowman & Littlefield Publishing Group, Inc.
4501 Forbes Boulevard, Suite 200, Lanham, Maryland 20706
www.rowman.com

6 Tinworth Street, London SE11 5AL

British Library Cataloguing in Publication Information Available

Library of Congress Cataloging-in-Publication Data

Names: Gordon, Randy, author.
Title: Glove affair : my lifelong journey in the world of professional boxing /
  Randy Gordon.
Description: Lanham, Maryland : Rowman & Littlefield, 2019. | Includes index. |
  Description based on print version record and CIP data provided by
  publisher; resource not viewed.
Identifiers: LCCN 2018039638 (print) | LCCN 2018054680 (ebook) | ISBN
  9781538121139 (Electronic) | ISBN 9781538121122 (cloth : alk. paper)
Subjects: LCSH: Gordon, Randy. | Boxing—United States—History—20th
  century. | Boxers (Sports)—United States—Biography. |
  Sportscasters—United States—Biography.
Classification: LCC GV1132.G595 (ebook) | LCC GV1132.G595 A3 2019 (print) |
  DDC 796.83092 [B] —dc23
LC record available at https://lccn.loc.gov/2018039638

∞™ The paper used in this publication meets the minimum requirements of
American National Standard for Information Sciences—Permanence of Paper
for Printed Library Materials, ANSI/NISO Z39.48-1992.

Printed in the United States of America

CONTENTS

CONTENTS

FOREWORD

Tracy Morgan

It was the early seventies. As a kid growing up in the Bronx, New York (is there any other Bronx?), I started following the New York Yankees. For me, life was all about Willie Randolph, Thurman Munson, Reggie Jackson, Mickey Rivers, and Sparky Lyle. There was also boxing. Muhammad Ali had just done the impossible and whupped up on George Foreman to regain the heavyweight championship of the world.

Every kid in America—well, at least every one of my friends—wanted to be like Ali. We couldn't get enough of him. A bunch of us even rode on a subway just a few stops to Yankee Stadium on September 28, 1976, hoping to be able to sneak into Yankee Stadium to see the great Ali. That night, "The Greatest" was facing big, muscular Ken Norton for the third time. Norton had won the first fight, breaking Ali's jaw in the process. Ali won a decision in the rematch just six months later.

As luck would have it, the New York City police were on strike that night, and only a few higher-ranking men in blue uniforms could be seen. We successfully made it into Yankee Stadium, running past security who were too old or slow—or both—to do anything about it. It didn't matter that I watched Ali–Norton from a seat closer to the stadium's lights than a ringside seat. What mattered is that I was in the same stadium as Muhammad Ali.

If I wasn't a fight fan before, I was now. My love for boxing grew. I followed everybody: Larry Holmes, Marvelous Marvin Hagler, Aaron Pryor, Sugar Ray Leonard, Hector Camacho, Roberto Duran, Thomas Hearns, Mike Tyson. At the same time, I watched my boxing on television. And there was plenty to watch. All the networks had boxing. So did cable TV, which was growing rapidly. HBO, ESPN, the USA Network, the MSG Network.

Being a fight fan in the 1980s couldn't have been better! During those years, two of my favorite boxing announcers were ABC's Howard Cosell and NBC's Marv Albert. Gil Clancy of CBS was another favorite of mine. But on cable, my favorite was this pesky, energetic little guy who asked questions of fighters who would have probably slapped the toupee off the heads of anybody else. His name was Randy Gordon. He was so energetic he could make a double espresso look like a cup of water. He was so in your face you just expected him to get stomped on with his line of questioning.

"You keep getting fatter every fight!" I remember him saying to heavyweight James Broad, who looked at him incredulously and replied, "I promise to be lighter in my next fight."

I remember him saying to Aaron Pryor, after calling Pryor's only loss, "You've got to get a grasp on your life, Aaron. You've got to clean up your act."

At first, I thought Pryor was going to smack Randy. He didn't. He almost cried. Then he promised he would straighten out. From that moment, he actually did.

When I was 20 and turning much of my energy toward making people laugh, Randy was named boxing commissioner in New York. My favorite boxing announcer left the microphone to become a state regulator. He did the job with the same kind of passion he put into his announcing.

When he was through being commissioner, he picked up the microphone again. I met Randy a few days after meeting his longtime radio partner, former heavyweight contender Gentleman Gerry Cooney, in 2016. Cooney and I connected while sitting courtside at a Knicks game at Madison Square Garden. I felt Cooney's passion and warmth for people, and we connected immediately. Cooney told me about the radio shows he cohosts with Randy Gordon on SiriusXM and invited me to be an in-studio guest.

A few days later, I went to SiriusXM. There they were, tall Gerry and short Randy. Forget Arnold Schwarzenegger and Danny DeVito. Randy and Gerry are boxing's real-life twins. Gerry is about 6-foot-6, maybe a little taller. Randy is about 5-foot-6, probably a little shorter. But they are as real as real can get. In them, I find a deep passion for what they do. I'm that same way. I love making people laugh. So do they. They also love informing . . . and teaching . . . and telling stories. They have no trouble making fun of listeners who call their show with ludicrous statements. But they also poke fun at each other and even with themselves.

On that first day I joined them in studio, Randy said to me, "In *Rocky*, [trainer] Mickey said to Rocky, 'Women weaken legs.' Do you believe that's true, Tracy?" I just looked at Randy and said, "How the fuck is a big, strong, well-conditioned fighter, who runs mountains and spars and trains hard every day, gonna get weak legs from a little pussy?"

Gerry laughed. Randy more than laughed. He screamed with laughter. He was actually unable to say anything for at least a minute. He was laughing so hard that tears were pouring from his eyes. Now, that's laughing!

Soon after, I had Randy, his wife Roni, Gerry, and his wife Jennifer join me and my family in my box at Giants Stadium. As we sat back and watched the Giants win, we talked, joked, and told stories about everything. They asked me about my accident in 2014, and I gave them details—as much as I could remember.

It's been the love of my family and friends that got me through the ordeal. It's their love that brought me back and told the Good Man upstairs that it just wasn't my time to leave. That day, I told them my story, and Randy and Gerry told me theirs. Each is unique . . . amazing . . . riveting. Gerry's is detailed in these pages in the chapter titled "Gentleman Gerry." So is Randy's. Included is a horrific accident that almost took Randy's life when he was 10. Like me, that accident shaped his future and paved the road for his life in boxing.

I live for my beautiful family and my wonderful friends. I also love to make people laugh. Randy is so much the same kind of guy. He lives for his family and friends, and he loves talking to sports fans, especially ones who have a passion for the "Sweet Science."

Randy holds back nothing. He didn't as editor of *Ring Magazine*, he didn't as the commissioner of commissioners, he doesn't as a talk show host on Sirius-XM Radio, and he certainly holds nothing back in the pages you are about to read.

Who knows what the future would have held for Randy Gordon had he not been so severely injured when he was 10. Yet, because of those injuries, he was introduced to boxing. Because of that introduction, both the sport, and we, as fans, have been blessed by his presence. Because of that childhood introduction to boxing, it put Randy on the road to becoming one of the sport's great historians and storytellers. And that road led to us becoming friends.

Here now is my friend's *Glove Affair*.

ACKNOWLEDGMENTS

I started this book years ago, as one incredible boxing story after another fell into my lap. With the support and encouragement of my family, friends, and colleagues, *Glove Affair* has become a reality. So, to Shari, Andrew, Traci, Mel, Ali, Dave, Mikey, Michele, Greer, and Jon, thank you for all you did to encourage me, and to Jamie, Jack, Justin, Ryan, Emma, Spencer, Noah, Dylan, Remi, Sophie, Penelope, and Jessie for inspiring me. To Roni, you believed in me, you listened to me, you encouraged me, you helped me, you pushed me, you lifted me, and you said, "Yes, you can!" when I said "No, I can't!" But most of all, you never stopped loving me. Because of you, *Glove Affair* is here.

To my friends and colleagues, I can fill pages with your names and what you have meant in the writing of this work. You know who you are. I can never thank you enough.

To my mentors, Bert Randolph Sugar, Don Dunphy, Gil Clancy, Marty Glickman, and Bob Wolff, a big thanks for working with me and teaching me.

To Bob Gutkowski and Jim Zrake, thanks for having faith in me and always having my back.

To my agent, Doug Anton, thank you for everything, especially for finding literary agent Margaret O'Connor for me. Margaret, you are truly amazing. I can't thank you enough. Get ready for more books—including a sequel!

To my editor at Rowman & Littlefield, Christen Karniski: You played such a huge part in helping my lifetime dream become reality. Thanks for the edits and, most of all, your professionalism.

To Tracy Morgan, thanks for coming into my life and showing the love that exudes from you.

ACKNOWLEDGMENTS

To Scott Greenstein and Steve Cohen, thanks for giving "Gentleman Gerry" and I SiriusXM's *At the Fights* and being in our corner. And thanks to producer Josh Friedman, who is my control tower and talks me through every takeoff and landing. To our channel's executive producer, Marissa Rives, you've been there since our first "on the air" light went on in 2009. Thanks for helping Gerry Cooney and I grow as show hosts.

And to Irish Wayne Kelly, your fighting spirit drove me to finish this work. Yeh, "It's about time."

And then there's the following: Marc Abrams, Don Ackerman, Gene Aguilera, Dr. Yigal Aharon, Al Albert, Kenny Albert, Marv Albert, Steve Albert, Dr. David Anderson, Steve Anderson, Vito Antuofermo, Bill Apter, Michael Ares, Alexis Arguello Jr., Eric Armit, Teddy Atlas, Billy Backus, Joyce Baldinger, Scott Ballan, Iran Barkley, Larry Barnes, Josie Basilio, Steven Bass, Kenny Bayless, Bruce Beck, Bob Beegel, David Beilinson, Mark Beiro, Rick Belyea, Gerry Benjamin and "The Gang" from Henry Schein, Michael Bentt, Dr. Ed Berliner, Len Berman, Al Bernstein, Barak Bess, John Beyrooty, Frank Bilovsky, Dr. John Boccio, Dave Bontempo, Frans Botha, Riddick Bowe, Charlie and Wendy Braunstein, Mark Breland, Christie Brinkley, Ellen Bromsen, Rich and Jodie Brook, Ed Brophy, Dr. Bennett Brown, Marcus Browne, Joe Bruno, Michael Buffer, Johnny Bumphus, Rod Burns, Bob and Tara (Hupp) Calissendorff, Sway Calloway, Billy Calogero, Bernie Campbell, Brian Campbell, Bob Canobbio, Mike Carbone, Marcello and Elena Carnevali, Tom Casino, Bobby Cassidy, Jim Cassidy, Jermall and Jermell Charlo, Kathy Clancy, Ed Claudio, R. J. Clifford, Tom Clohessy, Steve Cofield, Dean Coleman, Peter and Gail Contini, Gerry Cooney, Chet Coppack, Mike Coppinger, Joe Cortez, Jim and Suzie Crawley, Bobby Czyz, Kerry Daigle, Matt Damrow, Tony Danza, Howard Davis, Jay Deas, Joe DeGuardia, Oscar De La Hoya, Matt Deutshch, Phil and Heidi Devine, David Diamanté, Lou DiBella, Pete DiDonato, Dr. Randy DiLorenzo, Joe DiMaggio, Isaac Dogboe, Eric Drath, Gary Dubin, John Duddy, Bob Duffy, Bob Dunphy, Tom and Fran Dunton, Kerry Duperval, Roberto Duran, Dino Duva, Kathy Duva, Ashenefe Edmund, Emma Elizondo, Lee Elman, Rick Encinosa, Stephen Espinoza, Benji Esteves, Marlene and Michael Falken, Steve Farhood, Matt Farrago, Dr. David Fastenberg, Darrell Felder, Glenn Feldman, Dr. Alan and Sandi Ferber, Bernard Fernandez, Monique Ferrer, Shelly and Beth Finkel, Charlie Fitch, Bill Fitts, Lyle Fitzsimmons, George Foreman, Andy Foster, Mike Francesca, Peter Frutkoff, Frankie G., Joe Gadigian, John Gallagher, Liz Gary, Frank Garza, Baker Geist, Anthony George, Thomas Gerbasi, Joan and Roy Gilbert, Gary Gittelsohn, Dr. Vincent Giovinazzo, Rick Glaser, Dr. Stu Goldfarb, Herb Goldman, Bobby Goodman,

ACKNOWLEDGMENTS

Helene Gordon, Jerry and Marcia Gordon, Alan Gotay, John Gotti Jr., Johnny Boy Gotti, Ross Greenburg, David Greisman, Lee Groves, Brad Gruber, Matt Gunn, Marvelous Marvin Hagler, Dr. Gary Hanfling, Gordon Hall, Chris Hammill, Matt Happaney, Heather Hardy, Will Hart, Henry Hascup, Tom Hauser, Jeff Hawkins, Larry Hazzard, Joe and Jean-Marie Beckmann Heaney, Karl Hegman, Joie Vitali-Hein, Ruth and Peter Heller, George Henningsen, Rich Hering, Jack and Audrey Hirsch, Steve Hirsch, Logan Hobson, Stan and Lu Hoffman, Larry Holmes, Evander Holyfield, Bernard Hopkins, Dr. Neal Houslanger, Carlos Hranicka, Cathy Hunt, Karen Hunter, Jarrett Hurd, IB-HOF, *Imus in the Morning*, Seth and Paula Ingram, Kevin Iole, Jerry Izenberg, Dr. Larry Jack, Brad Jacobs, Roland Jankelson, Charles Jay, Brad Johnson, Sandy Johnson, Junior Jones, Roy Jones, Dr. Barry Jordan, Mark Joseph, Anthony Joshua, Jeff Jowett, Jan and Helene Kahn, George Kalinsky, Jackie Kallen, Myron Kamil, Andy and Demetria Karakostas, Peter Karakostas, Sue Karol, Anthony Karperis, Michael Katz, Ron Katz, Marshall Kauffman, Max Kellerman, Jackie Kelly, Ryan Kelly, Steve Kim, Andy King, Don King, Dr. Osric King, Doris Kinigstein, Terry and Karen Kinigstein, Dr. Stu Kirschenbaum, Ira Klein, Tokyo Joe Koizumi, Mark Kriegel, Laurie Kriegsman, Dave LaGreca, Jim Lampley, Paul and Deb Langley, Don Langlieb, Juan LaPorte, Gabrielle LaSpisa, Dr. Bill and Melvina Lathan, Dan Lattanzio, Michele Lavina-Kelnhofer, Harold Lederman, Bob Leigh, Jimmy Lennon Jr., Sugar Ray Leonard, Bob Ley, Fred Liberatore, Sam Liebman, Brett Lipton, Ron Lipton, Rocky Lockridge, Tom Loeffler, Scott Lopeck, Frank LoTierzo, Joe Lozito, Steve Lulkoski, Darcy Maccarone, Paul Malignaggi, Ray Mancini, Louie Mango, Teddy Mann, Sal Marchiano, Mike Marley, Bert and Fabiola Marmorato, Diana Mason, Wallace Matthews, Rich Mauro, Holt McCallany, Jessica McCleary, Tresha McCormack, Seamus McDonagh, Bernard McGuirk, Ryan McKinnell, Vince McMahon, Ron McNair, Sterling McPherson, Dr. Charles Melone, Denise Menz, Arthur Mercante Jr., Alex Metz, Jordan Meyer, Matt Meyer, Barry Michael, Philip Michael, Larry Michaels, Jarrell Miller, Chuck Minker, Shelton Minor, Tim Moley, Dr. Larry and Ronni Mollick, Carl Moretti, Eddie Mustafa Muhammad, George Munch, Dr. Abbey Muneer, Jay Nady, Dr. Jim Nave, Steve Nelson, New Jersey Boxing Hall of Fame, Rock Newman, Marc Nuccitelli, Robert Orlando, Mike Ortega, Bob Ottone, Ira Packer, Rob and Lauryl Palatnick, Skyler Palatnick, Derek Panza, Steve and Colleen Patchin, Robbi Paterson, Drs. John and Liz Pellerito, J. Russell Peltz, Art Pelullo, Joe Pelullo, Jim Pepe, Thurman Perry, Steve Petramale, Joe Pezullo, Michelle Joy Phelps, Elvis Grant Phillips, Warren Pick, Alex Pierpaoli, Adam Piervincenzi, Steve Pinto, Samson Plotkin, Dr. Robert Polofsky, Brittney Pressley, Regis Prograis,

Lance Pugmire, Dr. Stan Rabinowitz, Dan Rafael, Tommy Rainone, Alex Ramos, Mauro Ranallo, Dennis Rappaport, Felix Rappaport, Mark Ratner, Jack Reiss, Akin Reyes, Kerry Rhodes, Ray Richards, Jacquie Richardson, Scott Rider, Ring 8, Ring 10, Freddie Roach, Dr. Liz Robb, John Robnett, Rochester Hall of Fame, Jenny Rodriguez, Rich Roessler, Gary Rosado, Don Rosen, Sam Rosen, Sid Rosenberg, Arnie "Tokyo" Rosenthal, Leo Roth, Andy Ruiz, Chris "Mad Dog" Russo, Mike Russo, Dr. Rufus Sadler, Sandy Samek, Joe Santarpia, Dan Sapen, Joe Santarpia, Dan Sapen, Richard Schaefer, Brett Schare, Danny Schiavone, Brian Schmitz, Dr. Paul Schneiderman, Steve Schrober, Richard Schwartz, Allan Scotto, John Scully, Ed Scuncio, Lord Sear, Bruce Seldon, Art Shamsky, Bruce and Dana Shapiro, Ben Sharav, Gary Shaw, Tom and Stefanie Sic, Stan and Ilene Siever, John Signorile, Jay and Veronica Silver, Bruce Silverglade, Dave Sims, Greg Sirb, Daniel Sisneros, Tony Sitoy, David Skurnik, Harmon and Lori Skurnik, Bonecrusher Smith, Craig and Donna Smith, Derek Smith, James "Smitty" Smith, Dr. Neil Smith, Renaldo "Mr." Snipes, Greg Sobol, Steve Solomon, Bob and Fran Soltz, Steve Somers, Ryan Songalia, Dave and Larry Sontag, Joel Spielfogel, Joe Spinelli, Eric Spitz, Doc Stanley, Jack Stanton, Richard Steele, Ron Scott Stevens, Frank Stallone, Alex Stone, Jamie Stuart, Suburban Eats, Mauricio Sulaiman, Dr. Robert Sunshine, Steve Taub, Katie Taylor, Luke Thomas, Pinklon Thomas, Barry Tompkins, Bruce Trampler, Al Trautwig, Bob Trieger, Gary and Angela Trovato, President Donald Trump*, Eddie Trunk, Ruby Tyrell, Mike Tyson, Kevin Van Meter, Mercedes Vasquez-Simmons, Frank and Viviana Vigliarolo, Marcos Villegas, Shelly Vincent, Brandon Wald, Farley Wald, Steve Waldman, George Ward, Donald Wardlow, Herb Washington, Tony Weeks, Steve Weisfeld, Dr. Geoff Weisman, Mike Weisman, Harold Weston Jr., Tom Whipple, Pernell Whitaker, Deontay Wilder, Dan Wilk, Chuck Williams, Tim Witherspoon, Warner Wolf, Michael Woods, Dan Wulkan, Matt Yano, Brett Yormark, Ray Young, and Jim Zrake.

For those of you not on this list, know I appreciate all of you, and thank you for being part of my "Glove Affair."

Yes, I interviewed our 45th president in the 1980s, when he was a casino owner and a boxing promoter!

1

THE ROCK
AND MR. BOXING

It was around 6:00 a.m. on Monday, September 1, 1969. I was headed into my third year in college and my second year of competitive amateur boxing. I had gotten up early that first morning of September to head out for a fast-paced three-mile run, then head down to the local pool for a few dozen laps and some pool aerobics. Before I left the house on Long Island, I went outside and picked up the morning's papers, which were delivered to my home and left on the front steps. It was a morning ritual for me, always an early riser, to go outside, to retrieve *Newsday* and the *New York Daily News*, then tiptoe into my parent's bedroom and leave the papers on my father's side of the bed. As I picked up the papers, I looked at the headlines on both of the papers. I couldn't believe my eyes.

"ROCKY MARCIANO DEAD AT 45" was the headline on the *Daily News*. The subheadline underneath read, "Former Heavyweight Champ Dies in Plane Crash."

I was stunned. I quickly took *Newsday* out of its protective plastic bag.

Newsday's headline was, "MARCIANO KILLED IN PLANE CRASH."

I was breathing harder than if I had just finished my three-mile run. I needed to share this horrible information with someone.

Dad!

Why not? It was only natural. My dad, Carl, was the one who had introduced me to boxing 10 years earlier. I needed to wake him. I *had* to wake him.

I quietly opened the door to my mom and dad's room, then entered. I walked around to my sleeping dad's side of the bed. I took another look at the *Newsday* headline, just to make sure I read it correctly. I did. I wished it wasn't true.

1

"Dad!" I whispered. He didn't budge. My second "Dad!" got him to open his eyes.

He looked at me and lifted his head off the pillow. He looked at the clock. It was just a few minutes past 6:00.

"What is it, Randy?" he questioned softly. "Is everything okay?"

"Dad, look at the headlines," I said. I showed him *Newsday*. Then I held up the *Daily News*.

"Good Lord!" he exclaimed. He said it a few more times. Rocky Marciano was one of my dad's favorite fighters.

Then he turned to my mom, Roberta.

"Honey, wake up!" he said, tapping her lightly on the shoulder. "Wake up!" She half-opened her eyes.

"Ughhh, what is it?" she mumbled, still half asleep. "What's going on?"

My dad took the papers from my hands and held them over my mom's face. "Look!" he said.

She opened her eyes to read. In a flash, the sleep left her. Her mouth fell open.

"Oh my . . ." She clamped her hands over her mouth before she could get another word out.

"Rocky is dead?" my father said, half asking and half in disbelief. "How could that be? He was still a young man. How'd he die?"

"He died in a plane crash, Dad," I said. The news hit home even harder. Dad worked for TWA. Among his positions was that of a test pilot.

He sprang up in bed and began reading one of the papers.

My mom rubbed the sleep from her eyes. I handed her the other paper.

"Rocky was in a Cessna 172 when it crashed into a cornfield in Newton, Iowa," said my dad. "It appears there was very bad weather."

He took a deep breath. You could see he was moved.

"Rocky was one of the greats," said my dad. "Next to Joe Louis, he may have been the greatest heavyweight of all time. And, guess what . . . today would have been Rocky's 46th birthday."

In 1969, there was no YouTube and no internet. My 10-year journey into boxing consisted of hearing stories from my dad and reading *Ring Magazine* and the local papers. I truly considered *Ring Magazine* to be, as founder Nat Fleischer called his publication, the "Bible of Boxing." In being the bible, I also looked at Fleischer to be the creator of all things boxing. His word was gospel. His word was pugilistic law.

The news of Marciano's death was nothing less than shocking. How could "The Rock" be gone? I couldn't believe it. I wanted to know more about Marciano. How great was he? Where did he fit in among the great heavyweights of the past? I decided I had to speak with Nat Fleischer himself. I decided to call him later that morning. Then, I decided I wouldn't give a secretary a chance to make up an excuse he was busy. I decided to go to his office and sit there for as long as I had to in order to meet him and talk with him.

The Ring offices were located in an old seven-story building at 120 W. 31st Street in New York City, just down the street from the current Madison Square Garden. They had been in the old Madison Square Garden on 49th Street for years, relocating after that MSG faced the wrecking ball and the current MSG was opened in 1968.

I was on a 7:30 Long Island Railroad into the city and got to the building shortly before 9:00 a.m. I checked the directory on the wall and quickly found what I was looking for: Ring Publishing Corp., 5th Fl.

I excitedly stepped into the small elevator behind me and pressed the button with the number five on it. Little did I know, but that elevator would take me up and down from *Ring*'s fifth floor offices thousands of times, beginning in another 10 years.

When the door opened, several odors were immediately evident. Cigars. Perfume. Cologne. Mold. Mildew.

"May I help you?" asked a woman in an office with a sliding window immediately on my right.

"Yes, I'm hoping to see Mr. Fleischer," I told her.

"Do you have an appointment with Mr. Fleischer?" the lady asked.

"No, I don't," I said. "But I have been reading *The Ring* since I was a child and . . ."

She cut me off.

"I'm sorry, young man, but if you don't have an appointment with Mr. Fleischer, there is no way you can see him. He is very busy."

I tried explaining my desire to speak with the founder of *The Ring*, but the lady kept telling me she was sorry, but without an appointment, I would not be able to see Nat Fleischer. Finally, in a stern voice she said, "Young man, I appreciate your enthusiasm, but Mr. Fleischer is very busy. There will be a TV crew coming in soon to interview him. I'm sure you heard that Rocky Marciano has died in a plane crash. Mr. Fleischer will be doing interviews all morning."

I sighed and nodded. Then I turned and went to press the button for the elevator. At that moment, the door to Nat Fleischer's office opened. Out walked the balding, short, roundish founder of *The Ring*, the man who began rating fighters, the man whose opinion in the sport was heard and worshipped the way Moses heard and worshipped his Lord in front of the burning bush more than 2,000 years ago.

My heart almost jumped out of my chest as I saw Fleischer, the man known throughout the fight game as "Mr. Boxing."

"Mr. Fleischer," I said, moving toward him. "Boxing lost such a great fighter last night. I am an avid reader of *The Ring*. I live on Long Island and just had to come in to meet you and talk to you. I know you're very busy, but if you can give me just five minutes, I would be honored."

He stared at me for a few moments. Those few moments seemed like an eternity. Then, he spoke.

"I'm sorry, I didn't catch your name, son," he said.

"It's Randy, sir. Randy Gordon," I replied nervously.

"Mr. Gordon, I would love to speak with you," he said. Turning to the receptionist, he said, "Milly, will you please show Mr. Gordon into my office? I must talk with Nat for a few moments."

Nat? I thought. *Nat must talk with Nat?* It's got to be Nat Loubet, the managing editor. He was Fleischer's son-in-law and the heir apparent to Fleischer's throne.

"Would that be Nat Loubet you're meeting with?" I asked, quickly realizing I was out of place for doing so. I quickly shook my head in the realization of the fact that I should not have asked the question.

"Yes it is," laughed the most respected boxing journalist in the world. Then he gave me a playful smack on the top of my head.

"Milly, take this young man into my office and give him a few copies of his favorite reading material."

We walked into a neat office with framed issues of *The Ring* hanging on the walls, along with photos of Nat Fleischer giving and receiving awards. There he was with Jack Dempsey, Henry Armstrong, Gene Tunney, Joe Louis, Willie Pep, Sugar Ray Robinson.

This was the office where, a little more than 10 years later, I would sit—at that very same desk—as editor in chief of the magazine Fleischer gave life to in 1922, and Bert Sugar and I would bring back from the dead in 1979.

I walked around the room. I looked at the photos. My love for the sport intensified with every minute I stayed there. Then, as I was looking at a photo of Nat Fleischer presenting an award to Rocky Marciano, the door leading from Loubet's office to the boxing equivalent of the Oval Office at the White House opened. In walked Fleischer. He saw me looking at the photo of him and Marciano.

"I was presenting Rocky with the 'Fighter of the Year' award at the Downtown Athletic Club," said Fleischer. He then motioned to the couch in his office.

"Sit, Mr. Gordon," he said. "Stay and talk about Rocky Marciano."

"Thank you, Mr. Fleischer," I said, adding, "Please call me Randy. Mr. Gordon is my father."

Then, showing a sense of humor, he said, "Then you can call me Nat. Mr. Fleischer is *my* father!"

I walked over and sat on the couch. He walked over and sat down a few feet away. Then he turned and asked, "So, do you think Marciano was the greatest heavyweight champion ever?"

He watched as I looked up, obviously in deep thought. He answered for me.

"Marciano was good, real good," said Fleischer. "He may have been the toughest heavyweight champion ever . . . the most determined . . . relentless . . . a banger . . . he could take a guy out with either hand."

Then he paused and took a deep breath.

"But he wasn't the best ever," said Fleischer. "Far from it."

As an avid reader of *The Ring* and Fleischer's editorials, I knew who his choice was for the best heavyweight of all time.

"I know who your choice is for the best, Nat," I said. "It's Jack Johnson."

He nodded.

"That's right, Randy," he said. "Johnson was one of a kind. He was big. He was fast. He could punch with both hands. He had a terrific defense. There has never been anybody like him. There probably never will be."

He then took a pad from the table in front of the couch and removed a gold pen from his shirt pocket and began to write.

"Here are the top 10 heavyweights of all time," Fleischer said to me.

It took him about one minute to write out his list, which he then handed to me. Here were his picks for the top 10 heavyweights of all time:

1. Jack Johnson
2. James J. Jeffries
3. Bob Fitzsimmons
4. Jack Dempsey
5. James J. Corbett
6. Joe Louis
7. Sam Langford
8. Gene Tunney

9. Max Schmeling
10. Rocky Marciano

I looked it over. I was surprised to see Marciano at number 10. I asked Fleischer why he had Marciano rated so low.

"It's not that he's low," explained Fleischer. "It's just that the ones above him were so great."

Just then, the TV crew arrived.

I stood up and said, "Thank you, Nat. I don't want to be in the way, so I'll just . . ."

"Ah, ah, ah, stay right where you are, Randy," said Fleischer, holding up his hands. "Stay! These nice people are from ABC News. They are going to interview me about the death of Rocky Marciano."

"Thank you, Nat," I replied. "If you don't mind, I'll stay quietly out of the way and listen."

Fleischer then winked at me and pointed back at the couch. I sat down and watched.

Only a few hours earlier, I had been stunned by the news of the death of Rocky Marciano. Now, here I was, in the personal office of the most famous boxing journalist in the world, the founder, owner, publisher, and editor in chief of *Ring Magazine*, Nat Fleischer.

As I sat and watched, about eight members of the ABC crew set up their lights, ran electric wiring around Fleischer's office floor and duct-taped it down, checked their cameras and microphones, and connected a small microphone to Fleischer's shirt. They then ran the wiring down the back of his shirt and out to a small box connected to the back of his pants. One of the technicians powdered Fleischer's nose and held a piece of white typing paper next to his face as they did a white balance, making sure there wasn't too much light on the subject, causing an on-screen glare. The interview was under way within a half hour of the crew showing up.

"What was your reaction when you heard that Rocky Marciano had been killed?" Fleischer was asked.

"Like everybody else, I was stunned," he said. "I still am."

"Describe Rocky Marciano the fighter, Mr. Fleischer," was the next question.

"He lived up to his nickname. He was a rock. A boulder. He was relentless. And tireless. His defense wasn't the best, but he didn't mind trading punches. With Rocky, it took only one shot. Just one!"

As Fleischer was interviewed, I stared at his list of top all-time heavyweights:

10. Rocky Marciano

It virtually jumped off the page at me.

I had long thought Marciano should have been in the top three, but that was from hearing my dad heap praise on him whenever we talked about the heavyweight champs. Having been an avid reader of *The Ring*, I knew where Nat Fleischer rated him.

After the interview, and after the camera crew had left, I said, "Thank you, Nat, for taking the time to meet me and letting me stay to watch your interview. Before I leave, can I ask you three things?"

"Sure, Randy, ask away," said Mr. Boxing.

"My first question is, 'Are the guys on your top-10 list who are above Marciano so much better? Shouldn't he be rated higher? He knocked out Louis, who you have at number six.'"

He looked at me and said, "Marciano is one of my all-time favorites. He had the biggest heart ever. Sure, he beat Louis, but Joe was a shell of himself then and still gave Marciano a rough time. Other guys he beat, like Jersey Joe Walcott and Archie Moore, were also past their prime."

I nodded my head.

"Muhammad Ali is in exile," I said. "If he didn't run into draft problems and was still fighting, do you think he would have become an all-time great?"

"Cassius Clay [Fleischer always referred to Ali—even rated him—as Cassius Clay] was a big, strong, lightning-quick heavyweight. But speed and agility is all he had. Anybody in my top 10 would have had an easy night with him."

I remained expressionless, not wanting to tell Nat Fleischer not only that I disagreed, but that he was completely wrong. Maybe another time I'd tell him, but not now.

"My last question, Nat, is 'How do I get a job as a boxing writer?' I want to be in the business. Where do I start?"

He placed a hand on my shoulder.

"Well, it helps to know somebody," he said, looking directly into my eyes. Then he smiled.

"You know me," he continued. "I will help you get your start."

"*You will?*" I blurted out with excitement.

"I will," he replied. "When do you graduate college?"

"In two years," I answered.

"Stay in touch," he told me. "Send me some of the articles you write for your college newspaper. When you graduate, you've got yourself a job."

Excitedly, I embraced the dean of all boxing writers.

"Thank you, Nat! Thank you!" I said.

CHAPTER 1

We shook hands and he walked me out of his office—to the elevator.

"Stay in touch, Randy," he said.

"I will, Nat, thank you again. Thank you so much."

The elevator door closed and we waved good-bye to one another.

During the next few months, I sent Nat Fleischer several articles I had written in my college paper. He always sent me back his thoughts and a critique on my articles; however, when that elevator door closed the day I first met him, we never saw one another—or spoke—again. A few months after that, he celebrated his 82nd birthday. That winter, he contracted pneumonia, and the battle took its toll. He began to need more rest and went into the office less frequently. By the following year, he hardly went in at all. His son-in-law, Nat Loubet, took over the reins of *The Ring*.

On June 25, 1972, a few weeks after I graduated college, Nat Fleischer went to that big arena in the sky. He was 84.

It was eerie, when, seven years later, I walked into that same office to team with Bert Randolph Sugar in rebuilding, revitalizing, reviving, and rejuvenating a near-bankrupt *Ring Magazine*, turning it into perhaps the finest, most respected, and widely read boxing magazine of all time.

During those *Ring* years, and in the decades since, I have watched Marciano's legacy become almost mythical. The old-timers I knew back then who knew Marciano, covered him, and used to tell me stories of the Rock are long gone.

I have been asked, as a former editor in chief of *The Ring*, to put together my list of top 10 heavyweights, just like Nat Fleischer did and just like Bert Sugar did. Joe Louis was number one on Sugar's list. Marciano was number six.

I have never done a top-10 list of heavyweight champions. Until now.

On the day I met Nat Fleischer in 1969, 22 men had held the heavyweight title, from John L. Sullivan to Joe Frazier and Jimmy Ellis. No wonder six of the 10 men Nat Fleischer had on his top-10 list were born prior to 1900.

Since the time I met Fleischer, 55 more men have held at least a piece of the heavyweight championship. My ratings look entirely different than Nat Fleischer's did. Even Mr. Boxing would have to make drastic changes to his list if he was around today.

Mine looks like this:

1. Muhammad Ali
2. Jack Johnson
3. Joe Louis
4. George Foreman

5. Joe Frazier
6. Evander Holyfield
7. Sonny Liston
8. Mike Tyson
9. Lennox Lewis
10. Rocky Marciano

I wonder what Nat Fleischer would say about this list? In the top spot, I have a man who Fleischer thought little of, other than to say, "Speed and agility is all he had." He never saw near enough of the man he called and rated as Cassius Clay. Sorry, Nat. Ali would have "whupped" the likes of Bob Fitzsimmons, James J. Jeffries, Jim Corbett, Gene Tunney, and Max Schmeling. He would have beaten the others, too.

My number seven is Sonny Liston. Fleischer despised him, and I think, wrongfully so. There is no way Liston was ever going to be put on a Nat Fleischer top-10 list, even if he felt, deep down, that Sonny belonged at the very top.

Wouldn't Fleischer have been surprised to see the pupil of one of his friends—Cus D'Amato—on my list. That pupil is Mike Tyson, who was three years old when I met Fleischer.

Then there's Rocky Marciano. I have him rated exactly where Mr. Boxing had him rated.

Had Nat Fleischer been able to see all the boxing that followed his departure, I have a feeling his list of the top 10 all-time heavyweights would be a lot different than the one he wrote out for me in 1969.

In fact, I wouldn't be surprised if his list looked a lot like mine!

2

GLOVE AFFAIR

It was Friday night, March 11, 1960. It was my 11th birthday. I had gone to dinner at a local restaurant earlier with my parents, Carl and Roberta, and my brother, Jerry. Afterward, we sat around the den and watched TV, talked, and played chess. My brother, who was five and a half, had gone to sleep. I played chess a lot in those days. There was little else I could do physically, as I was wheelchair bound.

Seven months earlier, I suffered third-degree burns on most of my right leg. The injury caused me to spend almost four months in the hospital, many of those early days at death's door.

As I slowly recovered, I got around in a wheelchair, and sometimes on crutches. My mom taught me to play chess. I then taught my best friend, Tommy, along with neighbors Gail, Garry, Glenn, and Joanie, how to play. Quite often, we'd have chess tournaments.

On the night of my 11th birthday, my dad watched a TV program with music, singers, and dancers as my mom and I played chess. I remember glancing at the dancers every now and then, thinking, "I wish I could get out of this wheelchair and move around like them." After the chess game (I remember my mom winning), my dad began changing channels on the TV. He stopped when he came to a boxing match.

"Wanna watch the fights with me?" he asked.

"Sure!" I replied, staring at two guys dance around one another, darting in and out, throwing punches as they moved. I had just finished watching dancers move around so gracefully, and now I was watching this ballet with bruises. For whatever reason, their speed, grace, and power captured me. It took my mind off the still-excruciating pain of my burn, even for a little while.

One of the fighters was named Denny Moyer. The other was Emile Griffith. The TV announcer was Don Dunphy. The fight was coming from Madison Square Garden in New York City. Amazingly and perhaps ironically, a decade later, Griffith would become the first big-name fighter I would meet—both he and Moyer would become friends of mine, and Don Dunphy would become my announcing mentor—and in no venue would I ever watch, cover, and announce more boxing than Madison Square Garden.

Griffith won this fight on a split decision, although I had no idea what ring announcer Johnny Addie meant when he said, "We have a split decision." At first, Addie announced the decision as unanimous (all three judges in favor of the same fighter). Moments later, after conferring with commission officials, Addie changed it to split decision (two of the three in favor of the same fighter). To me, it didn't matter who won or lost. Emile Griffith and Denny Moyer, with their vast boxing skills, had, for the last 40 minutes, removed me from the constant pain of my fire-ravaged leg.

Although I knew nothing about boxing, I wanted to see more of it. I wanted to learn what Don Dunphy—who I would announce fights with 20 years later—meant when he said things like "hook off the jab," "slipping a punch," "parrying a punch," "work on the inside," and "counterpunch."

So, every Friday night, I sat in front of the black and white television and watched the *Gillette Cavalcade of Boxing*. I didn't just watch boxing. I learned about boxing. I studied the sport. Every month, I'd head to Lily & Lou's, the local candy store, and plunk down my 50 cents for the magazine I would become editor in chief of almost 20 years later—*Ring Magazine*. Then I'd sit at the counter with a root beer and read the magazine from cover to cover.

With every passing week of televised boxing, I became more and more of a fan. With every passing month, I got my "boxing fix" from *Ring Magazine*.

Following the Griffith–Moyer fight that I watched on my birthday with my dad, my Friday evenings were spent getting my boxing education from Don Dunphy. From Dunphy I learned boxing jargon. I learned about styles. I learned who the pure boxers were and who were the sluggers. I watched Don Fullmer, Florentino Fernandez, Luis Rodriguez, Zora Folley, Dick Tiger, Joey Giardello, Gaspar Ortega, Willie Pastrano, Mauro Mina, Eddie Cotton, Gregorio Peralta, Carl "Bobo" Olson, Henry Hank, Yama Bahama, Joey Archer, Carlos Ortiz, George Chuvalo, Rocky Rivero, Wilbert "Skeeter" McClure, and a slew of other world-class fighters during the next several years as I went from being a casual fan to an avid fan.

Through 1960, 1961, and 1962, I only missed one televised fight. That one came on March 24, 1962. The reason I missed it is because the next morning was my Bar Mitzvah, and my parents wanted me to get to sleep earlier than a night of fight-watching would allow. As it turned out, the fight I missed was a welterweight title fight between the champion, Benny "Kid" Paret, and the number-one challenger, my favorite fighter, Emile Griffith. This was the third meeting between the two. Paret, who was then the champion, lost his title to Griffith via a highly competitive 13th-round knockout on April 1, 1961. He regained the crown in a rematch, winning a split decision six months later in Madison Square Garden.

In an emotionally charged rubber match, Griffith fought with a fury his co-manager and trainer, Hall of Famer Gil Clancy, said was "unlike anything I have ever seen." In the weeks leading up to the fight, Paret had challenged Griffith's manhood, calling him, among other things, a *maricon*, the Hispanic equal of faggot. In later years, Griffith stopped hiding the fact that he was a homosexual, but in 1962, homosexuals kept their sexual orientation a secret. When Griffith's secret was revealed to the world, Griffith told Clancy, "Benny is going to pay for that." He did. He paid with his life.

After an exhausting and grueling 11 rounds of action, Griffith was comfortably in the lead despite being dropped in the eighth round. Before the start of the 12th round, Griffith told Clancy in the corner, "I'm finishing it this round. I'm taking my title back."

The Virgin Island native with the V-shaped body then tore into Paret. After staggering him and trapping him in a corner, Griffith unloaded punch after punch on an out-on-his-feet Paret, who was being held up by the cornerpost. Referee Ruby Goldstein inexplicably froze and did nothing as Griffith landed 32 punches to the head. By the time Goldstein pulled Griffith off of Paret, it was far too late. Paret, removed from the ring via a gurney, was taken to a local Manhattan hospital.

I remember going to sleep that night thinking less about my Bar Mitzvah and the religious importance it meant—especially for my parents and grandparents—and more about the first televised boxing match in years I was missing.

Is Emile Griffith going to regain the title tonight? I wondered, as I drifted off to sleep.

The following day, even as aunts left lipstick marks all over my face and uncles handed checks and cash to me, I kept wondering who won the fight. I didn't find out until the next morning. That's when I retrieved Sunday's *Newsday* from the front steps. There, on the back page, was the horrible news. I cringed.

"Tragedy at The Garden. Paret in Coma."

I said a silent prayer for Paret. I think we all did. He took those prayers with him 10 days later.

While Paret's death saddened me, it didn't deter my interest in boxing. If anything, it piqued my interest. I wanted to know why Paret died. Did the three very tough fights he had in the previous 12 months to facing Griffith have anything to do with his death? I wanted to know if the ref could have prevented the tragic ending. I wanted to know what would become of my first sports idol, Emile Griffith. I began following the sport more than ever.

Almost six months to the day after the Griffith–Paret fight—on September 25, 1962—I listened to the radio call of the September 25, 1962, heavyweight title fight between the fast-handed and popular but soon-to-be ex-champ, Floyd Patterson, and the heavy-handed and scowling soon-to-be crowned king of the heavyweights, Sonny Liston.

The fight took place on a Tuesday night, and I remember my mother telling me, "You have school tomorrow. I don't want you staying up late to listen to the fight. There will be others."

Somehow, I convinced her to let me lay in my bed and listen on my transistor radio. She agreed, figuring I would fall asleep before the fight started, and would have to come in my room to turn the radio off. The next morning, before I left for school, she said, "I guess you never listened to the fight last night. I came into your room just past 11:00 and found the radio on your night table. It was turned off."

I looked at her, smiled, and said, "We both got our wish last night. You wanted me to go to sleep early, while I wanted to listen to the fight. Well, I did both."

"Huh, how's that possible?" asked Mom. "I expected you to be awake way past midnight."

"The fight was over in just two minutes, six seconds."

"It was?" she asked wide-eyed. She knew that Floyd Patterson had been added to my list of favorite fighters. "I guess that Sonny Liston character wasn't so powerful after all."

I looked at her and shook my head.

"Other way, Mom," I told her. "Sonny Liston is the new champ. He knocked out Patterson in the first round. The radio announcer was so excited that he said, 'Sonny Patterson is down!' I wasn't sure who knocked who down. But it was Patterson who went down and out."

I found the radio call beyond exciting. As I left for school, I knew I was now more than a fan of boxing. I was hooked. From that moment, at the age of 13½, I knew I wanted to do something in boxing. Maybe I'd write about it, maybe I'd announce it. Maybe I'd promote it. Maybe I'd manage a fighter or two. Or ref.

Or judge. Or even fight. But I knew this: The sport of boxing, in some capacity, was where I wanted to spend my life. I don't know why the Liston–Patterson fight did that to me. I just know that it did.

Throughout my high school years, I was a better student at baseball and boxing statistics than I was in statistical math and algebra. I also found the history of boxing much more interesting than the history of the Corinthians. English literature? Reading Jimmy Cannon, Lester Bromberg, Red Smith, and A. J. Liebling was much more interesting to me back then than Edgar Allen Poe, Ralph Waldo Emerson, Nathaniel Hawthorne, and Mark Twain (although I did enjoy the latter four during my college years). Of course, there was only one science I really cared for then, and it wasn't earth science. It was the "Sweet Science."

Study hall? That was the time not to do homework, but to read "Ring's around the World" in *Ring Magazine*. How else was I supposed to find out what was going on in boxing outside of the United States?

On more than one occasion, a teacher would remove me from the classroom and send me to the principal's office because I was reading *Ring Magazine* instead of the assigned schoolwork. The last time it happened was just before the first meeting between Sonny Liston and Cassius Clay in February 1964.

"When you're some bigshot in boxing, I'll call you up and tell you how proud I am of you," principal John London yelled at me during a visit to his office in February 1964. "But right now, you're a part of the class of '67, and there's a curriculum you are required to take. Reading *Ring Magazine* is not part of that curriculum. I will hold the magazine until after the last period. You can pick it up then."

As I left his office, Mr. London asked me, in a much calmer voice, "You don't really think this Cassius Clay kid has a prayer of beating Sonny Liston, do you?"

I turned and looked at Mr. London. He was smiling.

"This Clay kid. Do you think he can beat Liston?" he repeated.

"I do, Mr. London, I really do!" I said excitedly.

He placed a hand on my shoulder.

"Listen, Randy, I think it's great that you're so passionate about boxing and love reading and learning everything you can about it," Mr. London said. "Maybe one day you really will be some top writer or journalist. But in order to do that, you have to have at least a high school diploma and even a college degree. How about a little more time on schoolwork? Schoolwork, then *Ring Magazine*, okay?"

He patted me on the back and sent me on my way. He even gave back my *Ring Magazine*. It was his way of telling me he trusted me. I understood him perfectly and was never sent to his office again (well, at least not for reading *Ring Magazine* in class).

Following graduation from high school in 1967, I continued both my formal and boxing education. My formal education took place at Long Island University's Brooklyn campus (Barclays Center was erected about a half-mile down the road almost 40 years after my graduation), while my boxing education continued from a P.A.L. center in the sleepy north shore town on Long Island called Port Washington. It was there I began boxing as a 118-pounder, and it was there I became friends with three young men. One was Steve DeFlorio, a 126-pounder with a brutal left hook. Another was 147-pounder Antonio Iadanza, another brutal left-hooker. The third was Wayne Kelly, a rugged 175-pounder who had just finished a double tour of duty in Vietnam. Wayne and I didn't just become friends; we became like close brothers. Our adjoined lives are detailed in chapter 11.

I met Wayne, the Vietnam vet, only days after he returned from a year in the jungles of Southeast Asia. A more likable, funny, lovable, loyal, personable, and caring—yet tough, rugged, and screwed up—individual I have never met. The toughest fight of my life was not in any ring or even overcoming the injuries from my burns. It was helping Wayne overcome the demons of Vietnam that ravaged and tormented his soul for years.

As for Antonio, he was dark-haired and handsome, although his good looks belied his fighting ability. Among the four of us, he was the one who wanted to become a professional fighter. He won his share of amateur fights, and usually did it with his potent left hook. My nose can attest to his power! It was broken for the first time in 1970, by one of Antonio's bombs.

One evening, after getting my head handed to me in a round-robin sparring session, where we continually alternated sparring partners until we had done two rounds with each guy (being the biggest, Wayne usually fared best in these round-robin sessions, while me, being the smallest, usually came away with lumps, bumps, cuts, and bruises), the four of us headed down the block to the nearest bar for some cold beers. I looked forward to the icy cold mug, which I pressed against the developing mountain ranges under my eyes. While the four of us sat there, we noticed a group of four girls sitting at the far end of the bar.

As Antonio dabbed at a cut on his lip, Steve and I pressed our beer mugs against our bruised faces, and Wayne chugged his beer and awaited another, Antonio pointed out the girls.

"How 'bout I give it the ol' college try," he said to the three of us. "I'm gonna go set us up. How'd you like to be holding one of them as tight as you're holding your beer mugs?"

Wayne shrugged. He was happy with his beers. Steve and I didn't really care, as neither of us felt like doing much other than applying some soothing ice to our reddened faces. Despite his cut lip, Antonio's testosterone levels were sky high. He was going for it.

We watched as he strutted toward the girls, holding his beer mug in one hand and a napkin in the other, dabbing at his cut lip. We watched as he spoke, gesturing toward us. Then we watched as he raised his glass to them and turned around and headed back to us.

His body language said it all. He was just shot down. We were just shot down. The fact is, I didn't care. I hurt all over. My nose hurt. My forehead hurt. Even my earlobes hurt. I was quite happy and content holding my beer mug. My happiness continued after Antonio returned to his bar stool.

"Well, Romeo, wha'd they say?" I asked him.

The three of us looked at Antonio as he answered.

"They told me to fuck off!" he said. "Can you believe that!"

The three of us smiled as Antonio frowned. He wanted action. We wanted our beers. The beers won.

More than likely, had that scene been replayed just a few years later, Antonio would have gotten his way. That's because Antonio was soon to become a star. While training at Gleason's Gym, which was then located on 30th Street in Manhattan, a casting agent, searching for the look that Antonio possessed, handed him a round-trip ticket to Los Angeles. At first he thought it was a joke or thought the guy was trying to hustle him. The casting agent came close to getting smacked by one of Antonio's left hooks; however, Antonio kept his cool and listened instead of punched. The casting agent asked Antonio if he had any acting experience. Antonio told him he had (he embellished the fact that his acting experience consisted of a few lines in a play while in college). He would be flown to California, met at the airport, and driven to a studio, and would then read a few lines from a script for a new sitcom that was being developed.

The TV execs loved what they heard. Antonio was hired. The TV boys polished his name. He went from being Antonio Iadanza to Tony Danza. He would play the role of taxi driver Tony Banta on *Taxi*, which became an immediate hit.

The series, which ran from 1978 to 1983, made a star out of not only Antonio, but also Judd Hirsch, Danny DeVito, Marilu Henner, and Andy Kaufman—his colleagues on the show.

During the years Antonio (now only known as Tony) was filming *Taxi*, he realized the dream he had years earlier—to become a professional boxer. He turned pro in August 1976, landing his big left hook early for a first-round knockout victory.

After winning his eighth fight—a first-round knockout of Max Hord—in front of an adoring hometown crowd in Madison Square Garden's 5,000-seat arena, the Felt Forum, Tony threw a massive party at a New York City nightclub. During the party, Tony pulled Wayne and me to the side and said, "I have another fight lined up in two weeks. After that, I'm hanging up the gloves."

Seventeen days later, Tony fought well-traveled opponent Johnny Heard in Arizona. Tony stopped him in the third round. As he told us, true to his word, he then hung up his gloves. He retired from competitive boxing with a record of 9–3, with all nine wins coming by knockout.

Shortly after Danza launched his pro career, Wayne and I launched ours. He did so in March 1975, winning a four-round decision. I launched mine one year later. I have long compared the maiden voyage of the *Titanic* to my pro debut. On April 15, 1912, and March 31, 1976, respectively, we both sunk! The *Titanic* ran into an iceberg. I ran into a pair of right hands.

My love of boxing took me into the ring 39 times as an amateur, where I lost twice, both on decisions in the New York Golden Gloves. The last of those bouts came in early 1972. College graduation and getting a job followed. So did a bunch of pounds. I went from a skinny 118 pounds to a lean 148 pounds during the course of three and a half years. But the burning desire to compete hadn't left me. It hadn't left at all.

Soon after Wayne turned pro, I started to think about having a pro fight. I was assistant editor at a publishing company that put out a series of boxing and wrestling magazines, including *World Boxing, International Boxing, Big Book of Boxing, The Wrestler*, and *Inside Wrestling*. I decided to turn pro and cover my own fight. When word got around that I was going to have a fight, Don King's publicist, Murray Goodman, called me the "Fighter Writer." The moniker stuck.

During the last half of 1975, I trained. I trained hard. But as I later realized, I did everything wrong. Knowing myself as a bantamweight/super bantamweight (118 to 122 pounds), I decided to get back to that weight. I needed to drop 30 pounds. I struggled to make 135, although I did and should have stayed there. Then I weakened myself to make 130. The weight loss continued. I starved myself to make 126. I killed myself to make 122. That's the weight I came in at on March 31, 1976, at the Nassau Coliseum on Long Island.

I ate nothing but plain yogurt for the last two months, thinking I was reducing my weight correctly. In addition, I had no trainer working with me. I just went to the gym and worked out and pounded the heavy bag and speed bag. For an educated guy, I really did some dumb things.

I fought on the undercard of world-rated featherweight Walter Seeley's ninth-round disqualification win against Natalio Jiminez. I shared a dressing room with a few of the other undercard fighters. One of them was Wayne Kelly, who was fighting with a severe sprain in his left wrist, an injury he hid from the New York State Athletic Commission.

My opponent, Gerald Odum, was a last-minute substitute. My original opponent, Seymour Sheppard, had pulled out a day before the bout, and local promoters Jimmy Winters and Gene Moore had to scramble to find a replacement. They came up with Odum, a local truck driver who was looking to have a professional fight.

In 1976, weigh-ins were held on the day of the fight. That was changed about 10 years later, as commission doctors agreed that drastic weight loss weakens a fighter, especially ones who try to lose a few pounds on the day of the event. So, ever since, weigh-ins are held the day before the fight. But, on Wednesday, March 31, 1976, we weighed in on the day of the fight. I weighed in at 122. My opponent, Gerald Odum, weighed in a few hours later. Because Odum was a last-minute sub, there were medicals for him to do and paperwork to fill out. I was told he'd be weighed in later. I wasn't hanging around the commission office waiting for "later," so I left. Promoters Winters and Moore said they'd check Odum's weight.

My first look at him was in the ring that night. When his robe was removed, he was chiseled. I weighed 122 soaking wet. He was announced at 128. He looked larger—a lot larger! When I ran into him at a fight card a few months later, he told me his weight that night was actually 138. He said only Gene Moore weighed him in—no one from the commission.

"I was told," he admitted, "that I should say I weighed 128, otherwise there would be no fight." Odum said that when he inquired about my weight he was told, "Gordon weighs around 130."

The size and weight were evident. I was a drained and weak 122 pounds. He was a cut and ready 138. I was a junior featherweight fighting a guy *four* weight divisions up.

I chased him around the ring in the first round. I nailed him with a jab on his left eye late in the round, and it stung him. A follow-up right hurt him. The few times he caught me with his jab and right cross I was unfazed, although each time I was able to roll with the punch. Unfortunately, I couldn't finish him, and the round ended. The scorecards were marked. Round one was in the books. I was given the round on all three scorecards.

Then, the *Titanic* ran into the iceberg.

I was doing okay, even winning round two, when Odum planted his feet and let his right hand go. It caught me flush on the point of the chin. The *Titanic* was doing okay as well, steaming across the North Atlantic. Then it got caught with a knockout blow.

I remember seeing a flash of light. My iceberg. That's all I remember. The films show me still fighting back. But Odum could see I was stunned. He stepped into a right uppercut. *Boom!* Again on the chin. I fell backward, headed for the ring floor. The *Titanic* fought back, too, before heading for the ocean floor. The *Titanic*'s maiden voyage was her last. My maiden voyage into the professional prize ring as a professional was also my last.

The time: 2:16 of the second round. The winner, in his pro debut: Gerald Odum. I have long heard that a fighter who gets KO'd never sees or remembers the knockout punch. I can attest to that!

On the same card, Wayne, unable to use his left hand, dropped a four-round decision to Al Ware. We were two pretty dejected guys in the dressing room that night. We each talked about getting a rematch. Neither of us ever did. Wayne tried, but promoters only used Al Ware as an opponent, so he retired after three more fights. I tried, as well, but my wife said for me to have a rematch with Odum, I'd have to get past her first. I would have preferred Odum. He would have been easier!

My love affair with this crazy and beautiful sport began when I was that 11-year-old wheelchair-bound boy and has grown stronger with every passing day. By the time I was in college, I knew I'd be involved in some way. But *this* involved?

When I was commissioner, I was asked by Alan Taylor, who owned a successful public relations firm that handled many of the day's largest boxing events, "What do you see yourself doing when your days as commissioner end?" As I absorbed his question, he added quickly, "And rest assured, they *will* end."

I had no definitive answer to his question. I did know, however, that whatever I did, it would have to be boxing related. When I told him that, when I told him how in love with boxing I have always been and always would be, he responded, "You are a very popular commissioner and a very good one. But still, you're going to have to grow up one day and move on."

Well, I have moved on and I have gotten older, but in the mind of Alan Taylor, I haven't grown up. I'm still involved in boxing. Sorry, Alan. I'm addicted. I'm hopelessly in love with the sport. I still read every word about boxing I can find. I read every press release, every article, every column, every website, every result. If it's boxing related, I not only read it, but also look at it. I study it. I watch it. I listen to it. That's what you do when, as I mentioned before, you just happen to be the luckiest, most fortunate fight fan ever born.

My love affair with the "Sweet Science" was a birthday present I received in 1960. Unlike a new pair of shoes, which a kid outgrows, I have never outgrown the sport of boxing. Nor has the sport grown old on me. Those young fighters I watched on my birthday that year—Emile Griffith and Denny Moyer—became two of my closest friends. Emile's manager/trainer, Gil Clancy, became my guru, my teacher, my confidante. The TV announcer, Don Dunphy, schooled me in boxing broadcasting.

I met Cassius Clay when I was 14 and years later became friends with Muhammad Ali. I even ran the hills of Deer Lake, Pennsylvania, with him. I also became close friends with Joe Frazier and had a lot to do with the two of them shaking hands in love and respect toward the end of their lives.

I am a former president of the Association of Boxing Commissions and was elected to both the New Jersey Boxing Hall of Fame and New York State Boxing Hall of Fame. I've refereed a world title fight, and I became the first commissioner to have three female judges work together on a fight (Melvina Lathan, Carol Castellano, and Eva Shain).

Then there are the boxing shows I host with Gerry Cooney on SiriusXM Radio. For a fight fan, it just doesn't get better than this!

All that, and more, all because I watched a boxing match on my birthday in 1960.

One of my biggest joys came in 1981, when I was the color analyst for ESPN's Top Rank Boxing. The day after the show, I received a call in my office at *The Ring*. It was from John London, my former high school principal who always dealt fairly with the teenaged boxing fan who kept getting sent into his office for studying more about heavyweight Sir Henry Cooper and boxing records than King Henry VIII and statistics.

"I told you that when you're some big shot in boxing I'd call you up and tell you I'm very proud of you," said my former principal. "I watched you last night on ESPN. I really enjoyed the show." Then he added, "I always hoped you'd wind up doing something in boxing. I'm glad you studied the sport as hard and diligently as you did." We both enjoyed the laugh.

Mr. London may have been the first person, outside of my parents, who truly felt my passion for boxing.

He knew a glove affair when he saw one.

3

EL FLACO EXPLOSIVO

Managua, Nicaragua. It sits on the isthmus (a strip of land that connects two larger land masses) joining Mexico with South America. Directly to its south on the isthmus is Costa Rica. To its north is Honduras. It is bordered by the Pacific Ocean to the west and the Caribbean Ocean to the east. Approximately 800 miles to the north is the island of Cuba. Today, the population of Nicaragua is a little more than 6 million. In Managua, the capital, that number is close to 2 million. In 1972, those numbers were approximately 3 million and 400,000, respectively.

It was almost half-past midnight on Saturday, December 23, 1972. The night was hot, but in Managua, hot is commonplace. Alexis Arguello and his wife, Silvia, were at home in bed. In an adjacent room slept their infant son, Alexis Jr. As Silvia and little Alexis slept, Alexis Sr. turned. And turned. Something was bothering him, but he didn't know what it was that was keeping him awake.

Arguello was a skinny, 20-year-old boxer with unlimited potential. No one could have foreseen that he would go on to become the greatest fighter ever from Nicaragua, a three-division champion, one of the greatest fighters ever, a Hall of Famer, and the mayor of Managua, as well.

The future Hall of Famer had gone for a long run in the morning, about 18 hours earlier. In the early evening hours, he decided to put in his favorite run—pulling Alexis Jr. in his red American Flyer—around the neighborhood. They'd run past vacant lots with tents, small shanties with makeshift tin roofs, and small, quaint two- and three-bedroom homes, some with as many as one dozen people living there. Chicken-wire fences kept hens, pigs, and goats on many of the properties, while dogs roamed the neighborhood, scouring garbage cans for food.

Arguello was the hope of the neighborhood, the kid who would beat the odds and fight his way out of the impoverished streets of Managua. Although just 20, he had already been a pro for four years. He had won 23 of his 26 matches. All but one took place in Nicaragua. Of his 26 matches, 24 took place in his hometown of Managua. Nineteen of his victims never made it to the final bell. Seven of them exited in the first round. One of his losses came when he was 16. Another came when he was 19. To say he had become a local favorite is a massive understatement.

He began 1972 by losing for just the third time. When I asked him about that fight, he shook his right hand and said, "I can still feel the pain. It was in the first round. I threw a body shot. My opponent [Jorge Reyes] blocked it on his elbow. My hand broke." Arguello fought through the pain until the sixth round. That's when the referee had seen enough of a one-handed fighter. He also knew the incredible prospect Arguello was, so he mercifully ended Arguello's evening.

The hand injury kept Arguello out of action for the next eight months. When he returned, he did so looking more powerful than ever. He fought once each in the last four months of the year, knocking out each opponent within three rounds. Three of the fights were at Arena Kennedy in Managua. A third was where the local soccer team played—Estadio Cranshaw.

The last of those four fights took place on December 17, 1972. Arguello looked awesome in stopping his foe midway through the third round. He took no time off. He was back in the gym the following day. His next match was about a month away, again in Managua. He wanted to stay busy in 1973, fighting as much as he could, learning as much as he could, preparing himself for the day he'd fight for the title; however, with Christmas coming up, Arguello decided to only do roadwork during the holiday weekend. He planned on returning to the gym the day after Christmas.

It was Friday night, December 22. Arguello's tree was up and wreaths hung on the walls. He loved being around the house, helping Silvia care for little Alexis. After their father–son "run" through the neighborhood, Alexis gave his son a bath, dressed him in light pajamas, and, together with Silvia, put him to sleep.

Shortly before turning out the lights and heading off to sleep with Silvia, the Arguellos stood in front of their house holding hands, looking out on the holiday lights that lit their neighborhood. The picture was one of serenity, peacefulness, happiness, and dreams to be fulfilled.

Although an upbeat and positive person, Alexis was uncomfortable and uncharacteristically jumpy this night, maybe as jumpy as the large number of barking dogs in his neighborhood. As Silvia talked, Alexis' eyes darted back and forth, as if he were looking for something.

"What is it, Alexis?" she asked him. It would be the first of several times during the evening she'd ask him that question.

"I don't know, Silvia," he said. "The night feels strange. The air has a smell to it. I don't know what it is. Do you feel it, too?"

"*Usted este entrenando muy duro,*" she told him. "You are training too hard."

He shook his head and together they headed back into the house. He really didn't think his training was what was bothering him. Arguello was in the best shape of his life. It was something else. He just didn't know what that something else was.

Silvia fell asleep in her husband's arms, knowing that was as close as she'd get to him before his fight in a few weeks. Arguello was an old-school fighter who believed in training hard, eating right, getting plenty of rest, and practicing celibacy while in training.

As Silvia slept soundly, Alexis laid awake, wiping sweat from his forehead. Nicaraguan Decembers are usually one of the country's driest months, but Arguello recalled that night as being "very muggy."

For a few hours, Arguello listened to what seemed like every dog in the neighborhood barking. Endlessly. He also heard chickens clucking away and the "baaaaah" of many of the sheep in the neighborhood.

Do they make this kind of noise every night? Arguello asked himself. *Why have I never heard this racket before? Do I sleep that soundly that I never hear this?*

Shortly after midnight and totally unable to sleep, Arguello got up to check on his son, who he could hear turning uncomfortably. As he sat up in his bed, sweat rolled down his forehead. He lightly touched his wife's cheek. She was also sweating. When he checked on his son, he found him sweaty, as well. Even for this native of Managua, it was unusually humid and uncomfortable.

Other than the miserable heat, humidity, and chorus of animals, Arguello still felt something was wrong, something amiss. He didn't know what it was, but he just knew something was not right. He lightly touched his wife on her arm. She kept sleeping. He lightly tapped her arm again. She awakened.

"What is it, Alexis?" she asked her husband.

"I think the three of us should sleep in here tonight," he said. An uneasy feeling grabbed at him. He knew there was a reason they should all sleep together, but he just didn't know what the reason was. It was that same uneasiness that had engulfed him all night. He just wished he had an answer to why he was feeling this way.

"What is it, Alexis?" Silvia asked him again. "What is wrong?"

Arguello didn't know the answer to his wife's question. He slowly shook his head and shrugged his shoulders.

"I remember thinking, 'We must stay together tonight,'" he told me eight years after that night.

In 1980, he said to me, "To this day, I don't know what made me want to do that. It was just a feeling I had. It wasn't a feeling that something bad was going to happen. It was just a feeling that the three of us had to be together." The strange, uneasy feeling something was not right was the same feeling the animals were having.

It was a feeling that saved their lives.

Arguello and his wife arose from their bed. Alexis went into his son's room and gently lifted little Alexis. He carried him back to the master bedroom. He turned a small nightstand fan on. It began humming gently. Then he moved the switch to "high."

His wife placed a sheet on her son, who was between the two of them. She and Alexis were too hot to get under the sheet, so they lay there, on their backs, sweating. As they did, they whispered, so as not to awaken their son.

"Why are so many dogs barking tonight? Why are the animals so restless?" Arguello asked, knowing full well that his wife didn't have the answer but unaware she was thinking the same thing.

As Silvia started to speak, a slight shaking of the house could be felt. It was 12:29 a.m. Quickly, the shaking intensified. Then came a roar—a loud, deafening roar. Alexis described the roar as the kind of noise you hear when you are sitting in an airplane on the runway, as the engines are being throttled to takeoff power.

"What is that, Alexis?" Silvia asked.

The future world champion in three weight divisions stared through the darkness and listened as the roar grew louder and closer and angrier. His first thought was that a plane was falling from the sky, hurtling right toward them. The roar grew louder and louder, stronger and stronger, scarier and scarier. Then, he heard an explosion a short distance away. Not only were animals in full audio, but people were screaming, as well. They were screams of horror. And death. As the house shook even more violently and the roar continued to intensify, Arguello realized what it was.

"Earthquake!" he screamed.

He heard his small home beginning to crack and crumble. He said the cracking of beams, walls, and boards in his home sounded like lightning. He took a pillow in one arm and flung his muscular 120-pound body over his son and wife, pulling them in close. He put the pillow over their heads. The sound of falling walls and ceilings, as well as shattering glass, all but drowned out their cries, screams, and prayers.

Explosion after explosion was heard. Some sounded far off. Others sounded a few yards away. Arguello remembers hearing barnyard animals scream in death as heavy equipment fell on them and many of them fell into faults and crevasses that had opened in the ground.

It was over quickly. A minute or two. It seemed like an eternity. As fast as the roar seemed to come on, it stopped. The rumbling ceased. Arguello removed the pillow from on top of them and looked up. His wife and son were crying.

"It is over. We are safe," he said. "Let me go outside and see what damage was done." He pushed aside a ceiling beam that was hanging two feet from the bed.

As he walked to the doorway and prepared to step into the hallway, he stopped in his tracks. His next step would have taken him outside. There was no hallway. There was nothing. The bedroom he was just in with Silvia and Alexis Jr. was all that remained of his house. Everything else had collapsed. Looking outside and toward the horizon, all he could see was flames and, through the light they created, clouds of smoke.

Managua, the capital of Nicaragua, home to approximately 400,000 of his countrymen, was, as Alexis Arguello knew it, gone, destroyed by a 6.2 magnitude earthquake. By earthquake standards, 6.2 was far from the worst ever recorded; however, because this took place more than five kilometers (3.1 miles) underground, unlike many others that are quite deeper, the rumbling and shaking was much more intense, and the old, poorly constructed buildings, houses, and streets of Managua collapsed. Gas lines exploded. Water mains split. Electricity went out.

Arguello stepped outside the bedroom and toward the area that used to be his living room. All that was there now was dirt, bricks, and ruins. His roof, which had fallen in, rested atop his couch. He spotted a broken lamp and a red wagon. It was crushed like a soda can by a falling beam. His house was gone. As he looked into the flame-and-explosion-lit night, his neighborhood was also gone. Even the streets on which he jogged were gone, turned into crevasses, gullies, and canyons.

He spotted an older neighbor, staggering through rubble, perhaps 30 yards away. Arguello called out to him. The man turned to look at him, then stumbled and fell facedown. Arguello ran to help him. When Arguello got there and rolled the man over, he noticed the stump of a right arm—it had been severed at mid-arm when a ceiling girder crashed down on it. Blood poured out of the gaping wound. Arguello pulled off his sweat-drenched undershirt and ripped it, using a long strip to tie a tourniquet above the site of the amputation.

From both near and far, explosions tore through the night. Piercing screams and frantic cries for help sent chills down the young fighter's back. Bloodied neighbors staggered aimlessly, either too badly injured or too much in shock to understand what had just occurred.

Alexis looked around and saw nothing but devastation. He remembered having seen photos of Hiroshima and Nagasaki after they had been leveled by atomic weapons 27 years earlier. His Managua looked no different.

For about 45 minutes after the initial tremor, Arguello ran around his leveled neighborhood, helping countless injured friends and neighbors. Then, the ground shook violently again. It was an aftershock of 5.0 magnitude. Buildings that were swaying and buckled either collapsed or swayed or buckled further. Minutes later came a 5.2 aftershock. Buildings and homes—what was left of them—continued to fall and explode. Hell had come to Managua.

Houses had crumbled. Buildings had tumbled. All four of Managua's hospitals had been rendered unserviceable. Fires burned out of control for weeks, as all of Managua's fire departments had been destroyed. The figures were staggering, as 90 percent of Managua had been destroyed. Almost 70 percent of its population had been left homeless. About 7,000 had been killed and 20,000 injured.

Animals, it is said, feel an earthquake coming on. The animals in Alexis Arguello's neighborhood felt it and spent the evening crying out to their owners. No one listened to them. No one except Alexis Arguello.

Rescue efforts went on for days. Cleanup efforts went on for years. Nicaragua, under the leadership of President Anastasio Somoza—one of the most corrupt individuals ever to hold such a position—was in financial shambles. Monies and financial gifts given to Nicaragua had been used by the Somoza family and insiders for personal gain, profit, and benefit. If you weren't part of what was facetiously called the "Chosen Somozans," it was too bad.

Residents of Managua, known as Managuenses, became victims of the earthquake, as little help from the Somoza-led government was available. While almost 7,000 were killed in the immediate earthquake, several thousand more perished in the days following the catastrophe, as no hospital or emergency services were available, nor were medical supplies or even drinking water.

Aid came from dozens of countries. Yet, because of the virtual destruction of the runways at Managua's airport, that aid had to be flown into surrounding areas, then trucked into Managua. Because of damage to all major roads leading in and out of Managua, that aid then took days to get to the needy populace, rather than hours. Helicopters were the primary source of aid, dropping off supplies and doctors. Unfortunately, many of the supplies could not be used. Well-intentioned people gave items to which they gave no thought, for example, winter clothes and frozen meals. Nicaragua is a country with a tropical climate with no need for winter clothes, and a lack of electricity rendered frozen meals useless.

Baseball legend Roberto Clemente's name will be forever linked with the tragedy of the Managua earthquake. Clemente, of Puerto Rico, was one of the most gifted baseball players ever. Clemente played exclusively for the Pittsburgh Pirates from 1955 to 1972. On the final day of the 1972 season, he doubled off left-hander Jon Matlack of the New York Mets. The hit was the 3000th of his incredible career.

In the offseason, Clemente did vast amounts of charity and volunteer work. When he heard of the earthquake and its massive destruction, he organized relief flights to bring aid to the victims. Clemente sent three planes with relief packages, carrying everything from cash, scissors, gauze, and tape to bread, water, blankets, and clothes. He was incensed when inside sources told him corrupt officials from the Somoza regime kept most of the relief aid for themselves, family, and friends.

Furious, he arranged for a fourth flight to leave San Juan, Puerto Rico, for Managua, Nicaragua. He reasoned that even the most corrupt government wasn't going to steal from one of Major League Baseball's biggest stars.

"If they steal from me, then the whole world will know about it," Clemente had said.

On December 31, 1972, Clemente climbed aboard a four-engine DC-7 he had chartered to take him and a friend, along with tons of supplies, to Nicaragua. The plane had numerous problems, one of which was a faulty right inboard engine. In addition, the aircraft had not been flown in four months. Even worse was the fact that the copilot and flight engineer were not qualified to be operating such an aircraft. On top of it all was the fact that this less-than-perfect flying machine with two unqualified pilots was overloaded by 4,200 pounds.

A first attempt at takeoff failed. The plane could not get enough power or speed to become airborne and had to slam on its brakes near the end of the runway. It then turned around for a second attempt at takeoff. This time, it was sent to a longer runway.

On its second attempt, the plane used just about all of the 8,000 allotted feet of runway to become airborne. It rose slowly. Suddenly, the right inboard engine failed. A moment later, the left inboard engine failed. The pilot banked sharply to the left in an attempt to get back to the airport; however, with only two engines working, the drastically overweight aircraft began losing altitude quickly. The pilot radioed that he was going to try and make it back to the field. It was the wrong move. Had the pilot accepted the fact they were going down and not attempted to turn the aircraft around with so much weight and not near enough power, he probably could have done a belly landing in the water, sparing the plane from destruction and saving all five men aboard. But it was not to be. In banking to the left, the plane lost altitude quickly. The pilot then lost control of his craft. According to eyewitnesses, it plummeted almost upside down into the sea, about a mile and a half from the luxury apartments and condos of Isle Verde. All five aboard were killed. The body of Roberto Clemente was never recovered.

It was later revealed that Clemente knew of the plane's problems. Nonetheless, he was so determined to help the victims of Managua's earthquake and just as determined to show the unscrupulous Somoza regime that they could not continue to do what they were doing and get away with it that he let his emotions cloud his judgment.

As a way to thank Clemente for his undying love and support for the people of Nicaragua, a baseball stadium in Masaya, a short drive from Managua, was named in his honor. It is called Estadio Roberto Clemente. It is where Arguello insisted on fighting once he fulfilled his contract with the local promoters, to whom he owed four more fights. All four would take place in one of the few structures in Managua that withstood the earthquake—Arena Kennedy.

For one straight week, Arguello led rescue teams as they pulled survivors from beneath tons of rubble. He worked tirelessly, almost machine-like, as days became nights and nights became days. He crawled across fallen rooftops and even under them, listening for signs of life. When he heard anything that sounded like life—a whimper, cry, groan, moan, or gasp—he'd yell "*Venido aqui ahora!*" ("Come here now!"). Neighbors would come running with shovels, picks, crowbars, and any other equipment they could use to free their trapped countrymen.

Rescue efforts eventually turned into cleanup efforts. After almost two weeks of nonstop work, with cuts all over his arms, back, stomach, and legs, and having saved hundreds of his countrymen, Arguello headed to meet up with Silvia and Alexis Jr., who were staying with friends in their home in a section of Managua that had not been leveled by the quake. It was time to get back in training.

Arguello rested for the next few days. But "resting" for Arguello meant spending "only" eight or nine hours per day assisting in the massive cleanup efforts, rather than the 20 per day he had been putting in. Then it was back to the gym to resume the career that would carry him to international celebrity status.

Arguello had tried to get a rematch with Jorge Reyes, against whom he had lost to on the broken hand one year earlier. When Reyes turned him down, Arguello tried for—and got—Fernando Fernandez, who had stopped Reyes a few years earlier. To Arguello, it would mean more than just another win. To beat a guy who had KO'd the guy who beat you, it would be like erasing a loss.

On February 24, 1973, a capacity hometown crowd turned out in Arena Kennedy to watch their ray of hope, the man they called "El Flaco Explosivo— "The Explosive Thin Man"—begin 1973 with a second-round stoppage of Fernandez.

In the next four months, Arguello fought and won three more fights. In August came the opening of the arena in Masaya dedicated to Roberto Clemente. Naturally, Nicaragua's popular and fast-rising star, Alexis Arguello, was in the main event. His opponent was Mexico's inexperienced but hard-hitting Nacho Lomeli, who brought a 3–1–1 record into the ring. All three victories had been by knockout.

In the fight's opening moments, Lomeli caught Arguello with a booming overhand right, sending the localite to the canvas. On his back, Arguello pushed himself into a seated position, then shook his head to clear the residue of the Mexican's cannon shot of a right.

He arose and the referee wiped the gloves on his shirt, while looking into Arguello's eyes. They were clear. He brought his hands into the boxing position, and the ref motioned for the men to resume action.

Lomeli tore into Arguello. As the Mexican launched another overhand right, Arguello slid his body to the left and away from the intended knockout punch and crashed a powerful left hook to the jaw. Lomeli crumpled to the floor, where the referee counted him out. Arguello had himself his 28th victory and his 16th knockout, with half of them coming in the first round.

Two months later, Arguello registered his fourth knockout in a row, dropping down Mexico's Sigfredo Rodriguez seven times on the way to a ninth-round knockout.

The following month, Arguello opened up the new Estadio Roberto Clemente in front of a capacity crowd. His opponent was former World Boxing Council featherweight champion Jose Legra of Spain, who brought with him an incredible record of 133–10–4, including 50 knockouts. Arguello was 22, and considered among the top contenders in the featherweight division. His record stood at 29–3, with 23 knockouts.

Legra, 31, was hoping to not only beat Arguello, but also beat him convincingly. Such a victory would almost certainly propel him into another world title fight. He planned on using his fast hands and even faster legs to get in on the local hero, score, and get out before Arguello knew what hit him. He was aware of Arguello's power. What he was totally unaware of, however, was Arguello's speed, especially in combination punching. When the 5-foot-10 El Flaco Explosivo threw punches, it wasn't one at a time. A long, punishing jab was usually followed by a crushing right hand. Behind that was usually a hook to the head and a follow-up and wicked left hook to the liver.

Following the national anthems of Spain and Nicaragua, the fight was under way. Legra came out behind a probing jab and dancing feet. He wasn't called "Pocket Cassius Clay" for nothing. He had been boxing pro since 1963, and had idolized the future heavyweight champion since he first saw him compete as a light heavyweight in the 1960 Olympics in Rome.

Arguello, however, knew what to expect from Legra. On one of the former featherweight champ's first attempts to score with the jab, Arguello countered with a sharp, perfectly timed right to the chin. Most fighters would have stopped right there. Arguello wasn't most fighters. A left hook to the head followed. Before Legra could even react, Arguello sunk a left hook to the liver. Legra dropped to one knee as the ref began to count. When he arose, Arguello was all over him.

As Legra covered up from the expected onslaught, Arguello picked his shots. He banged both hands to the body. Legra moaned as a few of his ribs cracked from the impact. As he dropped his hands to cover his sides from the cannon shots that were breaking him in half, Arguello fired a right uppercut up the middle.

Boom! It landed on Legra's chin. His head snapped upward. A follow-up left hook was the coup de grace. Down went the former champion. The referee didn't bother counting. Arguello had himself his ninth first-round knockout and the most impressive victory of his career. Legra, so soundly beaten, hung up his gloves. He was later asked if he'd consider coming back after a short rest.

"What for?" he asked. "To have a rematch with Arguello in a year? He's only going to be better in a year. It's time to move on." Legra kept true to his words. He retired from active competition after taking the short, vicious beating from Arguello.

Next up for Arguello was 27-year-old Raul Martinez Mora of Mexico. The fight would take place on January 12, 1974, seven weeks after the quick dispatch of Legra. Once again, Estadio Roberto Clemente would be the venue.

Unlike Legra, the gutsy Mexican elected to engage Arguello in a shot-for-shot slugfest. Bad idea. Arguello electrified the locals with yet another first-round ending, knocking Mora unconscious with a crushing left hook to the liver, followed by another hook, this one to the head.

A few days after the bout, Arguello was called by the local promoter. Arguello loved staying busy and thought this was a call regarding his next local fight. The call was indeed about his next fight, but there was nothing local about it.

"You are ready," said the promoter.

"Ready for what?" asked Alexis.

"Ready for a shot at the title," he was told.

"What title? When? Where?" Arguello inquired.

The promoter quickly answered two of Arguello's questions.

"The WBA featherweight title. It's held by Ernesto Marcel. The fight will take place in Panama City."

"When is it?" asked Arguello. "I've never been outside of Nicaragua. Will I be able to have a real training camp and get some top sparring?"

The promoter swallowed hard. Then he paused. Arguello knew immediately there was a problem.

"Break it to me," said Arguello. "When is this fight, next week?"

Again, the promoter hesitated. Then he spoke.

"No, it's not next week. It's next month. February 16."

Arguello couldn't believe his ears. He had just one month to prepare for a world title challenge against one of the best champions in boxing—25-year-old Ernesto Marcel. On top of it all, he would be leaving the comfortable surroundings of his country and his fans for the first time. He would be going to not only the home of Marcel but also one of the most intimidating hometown arenas in the history of boxing—the Gimnasio Nuevo Panama.

The seating capacity for the semicircular steel and stone structure, which was built in the 1930s, was approximately 8,000. When popular Panamanians the likes of Roberto Duran (who had handed Marcel one of his four career losses four years earlier), Eusebio Pedroza, and Marcel fought, that 8,000 swelled to several thousand more, with hundreds pressed up against the ring during the course of the bout. The temperature in the packed arena was generally about 100 degrees. In the ring and under the lights, the temperature was closer to 130 degrees. Coming from Nicaragua, Arguello was used to heat. But he had never seen—or felt—anything like this.

Arguello did his best to prepare for his first title fight. He ran longer. He ran faster. He sparred more rounds. But he needed more than that. Marcel, who had been informed a month earlier that his next opponent might be Alexis Arguello, had already been preparing for several weeks for his taller, younger, more lethal opponent. His sparring partners had been tall and rangy, weighing as much as 140 pounds. Arguello was sparring with the same group of fighters he had always worked with. None weighed more than 126. Some were flyweights (112 pounds).

The champion weighed in at 125½ pounds, a half pound under the featherweight limit. Arguello, whose body had never seen 126 pounds, weighed in at 122½. That was a huge mistake, for in his dressing room deep in the bowels of the old arena, the temperature was no less than 110. By the time the fight started, Arguello had spent several hours in that room. What's the most time you ever spent in a sauna? Twenty minutes? A half hour? Picture spending several hours in there. Marcel? His room was equipped with two swivel fans, each blowing air over the ice stacked in front of them. The temperature in his dressing room never topped 75.

Marcel was sweating when he entered the ring in front of a deafening crowd. Arguello was not sweating—he was soaked.

"I felt like I had taken a shower in my boxing trunks and socks, then put my boxing shoes on," Arguello told me, adding, "I have never felt such heat."

Although Marcel won a 15-round unanimous decision that night, Arguello credits everything about it to making him into a complete fighter.

"The short notice, the training, the sparring, the preparation, the dressing room, the fight—everything made me smarter and stronger," Arguello said. He was also quick to add, "And better."

Following the action-packed 15-rounder, Marcel told the media, "I have always enjoyed boxing and came into the sport with a hunger for competition and to test myself. With this and three other successful defenses, I have surpassed even my wildest dreams." He then shocked everyone by announcing his retirement, doing what few champions have ever done in the long history of boxing—walking away while on top.

When asked his opinion on the future of the man he had just fought 15 hard rounds against, Marcel replied, "He punches hard with both hands and is relentless. One day he will fight again for the world title. Next time he will win it." He drew laughter when he said, "I'm just glad his opponent won't be me."

With Marcel's shocking retirement, the World Boxing Association wasted little time in filling his title. They selected Mexico's Ruben Olivares and Japan's Zensuke Utagawa to fight for the crown.

Utagawa was the Oriental and Pacific Boxing Federation featherweight champion. At 24, he was already a veteran of 31 fights. He was a smooth boxer with a sturdy chin. His four losses all had come via decision.

Olivares, 27, was the hard-hitting former world bantamweight champion, the owner of a 46–4 record, with 38 of his victories coming by knockout. To this day, he is easily one of Mexico's all-time top-10 fighters.

The fight, on July 9, 1974, at the Inglewood Forum, was a noncompetitive blowout. Olivares overwhelmed Utagawa from the opening bell, dropping him three times—the final right knocking him out cold—on the way to a seventh-round knockout.

Although it wasn't announced, a title fight between the new champion and Arguello was all but a done deal. Olivares's promoters wanted to keep their two-division champion busy and sharp, so they lined up two nontitle fights for him. The first of the two was only about seven weeks after the title victory over Utagawa. In that one, he blasted out opponent and fellow countryman Enrique Garcia in the fifth round of a scheduled 10-round bout. About five weeks later came another scheduled 10-rounder, this time against a Panamanian native who now made his home in Mexico City—Carlos Mendoza. It was almost the wrong fight to take. This was no mere opponent. This was no Enrique Garcia.

Carlos Mendoza is the answer to the boxing trivia question, "Against whom did Roberto Duran make his pro debut?" Yes, it was this Carlos Mendoza, who, on February 23, 1968, dropped a four-round decision to the future Hall of Famer.

Mendoza gave Olivares and his promoters—as well as WBA officials—quite a scare when he dropped the champion in the second round with a stiff combination. You can imagine how they all felt when a short right put Olivares on the floor again in round four.

"I told myself it was time to wake up," said Olivares after the second knockdown. Wake up he did.

He began to throw more punches and more power shots. Faced with the sudden Olivares barrage, Mendoza began to go on the defensive. When he did, Olivares stepped up the pace even more. Although Mendoza was doing a good job of blocking many of the punches, he couldn't block them all and began to wilt under the Olivares onslaught.

After being caught by a solid right midway through the sixth round, Mendoza sagged against the ropes, where Olivares pounded him unmercifully, prompting referee Ernesto Zacatecas to put an end to the fight.

Immediately after the fight, the WBA announced Olivares's next defense. The date: November 23, 1974. The place: The Forum in Los Angeles. The challenger: Alexis Arguello.

For Arguello, the news was what he had been hoping for. This time, he would have plenty of time to prepare for his title challenge, unlike the amateurish mini-camp he used to prepare for Marcel.

Arguello began training for Olivares in the summer. This time, unlike what happened to him for his fight against Marcel, the challenger intended to be ready on a moment's notice. As he trained, he knew that moment was coming. Soon.

When his phone finally rang, Arguello was already in title fight condition. As it turned out, he would need every hour, minute, second, and moment of his training. That's because the legendary Mexican who Arguello would be facing would also be in championship form.

A near-capacity crowd of 14,000 showed up at the Inglewood Forum to watch these two future Hall-of-Famers put on a featherweight classic. It was nothing less.

Olivares was a pint-size Joe Frazier. When the bell rang, he was in your face throwing punches. Arguello, with a height—and especially a reach—advantage over almost every one of his opponents, loved it when they brought the fight to him. It usually meant he'd get to go home early. Seventeen of his knockout victims were out of there before the end of the second round. He was hoping for the same result against Olivares. What he hoped for and what he got were two entirely different things. What this turned into was a long fight, a tough fight, a two-sided fight. It was a fight that tested both men's resolve. In the end, it also turned into one of the roughest, most grueling fights of Arguello's magnificent career.

Until the seventh round it had been a close fight. Then, Olivares began to close the distance. He began to find the range. Midway through the seventh, he pinned Arguello on the ropes and blasted away. Arguello was hit with body shots that surely would have dropped and stopped most other featherweights. Veteran referee Dick Young, who had officiated a few of Olivares's other fights, knew what the Mexican was capable of. He watched carefully as Olivares unloaded bomb after bomb on the challenger from Nicaragua.

The pro-Olivares crowd exploded as their hero moved in behind a fusillade of blows. A right to the face had Arguello in trouble, and he smartly tied up Olivares. Later, ref Young said if Arguello had taken a solid follow-up punch, he would have stopped the fight. But in the time it took to clinch, Arguello's head cleared. He fired combinations back, and Olivares ceased his onslaught for a few seconds. As he did, Arguello moved off the ropes and back to mid-ring. As the champion went after him, the bell ended the round. Arguello had survived his greatest crisis as a professional fighter. He had passed his biggest test.

For the first 12 rounds, this was as two-sided as a fight can get. The forever-pressuring champion kept the taller, rangier Arguello on the move, intent on breaking him down with wicked body shots and perfectly timed rights over the challenger's jab. Arguello's job was to keep the fight in mid-ring and the champion impaled on the end of his jab. Officially, Olivares was slightly in the lead as the bell ended the 12th round. The fight was still close enough for either man to win it on the scorecards. Years later, in talking about that fight, Arguello said, "There was no way I was letting that fight go to the cards. I was going to knock him out or get knocked out trying."

Olivares bolted off his stool to start the 13th round. So did Arguello. Both men looked surprisingly fresh, despite the fact they had just completed 12 rounds of action that would have worn most other fighters out.

Arguello missed a long left to the body and took a right to the head in return. He planted his feet and threw punches with everything inside him.

"I was looking for the knockout with every punch I threw," he told me at lunch in 1980, adding, "It was one of the few times I ever went out looking for an ending to the fight with every punch I threw. I didn't believe I'd be able to win a decision, so I came out blazing."

It didn't take long. Just 13 seconds into the round, Arguello threw a "text-book hook"—short, quick, and with perfect leverage and snap. It exploded off the right side of Olivares's jaw. The champion crashed to the canvas on his back. He rolled over almost immediately on all fours. Then he spit out his mouthpiece. He did so to buy himself more time.

Olivares struggled to his feet on unsteady legs at referee Dick Young's count of "eight." His spit-out mouthpiece then bought him a few more seconds, as ref Young bent over, picked it up, and placed it back in Olivares's mouth. He did so with ungloved hands and without rinsing it off, two procedures you will not see anywhere in today's boxing world; however, Olivares needed more than a few seconds.

On two good legs, a fighter was still overmatched against Arguello. On two unsteady legs, the situation was basically hopeless. For 12 rounds, Olivares had given perhaps the best effort of his brilliant career. But that brilliant effort came against a man who time would prove to be a great fighter, a man who always seemed to have something extra, a man the world came to know as "The Explosive Thin Man." Alexis Arguello had come into Olivares's backyard to take the title, and now victory was a punch away.

That punch was a right uppercut to the jaw. After the earlier knockdown, Olivares dove right back into action. He was a proud warrior, too proud to hold on and certainly too proud to run. If ever the expression "He went down with guns blazing" was true, it was now. For almost 30 seconds, Olivares blasted away with both hands. Arguello was glad to oblige him. He planted his feet and launched punches with everything he had inside of him. Then came that right uppercut.

Olivares fell facedown, then rolled onto his back at the ref's count of "two." He rolled back to his stomach and began to push himself onto his knees as the count hit "six."

It was taking all his remaining energy to rise from this knockdown. He had given all he had to give for 12 rounds and had nothing left to call upon. The initial knockdown, and now this one, had drained him.

"I heard the referee counting, but my legs just wouldn't work," Olivares told me when I spoke with him at the International Boxing Hall of Fame in June 2012.

"I lost my title in a great fight to a great fighter. I lost to a legend," said Olivares.

As the ref yelled "10," Olivares was on his feet but not ready to fight. The ref waved his hands and it was over. Alexis Arguello was finally a champion.

A few days later, after a quick trip home to Nicaragua to meet with President Somoza and accept the adulation of his countrymen, Arguello flew to New York City for a meet and greet luncheon at Gallagher's Steakhouse with internationally renowned boxing writers. The veterans were all there: Dave Anderson, Reg Gutteridge, Barney Nagler, Red Smith, Phil Pepe, Michael Katz, Budd Schulberg, Ed Schuyler, Nat Loubet, Bob Waters, Pat Putnam, and Dick Young represented almost every major newspaper and media outlet there was. Former-light-heavyweight-champ-turned-journalist Jose Torres was there, too. Four of them—Budd Schulberg, Dave Anderson, Red Smith, and Michael Katz—are now in the International Boxing Hall of Fame. And there I was. Me. Pre-*Ring*, pre-ESPN, pre-commissioner me.

I had convinced my cheapskate boss, Stanley Weston, to allow me to go to the meet and greet. Usually, when I went to a boxing press conference, it was against ol' Stanley's wishes. What I would do was make up a story about having an appointment with a doctor or dentist. But in the few weeks prior to the Arguello meet and greet, I had gone to several "doctor and dentist appointments." Another one just wasn't going to fly. So, I had to tell Weston my intentions.

"I'd like to go meet the new featherweight champion," I said.

"Oh, the guy who just beat Olivares?" he asked.

"Yes, his name is Alexis Arguello," I told him.

"How would he do against Willie Pep?" Weston asked. "Against Sandy Saddler? Against Henry Armstrong?"

"I think he'd give 'em all a good fight," I replied. "But that's only from what I've heard. I have never seen him fight. But from what I've heard, I know I want to meet him."

"Let me tell you how he'd do against Pep, Saddler, and Armstrong," Weston replied in his sarcastic, know-it-all demeanor. "He'd lose to each one of them. Armstrong would outpunch him, Pep would outbox him, and Saddler would totally outclass him." He continued, "You think everybody around today is great. Nobody around today could even be a sparring partner for the fighters of 30 years ago. That includes your great Alexis Arguello." Then he said, "But if you feel you have to meet him, you can go. Just make sure all your stories are in on time." That's all I had to hear. I was off to New York City to meet a future legend.

I got to the famed steak house at the same time Arguello's limousine was pulling up. Although I had probably known more about boxing than most—if not all—of the writers who were going to be at the meet and greet, I would not have known what Arguello looked like had I not seen the photos sent to the magazine by our West Coast photographer immediately after the fight. When he stepped out of the limo, I recognized him right away.

It was late November, and the temperature in New York City was in the upper 40s—a far cry from what the temperature was in Arguello's home in Managua. Our eyes locked as he stepped out. I smiled at him respectfully. He smiled back.

"*Campeon,*" I said. "*Es frio, no?*"

He was thrilled to hear Spanish being spoken to him. He fired off a volley of words at me. I shrugged and shook my head.

"*Poquito Espanol,*" I said. "*Muy poquito.*"

He laughed and put his right arm around my shoulders.

"Is no problem," he said. "You are the first friend I have in New York. You teach me English. I teach you Espanol." His English was a lot better than my Spanish.

"*Bueno,*" I said. "*Muy bueno.*" We both laughed.

He asked me my name. I said "Randy." He repeated it perfectly. Then he said, "I am Alexis." He extended his right hand. We officially greeted one another. Then he opened the door to the steak house and said, "You go, my friend." I thanked him but shook my head.

"Champions first," I said. He smiled, then stepped inside. As I followed him, I saw writers I knew from seeing them at ringside and/or their pictures attached to their columns. On my left stood Bob Waters, my favorite boxing writer. He wrote for *Newsday*, the large, daily newspaper on Long Island. Next to him was *New York Daily News* columnist Dick Young. Hanging up their coats next to them was the vaunted trio from the *New York Times*—Red Smith, Dave Anderson, and Michael Katz. Syndicated columnists Barney Nagler and Jerry Izenberg chatted nearby.

In 1974, there was no cable television. No texting. There was no internet. There was no Facebook, Twitter, or Instagram. Boxing fans got their information from newspapers and magazines. These were the guys who brought fans the information New York was still a major fight town and these guys were the heavyweight writers.

When a publicist introduced Arguello to the assembled media, it was mentioned that he was learning English and would now do his best to say a few words to them. The new featherweight champion then stood up. A microphone was in his hands. A translator was at his side.

"I want to thank you all for coming," he said with unexpected sharpness and clarity for a man who was learning to speak English.

"My name is Alexis Arguello, and I be the new featherweight champion. I like the way that sounds. The new featherweight champion." He laughed at his humor.

The crowd of media laughed even louder. Arguello looked around the room and smiled that warm smile of his. The hardened, grizzled boxing writers smiled right back. They loved him from the start.

Then, Arguello said, "I am so happy to be here and meet new friends. . . ." He pointed to me and continued, "Like my new friend, Randy." Everyone in the room turned to look at me. Nobody knew who I was. But there was Arguello, telling everyone I was his new friend. Later, many of the writers came over to introduce themselves.

The meet and greet had gone on longer than I had figured. There would be no running out, no jumping on a train back to Long Island and getting back to work, where Stanley Weston had told me he expected me to be before 5:00.

"Go to the press conference, say hello to the new champion, then get back in here!" were his exact words.

There was no way I could run out on my new friend, Alexis. So I waited until all the writers were through doing their interviews, some one-on-one chats. When they were finished, I walked up to Alexis.

He put his left hand on my shoulder and said, "Randy, my friend. Thank you for coming here today. I hope to see you soon." Few people ever mean that when they say it. Alexis Arguello meant it, as I found out during the next 35 years.

Then, in broken English, he said, "My best [he meant favorite] expression is, '*Vaya con Dios*.' It means for God to go with you."

I asked him to repeat the expression. He did. Then I repeated it. Flawlessly.

"Very good," said Arguello. "Until the next time we meet." He clasped my right hand with both of his. Then he bowed. I bowed right back.

"Vaya con Dios," I said to him.

"And to you, too," he replied. "Vaya con Dios."

I smiled as I walked away. I smiled on the train ride home, despite thinking Stanley Weston was going to be furious with me in the morning.

I was still smiling when I walked into the office the next morning. I was there before the boss. When he walked in, he wasn't smiling. He put his coat in his office and strolled into the outer office where I sat at my typewriter (remember, no computers then!). In front of the five other writers he said, "So, how was it meeting the legendary Alexis Whateverhisnameis?"

"It was real nice," I said. "I think he's going to be a great champion."

"Remember what I said," Weston replied. "Armstrong, Saddler, and Pep. Those were featherweight champions. By next year, your Flaco Explosivo, or whatever you call him, will be an ex-champion and nobody but you will remember this guy."

"You'll see, Mr. Weston," I replied. "He's gonna be great."

"You don't know what great is! There will never be another Armstrong, Pep or Saddler," he said. "Remember that! Now get to work." He looked around the office.

"All of you!" he shouted.

I smiled at him. He tried not to show it, but he was holding back a smile, too. In me, he saw himself in his 20s, a young man with a dream of the future and a passion for boxing. He had known Armstrong, Pep, and Saddler when they were champions. I didn't meet any of them until their final years. Weston knew I was every bit as excited to meet Arguello as he was when he first met Armstrong, Pep, and Saddler. He didn't know what went on at the meet and greet, but he didn't need to know, nor did I have to tell him. He could see it in my eyes. He knew and respected my feelings but couldn't tell me so. His allowing me to go to the press outing, along with his ever-so-slight smile gave him away, though. That's who he was.

During the next five years, I went to almost every boxing match in the New York/New Jersey/Philadelphia area. Weston didn't care what we did at night, as long as we were in the office, earning our $15,000 salaries, in the daytime. Rarely did he allow any of us to go to press conferences, which were held at noon and generally meant taking the day off.

There was one fighter, however, Weston always allowed me to take off for: Alexis Arguello. He knew what Arguello meant to me. As always, however, he couldn't bring himself to say it.

Somehow, however, in the next five years, as Arguello defended the featherweight title, then moved up to win the junior lightweight title and defend it, then moved up to win the lightweight title, I had a feeling my boss was ready to tag a fourth name onto his trio of legendary fighters.

That name was Alexis Arguello.

El Flaco Explosivo.

4

THE RING

It was Monday, December 3, 1979. I had gotten into the office early, partly because of the amount of work I had in front of me, partly from excitement.

The excitement was left over from three nights earlier, when a new king of the welterweights was crowned. The amount of work was because of that coronation. The crown, of not only the welterweight division, but also perhaps the entire sport, was now on the head of the heir apparent to Muhammad Ali. Sugar Ray Leonard was the newly crowned "Prince of Pugilism."

Cover stories had to be written. Photo shoots with the charismatic new champion had to be set up. Story angles had to be conceived ("The One Man Sugar Ray Leonard Must Not Fight" and "Roberto Duran Wants 147 Pounds of Sugar" were two I came up with right away).

In my office at *The Ring*—one-half block from Madison Square Garden at 120 W. 31st Street—I pored over photos of Sugar Ray Leonard. There were poses. Head shots. Tight face shots. Black and whites. Color shots. There must have been 200 overall.

As I was looking at a possible cover shot of Leonard, I heard a commotion in the hall. Spanish was being spoken. Fast Spanish. Two of the voices belonged to *Ring* staffers Jenny and Nancy, who worked in our supply room, where back issues of *Ring Magazine* were kept, along with *Ring* T-shirts, *Ring* hats, *Ring* sweatshirts, and the *Ring Record Book* (where was the internet when I needed it!!!).

Jenny and Nancy were both in their early 20s. Both were attractive. Both were Puerto Rican. They were standing near the elevator when it opened, allowing its two occupants—Gregorio Benitez and his son, Wilfred—to get off.

Wilfred was the reason I was looking at photos of Sugar Ray Leonard. It was Wilfred whom Leonard had beaten three nights earlier in Las Vegas, Nevada. Leonard had stopped him in the 15th round to claim the World Boxing Council welterweight championship. The Benitezes had flown to New York on Sunday but missed the last flight to Puerto Rico. So, they decided to stay at the Penta Hotel across from Madison Square Garden, visit our office on Monday morning, and take an early afternoon flight to Puerto Rico.

When they stepped off the elevator, they ran right into the two Puerto Rican lovelies. Although there were only four of them, it sounded like the Puerto Rican Day Parade was taking place outside my door.

I got up from my desk and walked to my office door. Two offices over, Bert Sugar was doing the same thing. We stepped into the hall at the same time. Both of us were about to tell Jenny and Nancy to keep it down. Then we saw who they were talking to.

Wilfred was just 21 years old and an idol in Puerto Rico. Three and a half years earlier, Benitez became the youngest champion in boxing history, when—at 17½—he won a split decision against the legendary Antonio Cervantes for the junior welterweight championship. In January 1979, he became welterweight champion at the age of 20, when he defeated Carlos Palomino. Two months later, he made his first successful defense of the title, winning a decision against Harold Weston Jr.

As talks grew about a mega-dollar defense against the fast-rising Leonard, Papa Gregorio made a decision. He decided to keep his son on the sidelines. He was an inveterate gambler at racetracks, and he knew a match against Leonard would pay them at least $1 million. He didn't want to risk losing to a top contender for less. Thus, the decision he made was to keep Wilfred inactive until the fight against Leonard materialized. So, after the bout against Weston in March 1979, Wilfred trained but didn't fight. Meanwhile, Leonard fought. And fought. And fought. In 1979, Sugar Ray took on—and beat—tough, talented fighters. Names like Johnny Gant, Fernand Marcotte, Daniel Gonzalez, Adolfo Viruet, Marcos Geraldo, Tony Chiaverini, Pete Ranzany, and Andy Price gave Leonard the work and experience he would need to beat the gifted but inactive Benitez on November 30.

Bert and I greeted the Benitezes, and we spoke in the hall for a few minutes. Then Bert invited them into his office.

"We'd love to stay," said Papa Gregorio, "but we have a plane to catch. We just came to say hello." Then he asked, "Is there any chance we can get a *Ring* T-shirt and maybe a *Ring* hat? We'll show them off proudly!"

"Sure!" exclaimed Bert. "They run a little small, so why don't you try a few on." Then he added, "Wilfred, when you find one that fits you, come back here so we can get a photo of you, Nancy, and Jenny wearing *Ring* shirts." With that, Gregorio, Wilfred, Nancy, and Jenny took off for the back to "shop." Little did we know how much shopping Gregorio would do.

A few moments later, Wilfred came back wearing a *Ring* shirt. Nancy and Jenny also donned *Ring* shirts. Our in-house photographers, Jackie Goodman and Shelton Minor, took them both into the art department, placed them in front of the "photo wall"—a pale blue wall where they took poses and head shots—and began snapping away. As they did, Gregorio, who had been holding a folded canvas shopping bag, unfurled the bag. In the time frame of perhaps 10 minutes, he began tossing in *Ring Record Books*, T-shirts, sweatshirts, key rings, hats, and magazines. Two of our stock boys later told us Gregorio had said to them, "Bert said it would be okay if I fill the bag with some *Ring* merchandise." So, they allowed him to do so. They even helped him! When the bag was over-flowing, Papa Benitez headed to the elevator.

"Wilfred, *vamanos!*" we heard Papa Benitez shout to his son as the elevator door slid open.

"*Un momento*, Papa," the former welterweight champion of the world shouted back. "*Un mas photo*. Un mas photo."

Bert and I were still in the art department, watching as Jackie finished taking photos of the young former champ. Neither of us saw Papa Benitez leaving with so much merchandise—until it was too late.

We thanked Wilfred for visiting us and walked him to the elevator. His father was standing nervously in the elevator, holding the door open. The shopping bag was on the floor inside the elevator, out of sight from Bert and me. As we approached the elevator, the elder Benitez tossed a nervous look our way, thanked us for everything, and then pulled Wilfred inside the elevator. The door closed, and they were gone. Within seconds, one of the stock boys who had assisted Papa Benitez in filling his bag headed into the bathroom next to the elevator.

"That was nice of you to let Mr. Benitez take all that merchandise, Bert," said Luis.

Bert and I looked at one another.

"What do you mean, '*all* that merchandise'?" Bert asked Luis in a loud voice.

"He filled up a canvas bag he had," Luis replied.

"Filled it up? What did he fill it up with?" Bert screamed.

"Record books, T-shirts, hats, back issues of *Ring*, new issues of *Ring*, key chains, sweatshirts . . . everything," answered Luis.

"Why did you let him do that?" Bert hollered at Luis. "Why? Tell me why?"

Luis shrugged his shoulders. "He said you told him it would be okay to fill up his bag with as much as he wanted."

Bert pulled the black fedora off of his head with his right hand and slapped it several times off his right thigh, all the while shouting, "THAT SON OF A BITCH! THAT NO GOOD SON OF A BITCH! I'LL KILL HIM! I'M GOING AFTER HIM. AND WHEN I CATCH HIM I WILL KILL HIM!"

I reminded Bert that by the time the painfully slow elevator came back to our floor and took him back down, the Benitezes would probably be back in their hotel—maybe even in a cab.

Suddenly, Bert's eyes opened wide.

"I can still get the son of a bitch!" Bert said. He turned and ran into his office. Next to his desk, he opened the window and leaned out. He looked down five floors to the street. It was perfect timing.

"Here they come, walking out of the building!" said Bert excitedly. Bert pulled his head back inside. He quickly looked to his right, obviously searching for something. He saw nothing. Then he looked to his left.

"AHA!" he roared. He grabbed an old, broken typewriter, which had been on the floor at the side of his desk for the five months I had been at *The Ring* and had probably been there for quite a while before that. Holding it with two hands, he once again leaned out the window.

"What are you doing with that typewriter, Bert?" I shouted at him.

"I'm gonna kill that crook!" he replied. "He just robbed us, now I'm gonna kill him!"

Bert really meant it. He was about to drop the typewriter on Gregorio Benitez's head.

I remember thinking, "If it hits him—or anybody else—it'll definitely kill them!"

"BERT, DON'T!" I screamed at him. "DON'T DO IT!"

I was too far away to jump on Bert and perhaps grab the typewriter. All I could do was open the window I was close to and shout a warning to the Benitezes. Quickly, I lifted the window and leaned out. There were the Benitezes. They were just past the window I was leaning out of and just about under Bert's. As I was about to yell, Bert shouted, "GREGORIO! GREGORIO! UP HERE, YOU CROOK!"

Gregorio and Wilfred looked up. As they did, Bert released the typewriter. I felt my heart racing. Was I about to see a man get his skull crushed? Was Bert about to murder a man? The typewriter plummeted. Bert's skills were as a writer, not as a bombardier, thank heaven. The typewriter slammed into the pavement perhaps six feet behind them. For a moment, they were frozen. Perhaps they realized what that old Remington would have done had it hit them. Then, together, they burst into laughter as Bert shouted, "I SHOULD HAVE HIT YOU, YOU SON OF A BITCH!" He shook his right fist at Gregorio and cursed him out as father and son walked away, laughing.

"*Gracias*, Señor Sugar. *Muchos* gracias!" shouted Gregorio. "I see you soon. Gracias."

"I'll kill him!" Bert continued to say. "I'm not through with him yet."

Bert had come close, but Gregorio escaped Bert's wrath. I breathed a sigh of relief. I could not believe how unbelievably close Bert had come to actually hitting—and perhaps killing—Papa Benitez.

The near-hit did allow the Benitezes to escape back to Puerto Rico with the pilfered merchandise. When their plane landed, Wilfred was met by family members and friends, who took him home.

Gregorio? He had a car service waiting for him. It took him—as well as Wilfred's $1 million purse and some *Ring Magazine* merchandise—to the local racetrack. By the time the last race was run, all Gregorio had to show for his afternoon was some *Ring Magazine* merchandise.

He had gambled away every penny of Wilfred's million-dollar purse.

When Bert Sugar heard the news of Gregorio's losing day at the track, he shook his head and smiled. Then he said, "Now I won't have to kill him. Wilfred will do that for me!"

Although our office was on 120 W. 31st Street, Bert and I spent much of our time planning the next magazine at a pub called O'Reilly's about 100 yards up the road. It was Bert's idea, not mine. It was a great idea. In that pub we held meetings; had parties; and did interviews with such boxing luminaries as Pinklon Thomas, Matthew Saad Muhammad, Randall "Tex" Cobb, Joe Frazier, Hector Camacho, Cus D'Amato, Jim Jacobs, Ray Arcel, Carlos Monzon, Floyd Patterson, and Jose Torres, and countless boxing journalists, including Budd Schulberg, Barney Nagler, Red Smith, Bob Waters, Dick Young, Jack Fiske, Jerry Izenberg, Jimmy Breslin, and Norman Mailer.

Most companies—and bosses—frown on employees drinking while on the job. Bert frowned if I didn't have at least one beer. It was in O'Reilly's Pub where we came up with many of our best story ideas, story lines, and covers. It was there that the idea was born for the greatest *Ring Magazine* cover of all time—the Thomas Hearns "Hitman" cover.

It was August 1980, and Hearns was fresh off his second-round destruction of Pipino Cuevas for the WBA welterweight title. He was 29–0, and on a course for a unification mega-fight against Sugar Ray Leonard. Sitting at a table with our art director, Richard Kubicz, and chief copy editor E. J. Gary, the conversation went like this:

Randy: "We should get Thomas Hearns on the cover. We can put him on as a hit man. It's his nickname. We can have him holding a handgun."

Bert: "Not a handgun. A tommy-gun!"

Randy: "Wearing a black suit."

Bert: "And one of my black fedoras."

Richard: "Perfect! I can see the cover in my head. Perfect!"

E. J.: "But where can we get a tommy-gun?"

We stopped to look at each other. Where, indeed, could we get a machine gun, a tommy-gun? For a moment, there was silence. Just then, I remembered—I had one in my basement.

Randy: "I've got one!"

Bert, E. J.: "You do?"

Randy: "I will bring it in tomorrow."

Bert: "This I have to see! All we need now is Thomas Hearns."

Randy: "I will call Emanuel Steward tonight. I believe he is bringing Hearns into New York City to meet with the media at a luncheon in Gallagher's Steakhouse next week. Maybe we can do a morning shoot before the luncheon."

Bert: "Set it up!"

One phone call to Steward was all it took.

"It will be an honor to have Tommy on the cover of *The Ring*," Steward said. "We'll start as early as you want. Our press luncheon is called for noon."

Hearns did the session in our studio against a light gray backdrop. Our biggest problem was this: getting Hearns to be serious, to look sinister, to look mean. He laughed and joked throughout the photo shoot. As digital cameras were still years away from consumer use, Jack Goodman took the photos with a Canon camera that used film. There was no way he could check any photos without developing the film. As he snapped away, Bert and I kept trying to get Hearns to give us a mean look. We told him, "Hit men holding machine guns sneer and scowl, not smile and laugh." It didn't work. The more he tried, the more he laughed. Dozens of poses and hundreds of pictures were wasted. Finally, as time was growing short before the press luncheon, I said, "Tommy, listen, here's what I want you to think. I want you to think of Sugar Ray Leonard. I want you to picture him standing right in front of you in the fight that will happen down the road." I continued, "I want you to see Leonard. I want you to think about Leonard. I want you to feel his presence. Show me how you are going to look at him. Show me!"

We physically positioned Hearns for the shot. Hearns would hold the tommy-gun in his right hand, his fist tight around the clip pointed up. The back of the gun would be pinned against his chest by his right elbow, and the gun would be pointed up. He was to stare at the camera—at Leonard.

He did what he had to do—for just a moment. Snap the picture! Quick! Then, just as Goodman snapped, Hearns laughed. I held my breath. The PR people with him were getting antsy. They had to get him to the press conference.

"Got it!" Goodman yelled. "I got it! I am sure of that! Nice job, Tommy!" He then took off for the darkroom to develop his pictures.

Hearns continued to smile. Bert and I went to the press conference with him. He smiled all 20 blocks in the limo ride uptown to Gallagher's.

Few of Goodman's photos were usable, at least in the context we needed then. But that last one was the winner. It was more than a winner. To this day, it remains the biggest selling *Ring Magazine* in history, and perhaps the most memorable. About 25 years later, *Ring Magazine* tried to do the same thing with Floyd Mayweather. It didn't have the same impact.

Unfortunately for Hearns, the cover had a negative impact among advertisers. As the cover was so sinister and almost scary, several advertisers either dropped Hearns or changed their mind about using him. Our fantastic cover cost the "Hitman" a great deal of money.

How much money?

"With the accounts Tommy lost, was dropped from, or didn't sign with, I'd say he lost a few hundred thousand," Steward told us soon after the December 1980 "hit man cover" hit the newsstands.

If only those advertisers knew how much Hearns had been laughing his way through the entire photo shoot.

One more thing: The tommy-gun belonged to my three-year-old daughter, Ali. It was a water pistol! I bought two of them so we could have water gun battles in the backyard earlier that summer.

As mentioned in "The Hat," Sugar's partners were Chicago businessman Nick Kladis, New York marketing executive Jim Bukata, and former New York Knicks superstar Dave DeBusschere. Kladis knew about supermarkets. Bukata knew about Marketing. DeBusschere knew about basketball. None of the three knew a thing about publishing. That was left to Sugar.

They should have kept it that way.

Sugar's drinking and cigar smoking was more act than reality. Oh, he smoked those cigars and he did indeed drink, but not as much as he led you to believe. I never saw him smoke cigar after cigar, although he enjoyed carrying an unlit one with him at all times. They were as much a part of his persona as his fedoras. He also knew how to nurse his drinks.

One night, at the cocktail hour at a Boxing Writer's Dinner, a friend said, "I'd better get my drinks now, before Bert Sugar and a bunch of the other writers show up and drink all the booze!" He laughed. But he really believed that was true. I knew it wasn't. So, I decided to count how many drinks Bert had that night.

After a few hours, my friend, who was sitting at the next table, motioned me to come over. I did. He whispered, "Your boss can really put those drinks down." We looked at Bert. He was holding a drink in one hand and a cigar in the other.

"How many drinks do you think he's had?" I asked.

"Fifteen? Maybe 20?" was his reply.

I had been counting, as I realized Bert's drinking and cigar puffing was (pun time!) blown out of proportion.

The drink was not his 15th or 20th. It was still his first! He held it the way he held his unlit cigar. By the end of the evening, many of the writers were blitzed. Not Bert. He had but three drinks—two of which he didn't finish.

Now Dave DeBusschere, he was another story. At *The Ring* holiday party at O'Reilly's in December 1979, DeBusschere showed up. The bartender told me he started—and finished—an entire bottle of scotch himself during the course of the next two hours.

In 1983, DeBusschere, Kladis, and Bukata—who were constantly in run-ins with Sugar—voted to oust "The Hat" and make me the editor in chief, despite the fact *The Ring* was making money.

Several months after Sugar's departure, DeBusschere came to me and asked about our monthly world ratings, which were sponsored by Budweiser. It was a sponsorship set up by Bert.

"How much is Budweiser paying us?" asked DeBusschere.

"They're paying us $12,000 per month," I told him. "I have a meeting with them next week. I am going to suggest they start doing the Budweiser 'Fighter of the Month' for another $8,000 per month. I am certain they will be up for it."

"I'll go in your place, Randy," he said. "I'll get them to pay $25,000 for both the ratings and the 'Fighter of the Month.'"

I shook my head.

"I have already had preliminary talks with them," I said. "They will not go for paying more than double what they pay now. They will go for $20,000. They won't go for $25,000. Believe me."

DeBusschere waved his hands as if to tell me I didn't know what I was talking about. "They'll pay whatever I ask them to pay," said DeBusschere. "I may ask for even more, and give them even more."

"Like what?" I questioned.

DeBusschere shrugged.

"I'll figure it out," he said. If he played basketball the way he attempted to make money for *The Ring*, he would have never made it to the NBA.

At lunch with a few executives of Budweiser, I heard later that he became loud and abusive, especially to a few fans who had requested his autograph. Then, when he *insisted* Budweiser pay *The Ring* $30,000 per month but couldn't tell them what they'd be getting in return for their money, they refused. DeBusschere killed the deal when he said, "If you don't pay us the $30,000, I am going to Coors! They'll be happy to work with us!"

Budweiser's answer to DeBusschere: "Go to Coors!" Their meeting was over. So was their sponsorship of the ratings.

Of course, DeBusschere didn't have Coors—or any other beer company—lined up. We had just lost our biggest advertiser. Despite the fact that DeBusschere's New York Knicks number 22 hung from the rafters in Madison Square Garden, it was DeBusschere himself who should have been hanging there.

In mid-October 1984, DeBusschere and Jim Bukata came into the office. They were there to let several people go. One of those people was Nigel Collins, whom I had hired a few years earlier to run *Boxing Illustrated*, one of the Ring Publishing Co.'s other boxing magazines.

I was in Atlantic City, doing commentary on a USA Network fight, as well as taking photos and doing an interview with Donald Trump (yes, *that* Donald Trump!) for the next month's magazine. When Collins was told he was being released, he threw me under the bus.

"He said, 'Why me? Randy is the one who's never here. He is out today, in Atlantic City doing one of his many TV gigs. He was out two days last week, too,'" according to Nat Loubet, the former publisher who was brought on as a consultant during the transition, which he said did not originally include me. The two days I was out the previous week weren't because of any "TV gigs"—I was out because of the birth of my daughter, Greer.

Conveniently—and wisely—Collins took that day off. To his credit, he steered *The Ring* as its editor for almost 20 years. In June 2015, he was inducted into the International Boxing Hall of Fame, alongside former *Ring Magazine* publishers Nat Fleischer, Bert Sugar, and even Stanley Weston, who purchased the old magazine in 1990, fulfilling his lifetime dream of being its owner.

I went to work as a boxing analyst for both the USA Network and the Madison Square Garden Network and was still at both positions in 1988, when the second most important phone call of my life—the first being from Bert Sugar nine years earlier—came. It was a call that saw me hang up my headset for several years and replace it with a badge. My New York vanity plates then went from THE RING and MSGBOXNG to NYSAC 1.

I was about to become Commissioner Gordon.

5

A CHOICE TO MAKE

With Al Bernstein going on vacation in the middle of October, ESPN had given me his assignments. That meant I'd be calling Top Rank Boxing shows every week, from September 16 through the end of October, with the exception of the September 23 show from Las Vegas. For me, being given the opportunity to call five straight ESPN shows and six of seven was a dream come true.

On September 16, working alongside Sal Marchiano from the Sands Hotel in Atlantic City, I called two ESPN title bouts. One bout was between unbeaten heavyweights James "Broadaxe" Broad and Randy Mack for the ESPN heavyweight championship. The other was between Robert Sawyer and Dick Eklund for the ESPN welterweight championship.

Sal picked me up as usual on 81st Street and Central Park West at 1:30. During the two-and-a-half-hour ride to Atlantic City down Garden State Parkway, Sal and I spent a lot of time talking about this date being the first anniversary of the Sugar Ray Leonard–Thomas Hearns classic in Las Vegas, of our memorable time at the fight, of our flight on the red-eye to Philadelphia, and of being presented No-Doz on the air by the main-event winner that night, Teddy Mann.

On the ride down, I said to Sal, "You know, I've been with ESPN almost two years, and I've never had anybody critique my work. The only person who has ever said anything to me was Bill Fitts (then the executive producer), who told me that you and I should try not to stray away from the action as we sometimes tend to do." I added, "Aside from that, he said I was doing a fine job. But that was about three months ago. I haven't heard anything since."

Sal smiled and shrugged his shoulders.

"Listen," he said. "You're working another show this month and all of October's shows, right?"

"Right," I replied.

"And I understand you're talking more money with them, right?"

"Right, again." I said.

"Then don't worry," Sal said. "I'm sure if ESPN was unhappy with you they would have let you know a long time ago. I'm also sure I would have heard something if they were unhappy with your work. Listen, if they want us to stick to the action, then stick to the action we will!"

That night, it was easy staying with the action because there was plenty of it. Broad captured the ESPN heavyweight crown with an eighth-round TKO of Mack, while Sawyer took the ESPN welterweight crown with a 12-round unanimous decision.

As Marchiano was signing off at the end of the evening, I thought what a great show it had been, of how Sal and I mixed very well, how we played off one another, how we stuck with the action, and that all shows should go as smooth and easy as this one. In my wildest dreams I never thought this would be the last ESPN show I would ever work with Sal.

As I sat in my den the following week and watched Marchiano and Bernstein from Las Vegas, I did my homework for the next show, the first of five successive weeks I'd be on ESPN. Next week's show would originate from on board the aircraft carrier USS *Yorktown*, which saw more than one year of hard combat in the South Pacific during World War II. The USS *Yorktown* was a floating museum, docked in the harbor in Charleston, South Carolina.

As I watched the bouts on ESPN, I prepared my notes. The main event featured budding star Robin Blake and his 12–0 record against Carlos Santana in a lightweight 10-rounder. Included in the seven other bouts was an eight-round contest between "Irish" Billy Collins Jr., a 9–0 junior middleweight out of Nashville, Tennessee, and Bennie Miller, of Savannah, Georgia. Both Blake and Collins had become regulars on ESPN and were attracting a large and faithful following.

To Bert Sugar's displeasure, I took the day off from *The Ring*. An early morning flight got me to Charleston just in time for the weigh-in, which was held in the century-old but charming hotel in which I was staying.

At the weigh-in I glanced at the bout sheet and noticed that Billy Collins's opponent was Rahim Tayib, not Bennie Miller, as was originally told to me. I stared at the name.

Rahim Tayib. I never saw the name before, despite the fact I read through hundreds of fight reports daily. I wondered why I had never heard of Tayib. A few minutes later, I found out why.

I walked around the room and spoke with each boxer, gathering bio information on the ones I had never interviewed before. After talking to several boxers, I came upon an African American boxer, sitting by himself in a corner.

"Good morning, I'm Randy Gordon of ESPN," I said. "Mind if I talk to you and get some bio information?"

"No, I don't mind," said the boxer.

Embarrassed that I didn't know who he was, I did what I always do when I'm not sure what a boxer's name is: I asked him, "Who are you boxing tonight?"

"I'm fighting him," said the boxer, pointing across the room. I turned and looked. He was pointing to Billy Collins. I whirled around. *This* was Rahim Tayib, the boxer I didn't know, the name I had never seen before. For a few seconds, I stared at him. Split-second flashbacks raced through my mind.

"Do I know you from somewhere?" I asked him. "Have we ever met before?"

"I don't think so," said Tayib.

I proceeded with the interview. As I did, scenes of Tayib in a ring flashed before my eyes. Each scene lasted a millisecond. As he talked, I jotted down his remarks; however, I wasn't listening to him. I was concentrating on his face. I knew his face. I just couldn't remember how I knew him or from where.

When I asked who would be working his corner, he pointed to a large, rotund man with glasses. My brow creased. I recognized his cornerman, too. I recalled seeing him only recently. More visions sped through my mind.

"Cooney," I said to myself. "It's Cooney, or Rooney, or something like that."

Turning to Tayib, I asked, "What's his name?"

"Mooney," said Tayib. "Joe Mooney."

More creases furrowed my brow. Then, *bingo!* I spun around and looked at Mooney. Then I turned back to Tayib. More pictures flashed into my mind. This time, the pictures stayed there. Now, in my head was Tayib, trying to escape from a hard-hitting opponent. There was Tayib, getting hit and going down. He's up. He's groggy. The ref is stopping it. I turned to look at Mooney again. Then, I turned back to the boxer.

"You're Eddie Flanning, the guy who lost to Jose Baret six nights ago in the Felt Forum at Madison Square Garden, aren't you?" I asked.

Looking like the kid caught with his hands in the cookie jar, the boxer began stuttering.

"I, uh, that was, uh, that wasn't me against Baret."

"It wasn't?" I asked, half in disbelief, half in surprise.

"No, it wasn't me," he said. "It was my twin brother, Eddie. I'm, uh, Anthony Flanning."

"Anthony Flanning?" I asked with surprise. "I thought you were Rahim Tayib."

"I, uh, I am. Rahim Tayib is my Muslim name. But Eddie Flanning is my, my uh, my brother."

I just looked at him with my mouth hanging open in disbelief.

"That was your twin brother?" I asked him.

He nodded.

"That's really something!" I exclaimed.

"What is?" he asked.

"The fact that your twin brother has a scar above his right eye in the same exact spot you do!" I said, pointing to his scar. "Are you guys twins, or are you clones?"

He stared at me with his mouth open, knowing he had just been caught cold. Yet, he continued to deny that the boxer in New York was him.

"I'm telling you," he insisted, "that the guy who lost in New York was Eddie Flanning. I'm Anthony Flanning. Honest!"

"Listen, I know it was you," I told him. Still, he continued to insist that he was Anthony Flanning and the boxer I saw lose six days earlier was his identical twin, Eddie.

At this point, I began to get irritated.

"Okay, I'm not sure if you're Eddie or Anthony or Rahim," I said. "But I do know that you're the same guy I saw fight six nights ago in the Felt Forum."

He started to speak, but I cut him off.

"Listen to me. You are under suspension in New York," I told him. "That means you're also under suspension all over the country. My guess is that the New York suspension is probably for 45 days. Take the suspension," I urged. "If you don't, if you decide to box here tonight, you'll most likely be facing a suspension of around six months or more all over the country. My advice to you is not to box tonight."

My words fell on deaf ears.

"I'm tellin' you," said the boxer, "that was my brother in New York."

I shook my head slowly.

"Have it your way," I told him. "Right now, you're facing only 39 more days of suspension. After you box tonight, you're gonna face a lot more than 39 days. Oh well. It's your problem, not mine."

Little did I know just whose problem it really was!

The kettle was boiling, and I was too naive and inexperienced to stay away from it.

I'm a journalist and this is a story, I thought. *I've uncovered something, and I'm going to follow up.*

The first thing I did was to alert my ESPN sidekick that night, Sam Rosen. Sam was doing his own interviewing of boxers at the weigh-in, and he had been ringside six nights before when Flanning had been drilled in the second round against hard-hitting Garden prospect Jose Baret.

The Garden was high on Baret's title chances and nicknamed him Jose "The Threat" Baret. Not nearly as optimistic on Baret's chances of becoming welterweight king as those at MSG Boxing, I nicknamed him Jose "Not Yet" Baret, a name that greatly displeased John F. X. Condon, vice president of MSG Boxing.

When I asked Rosen if Tayib looked familiar, he said, "Sure, he looks just like the guy who was knocked out a few nights ago by Jose Baret in the Felt Forum."

"He is the same guy," I told Rosen.

"Are you sure?" he asked.

"I'm sure, Sam," I said with conviction. "I don't know what's up with the different name, but I know that Eddie Flanning and Rahim Tayib are one and the same guy. This guy knows that Eddie Flanning is under suspension in New York, which means suspension all over the country." I continued, "A suspension in one state is recognized by all states. He wants to fight tonight, so he is fighting under an assumed name. When I pressed him, he claimed that Eddie Flanning is his twin brother."

"Wow!" exclaimed Sam. "Does anybody know this?"

"Not yet, they don't," I replied. "But I'm about to tell Top Rank and Jed [Drake, the ESPN producer]."

Drake was with us at the weigh-in, getting sound bites from Robin Blake and Carlos Santana. I went over to Drake and informed him of my discovery. He told me I should definitely mention it to Akbar Muhammad, Top Rank's executive vice president.

Muhammad showed shock and a real concern when I mentioned what I had uncovered. He told me to follow him. He was going to call Teddy Brenner, who was Top Rank's matchmaker. Standing next to him, I heard Muhammad's end of the conversation.

"Teddy, listen," said Muhammad. "Randy Gordon said that the guy who is boxing Billy Collins tonight was knocked out six nights ago in New York and is under suspension . . . uh, he fought, uh, Jose Baret in the Felt Forum and was stopped in the second round. Yeah, I know this is a different guy." Muhammad went on, "Well, Gordon insists this is not a different guy. Gordon claims his name is Ed Flanning and that Flanning and this guy, Rahim Tayib, are the same person. He says the fighter is under suspension and is not allowed to fight tonight. . . . He's right here. I'll put him on." His eyes told me Brenner was not in a good mood.

I swallowed hard, then took the phone from Muhammad. In the past two years, I had ingratiated myself to Brenner, the former matchmaker for Madison Square Garden. We would ride from New York City to Atlantic City via bus and fill the two and a half hours with boxing talk. Brenner is regarded by many as the best matchmaker in boxing history. Perhaps he was. But, in the past few months, I believed the matches he fed to ESPN were noncompetitive and one-sided, unworthy of being shown on the rapidly growing network. My opinions and commentary on a few of those matches had been too honest, open, and embarrassing to him.

On more than one occasion, Brenner had telephoned me the day after an ESPN show to blast me for knocking his (mis)matches. About two months earlier, I had told the television audience that ESPN favorite Kenny "Bang Bang" Bogner, with a 17–1–1 record, should have no trouble disposing of opponent Bobby Alexander, whose 13–9–1 record hid the fact he had won only two of his last 10 matches and been KO'd four times. The day after the Bogner–Alexander bout (which Bogner easily won on a fifth- round TKO after dropping Alexander in the first round and carrying him into the fifth), Brenner called me up at *Ring Magazine* in a rage.

"Where do you come off saying the things you said last night?" yelled Brenner.

"Like what?" I asked him.

"Like what?" he repeated. "Like saying Alexander's got no chin. How do you know he's got no chin?"

"Because it's a fact," I said. "He's got no chin. I know it."

"How do you know it?" Brenner challenged me. "Where do you come off saying a guy has no chin? Where? Huh?"

Boy, did I have an answer for him. Only one week before, I had been working out at Gleason's Gym, one block from my office. Alexander had been working out, too, and asked me if I wanted to spar. I happened to have my equipment with me, so I said yes. The two rounds of sparring we did showed me all I had to see and all I had to know about the 10-year professional veteran.

"I dropped him in sparring last week!" I told the steaming, future Hall of Fame matchmaker.

"You what?" shouted Brenner.

"I dropped him, knocked him down with a short right to the chin. If Alexis Arguello dropped him, then I wouldn't say he had no chin. But I decked him! Me!"

"And that gives you license to put down my matches on television?" growled Brenner.

"I was doing what I thought was right and truthful," I told him.

"Well, it *wasn't* right!" he yelled. "Don't let this kind of thing happen again!" He slammed down the phone.

That was eight weeks earlier. Now, I was about to get on the phone with Brenner again. As I took the phone from Muhammad, I thought, *How can Teddy be mad at me? Ed Flanning/Rahim Tayib is under suspension. Teddy will understand. I'm sure he will.*

I was never as wrong in believing anything in my life as I was with that thought.

"What the hell are you doing?" asked Brenner. He wasn't yelling, but he was angry.

"Rahim Tayib, the guy we got in with Billy Collins, is really Eddie Flanning," I told Brenner. "He was knocked out in the Felt Forum six nights ago by Jose Baret."

"So?" Brenner responded. At that point, I knew there was going to be trouble.

"Teddy!" I pleaded. "This guy is under . . ."

He cut me off.

"This guy is under nothing! It's probably not even the same boxer you think you saw in the Felt Forum."

"I know I saw him," I responded to Brenner. "Rahim Tayib and Eddie Flanning are one and the same person. He's under suspension and cannot fight."

"Who died and left you boss?" Brenner angrily asked me.

"Nobody," I replied. "It's just that he's suspended and can't fight tonight."

"And what if he does fight tonight?" Brenner asked me.

"If he fights, I'll mention it," I told Brenner. "I'll tell everybody he's fighting while under suspension."

"If you do, you're gone," he said. "You'll be through on ESPN!"

BOOM! That remark did it. Brenner had just set me off. He pushed my explode button.

"I don't work for Top Rank," I told him. "I don't work for you. I work for ESPN. The way I see it, you've got one of three choices. One: You kill the fight. Two: You sit Flanning down and come up with a last-minute substitute. Or three: You let the fight go on. But I'm telling you, if Flanning fights, I'm going to say something on ESPN."

I showed up at ringside at 6:30, 90 minutes before the opening bell for an undercard bout that would not be shown on ESPN. It wasn't long before Akbar Muhammad came over and sat down next to me. He put a hand on my shoulder and said, "Randy, we tried to get an opponent to replace Rahim Tayib today." I listened intently. He continued.

"We didn't have any luck." He sighed and shrugged his shoulders. "What we're gonna do is have Tayib go through with the fight and have the referee watch the situation very carefully. We're going on the belief that Tayib is the same guy you saw lose in New York."

"He *is* the same guy, Akbar," I said. "He is. Believe me."

With a reassuring pat on the hand, Akbar said, "We do believe you. I spoke to the referee. He'll be on top of things all the way. At the first sign of trouble, he'll stop the fight. He won't let Tayib get hurt. Trust me."

I looked Akbar in the eyes, shaking my head in disbelief. Despite the knowledge that Rahim Tayib was really Eddie Flanning and under suspension, Top Rank turned its promotional head and looked the other way.

"Akbar, you're doing the wrong thing," I said.

"Randy, as a friend, I'm asking you not to talk about this on the air. Please?"

"Akbar!" I said, raising my voice. I couldn't believe my ears. Not only was the fight going to be held, Top Rank was now asking me not to mention what I knew about Flanning/Tayib on the air.

"I can't hide the fact that Tayib was stopped last week in New York," I said. "Do you know how many top writers were at that bout? Every big gun in the New York area was there." I declared, "Every one of them will be watching tonight. Would the editor in chief of *The Ring* not remember a guy who fought in the main event of a fight he was ringside for just six nights earlier? Forget it. I have to mention it. I *will* mention it."

"They'll never suspect a thing," said Akbar. "I'll be willing to bet not one of them recognizes him. If you don't say anything, nobody will ever know. And if you do mention it, are you going to get an Emmy Award or a trophy or national acclaim for being a top reporter?" he asked. "Will mentioning this get you an appearance on *Nightline*? I don't think so. If you do mention it, all that will do is hurt Top Rank. That'll hurt me. Do you want to hurt me?"

"I don't want to hurt anybody, Akbar," I said. "But if I don't mention it, I'm the one who's gonna get hurt. If you scratch Flanning from the card, neither of us will get hurt. Please, Akbar. Do the right thing."

He shook his head slowly, shrugging his shoulders as he did.

"I can't, Rand. I just can't. It's too late to kill the fight or to make a change. I've gotta keep everything just the way it is now."

I looked Akbar straight in his eyes.

"You've gotta do what you've gotta do," I said. "I understand that. And you've gotta understand that I've gotta do what I've gotta do."

This was the toughest decision I ever had to make in my business life.

He lowered his eyes and nodded his head. He knew that what was to follow would not be fun.

The preliminary bouts were over. In the ring was unbeaten junior middle-weight Billy Collins Jr. and Eddie Flanning/Rahim Tayib. The cameras were ready. Our microphones were hot (television jargon meaning they were "on"). With ESPN in a commercial, Rosen and I waited for a cue from the control truck to begin announcing. I glanced at Akbar, who was sitting with us at ringside, two seats to our left. He folded his hands as if in prayer and beggingly mouthed the word, "Please?" It was his final plea for me not to mention Flanning/Tayib's loss in New York six nights earlier and subsequent mandatory medical suspension. Then, in our headsets, came the voice of the producer, Jed Drake.

"Stand by, guys. Ten seconds to you, Sam. Stand by . . . and 3, 2, 1 . . . GO SAM!"

"We're back live aboard the aircraft carrier USS *Yorktown*," announced Rosen in his unmistakable, booming voice, "docked in the harbor here in Charleston, South Carolina. For the introduction of our next bout, let's go up to ring announcer George Myers."

Myers introduced Tayib, then Collins. Then, Rosen took over.

"Irish Billy Collins, nine and oh," said Rosen. He then followed with a slower, more deliberate, "and Ra/HEEM Tah/EEB, from Savannah, Georgia."

"Or, whatever his name is," I said, looking at a wincing, cringing, Akbar Muhammad as I delivered the words.

"Well, there is a question, Randy," said Rosen, "because, I tell you, quite frankly, he looks exactly like a fighter I saw lose Friday night to Jose Baret at the Felt Forum at Madison Square Garden."

Akbar listened intently, wearing a pained expression as he did.

"At the weigh-in today, and everyone should know this," I reported, "the original opponent for Billy Collins—Benny Miller—pulled out when his wife said she'd leave him if he went through with the fight. Ed Flannigan . . ."

"Flanning," said Rosen, correcting me.

"Right, Flanning," I said. "Flanning was contacted to replace Miller. At the weigh-in I said to him, 'Aren't you Eddie Flanning, the guy who just lost six nights ago in the Felt Forum?' He just looked at me and said, 'Uh, uh, no, I'm Rahim Tayib.' In each of his eyes was written L-I-E."

With his elbows on the table in front of him, Akbar put his head in his hands and shook his head over and over. I had just told the world something he, Teddy Brenner, and Top Rank did not want disclosed. I looked at Rosen, then glanced at Akbar. Then I continued.

"I told Flanning, 'If you're lying, all the commissions are going to hear about this. You will be suspended for six months, nine months, maybe more.'"

For the remainder of the round, I did more than mention the issue. I beat it to death. By the time Collins stopped Flanning at 2:21 of the third round, every viewer knew the story of Ed Flanning/Rahim Tayib. Every single viewer. That includes Teddy Brenner.

Driving back to the hotel with Drake and Rosen, we talked about the show and how it had gone. To no one's surprise, the main event was won by Robin Blake on a unanimous decision against teenager Carlos Santana, who was boxing in his 16th bout of the year (fighters generally don't fight more than four or five times a year). The televised portion of the undercard also went very well.

"Nice show, guys," said Drake, who has had a wonderful career with ESPN. He is currently their vice president/executive producer in charge of sports programming. "You guys were hot, even if the main event didn't turn into the 'Fight of the Year.'" Then he added, "As for the Collins–Flanning fight, I thought you both handled the situation real well. You told the viewers what was going on, and nobody can ask for more than that."

It was 11:30 p.m., and we were hungry. After driving around for perhaps 20 minutes and finding nothing open (Charleston is definitely not New York City for staying up late!), we gave up thinking about food and headed back to the hotel.

As I was opening the door to my room, I heard my phone ringing. I hurried in to find friend and boxing manager Shelly Finkel on the other end.

"Hi, Randy, I watched the show tonight," said Finkel.

"Whaddya think, Fink?" I asked him.

"I think you're gonna get in trouble for doing what you did, for saying what you said about Collins's opponent, that's what I think," replied Finkel. "I think this whole thing is gonna blow up in your face. I hope I'm wrong, but I just have a bad feeling about it."

Coming from someone else, those words would not have bothered me. But from Finkel, one of the greatest managers/advisors ever to work in boxing, a wave of nausea came over me.

"Shelly, the guy was under suspension!" I said.

"You don't have to explain that to me," he replied.

You did the right thing. It's not me you have to explain anything to. It's Bob Arum and Teddy Brenner. And I don't think they are going to want to have anything explained! They put on a weekly boxing show for ESPN. They get paid to do so. The show is getting bigger and bigger. Sometimes, fights fall apart at the last minute, and substitutes have to be brought in. Top Rank is building Billy Collins, and they wanted him to fight. They didn't care who he fought, so they brought in a guy from Savannah, Georgia. It just so happened this guy from Savannah, Georgia, was a guy who was knocked out six nights earlier. If you take him off the card, Billy Collins, the kid Top Rank is so high on, doesn't get to fight. So they allowed the fight to go on, despite the fact they knew the facts. How does that make them look in ESPN's eyes? You embarrassed Top Rank. You rubbed their promotional face in it. No, they are not going to be happy!

I went to bed with Finkel's words on my mind: "This whole thing is gonna blow up in your face."

An early morning flight had me back in New York and in my office by 9:30 a.m., a few minutes ahead of Bert. When Bert arrived, I heard him ask Jenny, "Is Randy in yet?" as if punctuality were of great importance to him.

"He's in his office," she replied.

"Hmm, I'm impressed," said Bert. "Real impressed."

He walked into my office. Smoke from his ever-present cigar quickly clouded the room.

"Nice job last night," said Bert. "You certainly didn't pull any punches, did you?"

"You mean about Flanning?" I asked.

"About Flanning, about Rahim Tayib, about that whole situation," Bert said. "Have you had any repercussions about what you said?"

I looked at Bert and shook my head. "Nope. Nothing."

"You will," he said. "Trust me. You will."

"Great," I mumbled.

"Don't worry," he said, taking his cigar from his mouth and waving it through the air. "You did some great reporting last night. That's what counts. That's the bottom line. But as far as hearing from somebody at Top Rank, it's not a question of 'if.' It's a question of 'when.'" He turned and walked out of my office.

As he did, I buried my face in my hands as Bert's words joined with Shelly Finkel's ("This whole thing is gonna blow up in your face") in my mind.

I felt relieved, however, when the day ended without anyone from Top Rank or ESPN calling to reprimand me for my revelation to the viewing audience the night before. I was even more relieved when the days of the following week melted away with still no angry or condemning phone calls from either the promoter or the TV network. On Thursday afternoon, October 7, when I left for Atlantic City, the site of ESPN's next Top Rank Boxing show, I was sure that if anything would have blown up, it would have happened already. I was alone in my thinking, however. Both Finkel and Sugar were still telling me to expect fireworks.

Working with Steve Albert, the Atlantic City show went well. In the main event, Sean Mannion outpointed Rocky Fratto more than 10 rounds in a spirited junior middleweight bout, and Terrence Alli, appearing on ESPN for the second time, fought to an eighth-round draw against Thomas Baker. In the next nine years, Alli would appear on ESPN more than any other boxer. After the show, ESPN's producer, director, two of the cameramen, Albert, and myself went with Akbar to a nightclub in Atlantic City. There, we partied until 2:00 a.m.

The following week, I was back with Steve Albert, this time from Indianapolis, where former WBA light heavyweight champion Marvin Johnson was to face cross-town rival Alvino Manson. The hard-hitting Manson was fresh off a knockout victory in the finals of the light heavyweight division in ESPN's first tournament.

Albert was to pick me up in his car at 11:30 a.m. in front of my office at *Ring Magazine*, and together we'd head to the airport. At 11:15, I was sitting at my desk, editing copy, when Jenny informed me that there was a phone call for me.

"It's Bill Fitts from ESPN," she said.

"Fitts?" I repeated. "Bill Fitts?"

"That's right," she said. "From ESPN."

A nauseous feeling came over me. Having a root canal was less painful than getting a phone call from the usually nonpersonable executive producer of ESPN Sports, who many of us called "Wild Bill." I looked at the telephone, took a deep breath, and picked it up. My root canal was about to start. Without novocaine!

"Good morning, Bill," I answered.

Never known to be a warm individual, Fitts immediately began on a cold note. "Yeh, Randy, look," he said. "I've done some thinking, and I've got some bad news for you."

"Bad news?" I asked.

"Yeh, it's like this. After this month, I'm taking you off the air. You'll do tonight's show, next week's show in Las Vegas, and the 28th show in Atlantic City."

"Why, Bill?" I asked. "What's the reason for this? Everybody I've spoken to at ESPN has told me my work is fine. My producers have all been commending me after the shows on my work. Even you said I'm doing fine. Why are you taking me off the air?"

Upset at my prying question, he got angry and responded that it was because I was inconsistent.

"What do you mean I'm inconsistent?" I asked.

Fitts refused to give any further details, just telling me that he was the boss and that I was off the air. With that, Fitts hung up the phone.

I sat stunned and frozen, staring at the phone's receiver in my left hand. Was I dreaming? Did ESPN's executive producer just fire me?

Two weeks earlier, I had a choice to make. In life, we all have choices to make. My choice two weeks earlier was between my journalistic principles and making the promoter happy. It was a choice between right and wrong. Nothing more, nothing less. Had I said nothing, chances are no one would have ever known Rahim Tayib was really Ed Flanning, a fighter under suspension. It was a choice to make. Teddy Brenner had said that if I did what I believed to be the right thing—revealing Tayib's identity—I'd be "gone from ESPN." I weighed my options and I weighed the story. I was so against fighters getting stopped in one state, then moving on to fight in another state while under suspension. It was something I would attack years later, after I became head of the New York State Athletic Commission. I had a choice to make, and I didn't have time to get opinions and analyze the situation deeply. So, I made my choice to do my job as a broadcast journalist. I was comfortable with my decision then. I am comfortable with it today.

Now, a phone call from my boss at ESPN. Now, a verbal lashing. Now, my termination. Sugar and Finkel were right. The payment for making that choice was due. "Wild Bill" Fitts was sent to collect.

I picked up my travel bag, waved to Bert, who was on the phone, gave him a "see ya tomorrow," and headed for the elevator to meet Steve Albert.

I timed it perfectly. As I walked outside, Albert was pulling up in his gold LeMans. I wanted so badly to tell him about the phone call I just received but decided not to do so. It was one thing for me to be depressed while on the air, but I refused to take Albert down emotionally before the show by telling him the news.

On the plane to Indiana, I stared out the window, wondering why Bill Fitts had refused to elaborate or explain his decision to take me off the air at the end of the month—and how strange it was that ESPN was allowing me to call three more shows. After all, when a member of the electronic media is fired, that dismissal always comes at the end of the show and without his or her knowledge. The terminated employee does not get another chance to do another show and have the opportunity to rip into the company that has sent them packing. As confusing as the questions were, the craziest scenario was yet to come.

After landing, Steve and I headed to our hotel, where the weigh-in was being conducted for the fights that night. Following the weigh-in, Steve and I sat down with several of the fighters on the card and did taped interviews with them.

Afterward, we had lunch with the guys from the ESPN crew. There, I found out I didn't have much of an appetite. Still, I showed Albert and everyone else only my sunniest side. It was then off to my room for a shower, some paperwork, and a change of clothes. At 5:30, Steve and I headed to the decades-old Market Square Arena, site of the show.

As I took my seat at ringside in the still-empty arena, I was approached by Top Rank's then-assistant matchmaker, Bruce Trampler. Trampler was Teddy Brenner's right-hand man. Bruce and I had been friendly for years, and I figured he'd tell me the truth. I looked at him and motioned for him to step away from ringside, out of earshot of Steve Albert.

"Bruce, I've been fired by ESPN," I said.

"I've heard," said Trampler.

My brow creased. Trampler heard? Already? What did Fitts do? Did he hang up with me and call Teddy Brenner, who called Trampler in Indianapolis?

"What have you heard?" I asked Trampler.

"Well, it's like this," said Trampler. "ESPN has been real unhappy with the way you always talk about the Enswell device [a small, flat piece of metal used by cornermen to reduce swelling]. They think you may be getting a piece of the action in some way."

My eyes opened wide in amazement and my mouth fell open in shock. A stun gun could not have jolted me more.

"WHAT!" I blurted out. "That's preposterous! Of course I talk about the Enswell. It's a great piece of equipment. The Enswell is a part of this sport. It's the thing that kept Sugar Ray Leonard in the fight against Thomas Hearns and the device we see used every week on ESPN. How can I *not* talk about it?"

Trampler shrugged his shoulders and said, "You're right. You're absolutely right. But what can I tell you. This is not coming from me or from anybody at Top Rank. It's coming from ESPN."

I shook my head over and over in disbelief.

"I know it sounds crazy," said Trampler, "but it's the truth. To ESPN, it looks as if you're plugging the Enswell. I've tried to talk to them, but they just won't listen."

"Who did you speak to?" I asked Trampler.

"Well, uh, I'd rather not divulge that," said a floundering Trampler. "I don't want you singling out one person, when, in fact, it was a corporate decision."

I looked Trampler in the eyes. He looked down. I suspected right then that his story was pure fiction.

"Listen," said Trampler. "Just get out there and have a good show tonight. Maybe something can be worked out. C'mon." He patted my shoulder a few times.

"Sure," I said, exhaling the word as I walked back to ringside. "I'll have a great show!"

As I walked away from Trampler, I saw Akbar Muhammad on the far side of the arena. I headed over to him.

"Hi, Akbar, have you heard the news?" I asked.

"Yes, Randy, I just heard a few minutes ago. I was on the phone with Teddy and he said he had just heard."

"Bill Fitts called me at my office just before I left for the airport to break the news to me," I said. "Yet, when I asked him the reason, he refused to answer me. Did Teddy say he knew why I was fired?" I didn't tell Akbar I had just spoken to his Top Rank colleague, Bruce Trampler. I wanted to see if their stories matched.

"Teddy said he didn't know, other than the fact it came right from the top at ESPN."

I stared at him blankly, not knowing what to say.

"Tell you what," said Akbar. "Come with me. I'm gonna go call Scotty Connall [who was then the executive vice president of ESPN]. He'll tell me what's going on. Come with me."

I followed Akbar to the hall to a pay phone. He picked it up and began punching in lots of numbers.

"These calling cards are great," said Akbar.

"Good evening," he said. "I'd like to speak to Scotty Connall. This is Akbar Muhammad of Top Rank." A brief pause followed, then Akbar said, "Sure, I'll hold."

He covered the mouthpiece of the phone. At this point, all I had to go on was Fitts telling me I was gone but not telling me why, and Trampler telling me a ludicrous tale about me overpromoting the Enswell device. Now, Akbar was going to get me the entire story, or so I thought.

"I'm sure Scotty will be able to tell me what's going on," said Akbar. "I'm pretty tight with him and . . ." He pulled his hand off the mouthpiece.

"Hi, Scotty. Listen, I'm in Indianapolis for tonight's Top Rank Boxing show. I just heard the news about Randy Gordon being fired. What happened? Mmm-hmm. . . . Right. . . . No! . . . Get out of here! . . . Are you serious? . . . I can't believe it! . . . No wonder Bill Fitts couldn't tell Randy on the phone today! . . . Geez!" He took a deep breath and sighed.

"Scotty, don't you think Randy should know this? Isn't it only fair to tell him? . . . Mmm-hmm. . . . Mmm-hmm. . . . No, I don't mind. I'm close with him. I'll tell him. . . . Okay. . . . I'll tell him. . . . Bye."

I looked at Akbar, who was shaking his head as if in disbelief. He walked over to me and put an arm over my shoulder.

"Randy, you're not going to like this," said Akbar.

"I don't like this whole thing already, Akbar," I replied.

Standing in front of me, Akbar placed both hands on my shoulders. He looked me in the eyes and spoke.

"You're being taken off the air because . . ."

He hesitated.

"Go ahead," I told him.

He took a deep breath, then continued. "Because . . ." He stopped again, then he resumed. "Because ESPN doesn't like your on-camera appearance."

I didn't know whether to split my sides laughing or crying. *ESPN didn't like my on-camera appearance?* Who was Akbar kidding?

"I don't believe it!" I said, totally astounded. "I don't believe it."

"I know, Randy," said Akbar. "I wouldn't believe it either, if I hadn't just spoken to Scotty Connall on the phone."

I looked at my reflection in a glass door. I ran my hand through my hair, then touched my nose. Then, I gently ran my fingers across my cheeks and onto my chin.

"They don't like my on-camera appearance?" I questioned disbelievingly.

"I don't know what to say, Randy," shrugged Akbar, shaking his head. "I know it must hurt, hearing this kind of news. For some reason, though, ESPN just doesn't like . . ." He stopped and took a deep breath. Then he continued. "They don't like the way you look on camera. If you want, I'll get Connall back on so he can tell you himself." He pointed to the phone.

"It's 5:30," Akbar said, looking at his watch. "That means it's 6:30 back in Bristol. I don't know if he'll still be there. He said he was just leaving when I spoke to him a few seconds ago."

"Try him," I said.

Akbar went back to the phone. He looked uncomfortable as he punched in a series of numbers.

"Hello, this is Akbar Muhammad from Top Rank. Is Scotty Connall still in? . . . Oh, okay. Just tell him I called. Randy Gordon wanted to speak to him. Thank you." He hung up.

"We tried," he said.

"Yeh, we tried," I mumbled.

"I can't even imagine how you feel, Randy," said Akbar. "Getting fired for the reason I told you must be a tremendous blow to your ego. It would hurt anyone. I wish this hadn't happened, but it did. I wish this wasn't true, but it is."

True, my ass! I thought. *Something's going on here. Bruce has got one story and Akbar's got another. The story about ESPN thinking that I'm plugging the Enswell device just can't be true, and as sure as I'm standing here, neither can Akbar's story be true.*

I told Akbar I was going to the bathroom and I'd see him at ringside. He gave me a pat on the shoulder, just like Trampler did, and walked away. I walked slowly to the bathroom, stopped, turned around, watched Akbar disappear into the crowd that was filing in, then headed to the bank of telephones Akbar had just "called" Scotty Connall on. I was about to call ESPN.

Aware of what time it was, I called the newsroom, where an intern picked up.

"Hi, this is Randy Gordon," I said. "Do you know if Scotty Connall is still in?"

"Hi, Randy," said the intern. "I don't think he is, but hold on a second." A few moments later came a familiar voice.

"Marvin Johnson versus Alvino Manson? How many rounds do you think it will go?" The voice belonged to ESPN sportscaster Greg Gumbel. I recognized it right away.

"Hey, Greg," I cheerfully said. "I don't think it'll go too long. Johnson's a bomber and Manson's chin is shaky."

We talked for a few minutes, then Gumbel said, "I hear you're looking for Scotty."

"Yes, Greg, I am. Is he still there?"

"No, Rand, he's not."

I expected him to say, "He left less than 10 minutes ago." After all, he had just spoken to Akbar. Or did he?

"Do you have any idea when he left, Greg?" I inquired.

"Sure. He came into the newsroom over an hour ago and said good night. He was wearing his coat."

OVER AN HOUR AGO . . . OVER AN HOUR AGO . . . OVER AN HOUR AGO.

Gumbel's words reverberated through my brain like an echo through the Grand Canyon. If he left more than an hour ago, how could Akbar have just spoken to him? When I hung up with Gumbel, my body felt as if it had been given a massive injection of novocaine. I don't remember hanging up the phone, but I do remember how numb I felt as I headed toward my ESPN announce position at ringside.

What were they doing to me? Why could Fitts not explain why I was being taken off the air? Why did Trampler and Muhammad have entirely different stories? What was going on?

Despite feeling so numb and utterly confused, I forced myself to smile. There was no way I wanted Steve Albert to be dragged down by the pain I was in.

The show must go on, I thought. And go on it did. I was determined to have a good one.

I was not surprised how good Albert and I were that night. We were informative, concise, to the point, and, at times, funny. As Albert was signing off, I looked at him and smiled, knowing I had just given ESPN much more than the $250 they were paying me.

"Okay, guys, that's a wrap. We're clear. Nice show." Those words from producer Steve Anderson signified the end of the show. They were terribly painful for me. It was 11:00 p.m. Twelve hours earlier, I had been fired by the executive producer, who wouldn't give me a concrete reason for taking me off the air. I was fired, yet told I could still work three more shows. In radio and television, as I mentioned earlier, when you're fired by a station, you are not given another chance to go back on the air, not given that final opportunity to take venomous bites out of the station that just dismissed you. But here I was, fired by ESPN for no explainable reason, yet told I could work three more shows. Then there were the lies by Trampler and Muhammad. The entire thing just didn't make sense.

As I was reaching to remove my headset, I heard the voice of my producer. Steve Anderson said, "Randy, Bill Fitts called the truck a few minutes ago. He asked if you could give him a call tomorrow when you get back to the office." My body went limp from hearing that. Twelve hours earlier, Fitts had fired me. Why was he now requesting I call him when I got back to New York? I was more confused than ever.

"Is everything okay?" asked Albert, sensing—and seeing—the anguish within me.

"Steve, I was fired this morning," I told him.

Albert was speechless. I answered the questions he wanted to—but couldn't—ask.

"Bill Fitts called and fired me just a few minutes before you picked me up this morning. Don't ask why. I've been given three reasons by three different people. Fitts told me one thing. Bruce Trampler told me something entirely different. Akbar Muhammad had his own story. Nobody's story matches." I looked at Albert and shrugged.

"Why didn't you tell me?" Steve asked.

"I didn't want to upset you, didn't want you to feel bad for me and have it on your mind during the show," I answered.

Albert put a hand on my shoulder and said, "Thanks for thinking of me, Randy. I'm really sorry. Hey, how 'bout we go out with the crew and have a drink?"

"Thanks, Steve, but I'm gonna head back to the hotel. It might be better if I were alone tonight. I'm just not gonna be any fun to be around." I quickly gathered my notes and papers and headed for the door.

"I'll meet you back in your room," yelled Albert. "We'll talk."

I shook my head, took a deep breath, and walked out of the arena.

Stretched out on my bed, I stared at the ceiling. My thoughts raced back to the Kenny Bogner–Bobby Alexander fight, to the shouting matches with Teddy Brenner, to the Billy Collins–Eddie Flanning fight two weeks earlier, to Shelly Finkel's prophecy that this entire thing would "blow up in my face," to being fired by Bill Fitts 12 hours earlier, to the different stories by Trampler and Muhammad, to being told by producer Steve Anderson that Fitts had called the control truck less than 30 minutes ago, requesting I call him in the morning. What the hell was going on?

My thoughts were interrupted by three sharp knocks on my door. I looked at the door but didn't answer. The knocks came again.

A friendly voice followed.

"Come on, Randy! Open up! I know you're in there! Open up!"

It was Steve Albert.

"Go away!" I yelled.

KNOCK! KNOCK! KNOCK!

"Randy! Open up! Open the door!"

I turned away from the door and resumed staring at the ceiling. For the next few moments, it grew quiet outside my room. Then, I heard the door open to the room next to me, the room occupied by Steve Albert. He had given up trying to speak with me. At least I *thought* he had given up. A few seconds later, my telephone rang.

"Raaandeee," sang Albert in a soft voice. "Open the daw/awr. We've gotta taw/awk."

He had forced a smile out of me.

"You're persistent, aren't you?" I said.

"I figured you might need a shoulder to cry on," he said.

"I do," I replied. "Get over here!"

We talked for several hours. Although I was no closer to understanding the mechanics of my dismissal, the talk was therapeutic, making me feel a lot better.

"You had a choice to make," Albert told me. "It was compromise your journalistic principles or go with what was right and what you believed in. You made the correct decision. Don't ever doubt that fact." He continued, "And that was such a stand-up thing you did tonight—not telling me until after the show. I don't know how you kept it inside, knew what you knew, and still were able to have a tremendous show. You shouldn't be sad. You should be proud of the kind of man you are."

Albert's words made me feel better. When I put my head on my pillow that night, the small amount of doubt that perhaps what I did was wrong was gone. I didn't believe I was 75 percent right, or 85 percent, or 99 percent. I believed the choice I made was 100 percent the correct one.

Today, over 35 years later, I believe it more than ever.

6

TERRIBLE TEDDY, WILD BILL, AND UNSWERVING IRVING

My glum attitude returned the next morning, when, back in New York, I did as Bill Fitts requested and called him soon after walking into my office at *The Ring*. Before I could even settle in and make the call to Fitts, however, Jenny informed me I had an incoming call. It was *Newsday*'s TV/radio columnist, Stan Isaacs. Word of my dismissal from ESPN had gotten around fast, and Isaacs jumped on the story.

"Why do you think you've been taken off the air after two years of solid work?" Isaacs asked.

I told him I didn't know for sure but had an idea why.

"Was it revealing the attempted Ed Flanning/Rahim Tayib coverup?" he asked. "Top Rank was not too happy with you for that."

"I don't care if Top Rank didn't like it," I responded.

They can't tell me they didn't know that Rahim Tayib was really Ed Flanning, a fighter under suspension. They have two of the best matchmakers ever in the sport working together—Teddy Brenner and Bruce Trampler. They had to know Rahim Tayib was really Ed Flanning when they made the match. If they didn't know it then, they certainly knew it the morning of the fight, when I called them on it. Yet, Top Rank asked me not to mention it on the air. Am I wrong for not hiding the fact I knew who Tayib was? Am I wrong? I told Teddy Brenner he had three choices regarding Tayib. One was to kill the fight. Two was to get a last-minute replacement. Three was to let the fight go on. Brenner was so upset that I might mention it that he told me I would be gone from ESPN if I talked about it on the air. I told him "I don't work for Top Rank, I work for ESPN."

As I did on the USS *Yorktown*, I told the truth, or at least what I believed to be—and would soon find out was indeed—the truth. As I learned, telling the truth can often come back to hurt you.

After the interview with Isaacs, I had a meeting with Bert Sugar, planning our next magazine. Following that meeting, I headed back into my office to call "Wild Bill" Fitts. The call left me more confused and lost than a mouse in an intricate maze.

"Randy, you were very good last night," said Fitts. "In fact, you were better last night than you've ever been."

"Thank you, Bill," I said in a low, subdued voice.

"Listen," he continued. "I have an idea."

"What's your idea, Bill?" I asked, totally puzzled, unable to conjure up even the wildest thought on why Fitts had asked me to call and what his idea was.

"I've given this lots of thought," said Fitts. "I've decided to allow you to stay on the air, but in a different capacity."

Softly, I forced out, "Stay on? Different capacity?"

"That's right," said Fitts. "You've done some nice work in-studio for us on *SportsCenter Plus*, and I'm going to work out a schedule where you can come in and do some interviewing, previewing and reviewing major fights and putting together some magazine-type shows for us. Most of it will be boxing-oriented, but you'll also be working on some other sports. You've already covered the New York City Marathon, the NFL, and baseball for us, and you've done a nice job in all of your work. So, are you ready?"

Talk about playing with a guy's emotions. One day he's firing me, the next day he's asking me if I'd like to do in-studio work. So much for Enswell's endorsements and certainly a negative on-camera appearance. Whew!

"Sure, Bill, I'm ready," I said, totally perplexed and confused as to what was going on.

"Good. I'll be in touch as to when your first assignment is," he said without emotion. "Have a nice day. See you in Bristol."

Unfortunately, I never got near Bristol, Connecticut, again.

Shortly after the call from Fitts, I called Isaacs to inform him of my reinstatement. He called Fitts to discuss it. But, to him, the story wasn't about me being fired then reinstated in a different capacity. The story was about an announcer being fired for standing up to a boxing promoter and telling the truth about one of the promoter's fights on the air, then having the boxing promoter strong-arm the TV network into firing the announcer.

Stan Isaacs's column came out the following day. Fitts didn't enjoy any of it.

Wild Bill was back on the phone with me that day.

"I put you back on the air and this is what you do?" he yelled.

I attempted to explain.

"Bill, I spoke to Stan Isaacs before I spoke to . . ." He cut me off.

"I am so fed up with your wise ass attitude. You are through here. Through!"

I tried to tell him I looked forward to seeing him, but Wild Bill hung up. So, in the span of two days, I worked for ESPN, was fired by them, rehired, and fired again. An emotional roller coaster? Without question. It was the biggest one I had ever been on.

Although Bert Sugar and many friends inside both boxing and television sided with me, it still hurt being bounced from something I loved doing and for reporting on something I was right about. Maybe I should have kept quiet about Ed Flanning, but I would not have been right in doing so.

That night, shortly after dinner, I was sitting in my home office. I was feeling pretty low and must have shown it. My five-year-old daughter, Ali, saw me sitting there and came over to me. She stood next to me and asked, "Daddy, why do you look so sad?" I remember thinking, *What is the answer to my little girl's question? How do I tell her daddy just got fired for telling the truth?* I put my arms around her and held her tight as tears rolled down my face.

It had been a helluva couple of days: fired on Thursday morning, keeping it together to do one of my best shows for ESPN that night, rehired the same night, given a new assignment the following day, refired the very next day.

During the next few days, many newspapers wrote about my termination; however, I just wanted it all to end. I was gone from ESPN and would not be going back. No amount of media coverage would bring me back, either. I settled back into my job as editor of *The Ring*. In the back of my mind, however, I still wondered just how much Bob Arum and Teddy Brenner had to do with my dismissal.

About two weeks after my final dismissal by Wild Bill, I received a phone call that confirmed what I wanted to know. It was from veteran publicist Irving Rudd.

Rudd, who was in his 70s, was a longtime publicist in and around boxing. He had also been a press agent (he couldn't stand the term "public relations man") for the Dodgers and Yonkers Raceway. At the time, he was Top Rank's director of publicity. No one had more "ins" to the media than the man most insiders affectionately called "Unswerving Irving" and "Uncle Irving." He truly was like a favorite uncle. He called me at *Ring Magazine*.

"Uncle Irving is on the phone, Randy," buzzed copy editor Liz Gary, who was as much like a beloved little sister as she was a copy editor.

"Hello, Irving," I began. "To what do I owe the honor of this call?"

"Listen, Randy, I have to talk to you in private," Rudd began. "I am in a pay phone. I know the whole story of your dismissal from ESPN. How about we meet for lunch? You pick the place somewhere near you. It can't be anywhere near Top Rank's office [it's now in Las Vegas but was then in New York]."

"The Cosmic Coffee Shop. I have breakfast with Jim Jacobs there every week," I told him. "It's right next to my office."

"Okay, but are there a lot of boxing people who go in there?" he wanted to know, adding, "I don't want Bob [Arum] or Teddy [Brenner] to find out I was with you. They'd fire me . . . kill me. You and I are friends, and I want you to know for certain what you might already suspect."

We met an hour later for lunch at the Cosmic Diner on West 31st Street. Rudd, who always had a smile for everyone, was not smiling. He was nervous, jumpy, and jittery.

"Calm down, Irving, calm down," I implored him.

"I can't," said Rudd. "I'm so nervous somebody is gonna recognize us in here. I should have met you out on Long Island. I should have taken the LIRR and had you pick me up and take me back to your house."

"Irving, please calm down," I begged him. "Nobody is ever gonna know you're here."

He made sure of that. We sat at the last table in the back against an L-shaped wall. Rudd sat in the seat that was out of view from the door. Behind him were the single-occupancy restrooms. He planned on heading into whichever one was available if anyone from either boxing or Top Rank walked into the restaurant.

"I don't even want to think what would happen to me if I was seen with you," said Rudd.

"Is your body gonna be found in a landfill in Staten Island?" I asked.

"Don't joke!" he said seriously. "Don't joke!" I stared at him with an "Are you kidding?" kind of look.

"What is this all about, Irving?" I wanted to know.

"It's about Teddy Brenner. You've riled him up with your commentary, which, by the way, is terrific," he reported. "But you're too honest for his liking. If a guy with a losing record is fighting, you don't hide it. If a guy has a questionable chin, you say so. And when you went on the air with the news about Flanning—which Teddy knew right from the start—he was furious. Just furious!"

"Yeh, I think I pissed him off a bit!" I replied.

"You did," said Rudd. "And the more you pissed him off, the more you told the truth about what you were watching, the angrier he got. Teddy got all over Bob [Arum], dragging him into it. Once Bob got into it, you had problems."

"When did Arum get involved?" I asked Rudd.

"I guess it was about the time you said Bobby Alexander didn't have a chin. Teddy took that personally, as if you were telling the viewing audience, 'Top Rank is giving you a setup fight here, a guaranteed win for one of its house fighters against an opponent who will crumble the first time he gets hit solidly.'"

I understood. The match wasn't fixed, and Alexander wasn't being paid to take a dive. But he was brought in as the fodder, the way the Christians were brought in as fodder against the lions a few thousand years ago. It was entertainment, but the lions would always win. In this case, Alexander was one of the Christians, being fed to a Top Rank lion. Top Rank knew it, and I knew it. ESPN didn't know and neither did the viewing audience—until I informed them who was who.

"Teddy would come in the next morning and say, 'Fucking Gordon knows too much. He must know every fighter out there.' He told Bob [Arum], 'We have to sit him down and ask him to work with us, to temper how he phrases things.'"

"Why didn't they?" I asked.

"They were about to," explained Irving.

Teddy was gonna call you and invite you out to lunch. Then came the Flanning situation. Both Teddy and Bruce [Trampler] knew about Flanning. They just were hoping you wouldn't know. When you did, and when you called him, he lost it. He didn't really mean everything he said. He just didn't want you saying anything. When you fired back at him, then went on the air and hammered it home over and over, Teddy went wild. He was on the phone with Bob the whole show. The next morning, all he kept saying was, "Bob, we've got to get him off the air. He's killing us!"

"Did they call ESPN?" I asked.

"Yes, they spoke to Scotty Connall. Bob spoke to him," Irving stated.

He insisted ESPN take you off the fights. ESPN stuck up for you, said you were doing a good job. Bob reminded them how well Top Rank Boxing was doing on ESPN and said he'd pull the show off the network if they kept you on. ESPN wouldn't back down. Finally, ESPN agreed to have a "cooling off" period and agreed to take you off the fights for a few weeks but use you as an in-studio host. Unfortunately, Bill Fitts didn't want you to know that Top Rank was behind this move and didn't handle himself well on the phone with you. He lost his cool, the same way Teddy did. When you fired back in the media, ESPN couldn't take you back. They had to let you go. It was all an unfortunate situation.

I asked Rudd why both Bruce Trampler and Akbar Muhammad had different stories in regard to my dismissal. I told him about Akbar's call to Scotty Connall.

"That had to be hard to understand," said Rudd.

Both Trampler and Muhammad were in Indianapolis with you. Neither guy coordinated anything with the other guy. First Trampler called Teddy and asked how he should respond if you asked him any questions. Teddy was in a lousy mood and said, "I don't care what you tell him. He talks about the Enswell a lot. Tell him ESPN thinks he's got a piece of it. Tell him anything. Who cares what you tell him!"

"But what was with Akbar's story?" I inquired. "He told me ESPN didn't like my on-camera appearance. He said Scotty Connall told him that on the phone while I was standing next to him. I called ESPN right after. Connall had been gone for over an hour. What was with that?"

Rudd laughed.

"I was sitting next to Teddy when Trampler called, then, a few minutes later, Akbar," he revealed. "Teddy told Trampler to say anything and mentioned the Enswell. By the time Akbar called, asking the same question, Teddy was in a vile mood. He shouted, 'Who cares what you tell him! Tell him ESPN thought he was ugly. Who cares what you tell him!'"

I shook my head. I finally understood.

Then Rudd took a sip of his water, placed the glass down, and looked at me. He shook his head and spoke.

"You know what's ironic about this whole thing," he commented, saying it more as a statement than as a question.

"What's that, Irving?" I asked.

"Teddy really likes you," Rudd revealed.

He said the two of you guys used to ride on the bus down to Atlantic City on many occasions. He said the two hours went by so fast because of the great conversations you guys used to have. He said those were some of his fondest memories. He was distraught after he hung up with you when you were arguing with him about Flanning. He was distraught because he knew he was wrong and that you were right. He was also distraught because he likes you. Deep inside he really likes you. Maybe one day you two can patch things up.

"I doubt it," I said. "I really doubt it."

"Don't doubt anything," replied Rudd. "Life is strange. Don't doubt anything!"

A few weeks after being starched by Top Rank and Wild Bill, I received a call from Jim Zrake, head of sports at the USA Network, asking me if I'd like to sit in for their boxing analyst, Angelo Dundee, who was busy training Sugar Ray Leonard. Alongside golden-throated Al Trautwig, I called a fight card from Tampa, Florida. I remained as USA's color analyst for the next five and a half years. An appointment from Governor Mario M. Cuomo took me out of my TV analyst's seat and put me in the driver's seat as the top dog of boxing in New York state. The appointment made me, at 38, the youngest head of boxing's oldest state commission.

In 1995, I was with my family on vacation in Florida. On Monday, I would head back to work at the commission while my family stayed for another few days. I was booked on a 6:30 a.m. flight. While waiting behind one other customer as I returned my rental car, the door to the rental office slid open. A middle-aged man entered and got in line behind me.

The customer in front of me was having a problem with his bill. I waited patiently. The middle-aged man behind me had no choice. While waiting, I looked around the room. As I turned, I glanced at the man. His head was lowered. He was looking at the floor. I looked back at the desk but spun around toward the middle-aged man a moment later. I knew him. He knew me, too, but didn't want me to recognize him.

It was Wild Bill.

"Well, well, well," I said. "If it isn't my good friend, 'Wild Bill' Fitts. What better way to start your day than by running into an old friend, an old pal."

Of course, I was being more than facetious. The incident from 13 years earlier, not even a distant thought a moment ago, came rushing back.

The rental car sales rep looked up and gave us a smile as he saw two old friends getting reacquainted.

"It's so nice to see you, Bill," I said. "You look wonderful. What a pleasant surprise this is."

"Uh, hi, Randy, uh, how are you?" stammered Wild Bill. I stepped toward him, stopping only inches away. The urge to hit him was enormous. I hoped he would take a swing at me.

The rental car agent sensed something was wrong, and asked, "Is everything okay, gentlemen?"

"Yes, everything is fine," said Wild Bill.

A moment later, it was my turn at the counter. As the agent said, "Next in line," and looked at me, Wild Bill said, "I've gotta go outside for a second. I'll be right back."

I whirled around.

"Don't go anywhere, Bill. It's been so long. We have to talk. How's the job? The family?"

The agent squinted his eyes. You could see he was wondering just what was going on.

"You're a state commissioner, now, huh?" said Wild Bill, attempting to diffuse the bomb about to explode in front of him.

"Governor Cuomo made a perfect move in choosing you to be commissioner," he continued. He was also doing a great job in taking the fight out of me. His remarks made me think, *Don't hit him. Don't get in trouble here. Remember, you're a public official.* But then, in a flash, my thinking turned 180 degrees.

This is the asshole who made your life miserable in October 1982. This is the guy responsible for your five-year-old daughter asking, 'Daddy, why are you so sad?' I am going to provoke him into a fight.

The agent's voice interrupted my thinking.

"All done, Mr. Gordon," he said. "The next bus to the terminals will be here momentarily."

Then the agent motioned for Fitts to step to the counter. Wild Bill looked at me and smiled nervously.

"Well, it's been nice seeing you, Randy," he said. I shook my head.

"I'll wait for you to finish, Billy," I said sarcastically. "I'll ride the bus with you." I smiled. The agent smiled at the two friends he saw reunited in his office.

As the agent processed Fitts's papers, I slapped my old boss on the back a few times.

"Damn, it sure is good seeing you, Fittsie," I said. I stood right next to him. Beads of sweat were on his brow. I was wondering what he was thinking.

"That's it, Mr. Fitts, all done," the agent said. "The bus is pulling in now. Have a nice trip, gentlemen. Great to see two longtime friends meet up like this."

"It sure is," I remarked. I turned to Wild Bill and asked, "Isn't it, Bill?" With a sick-to-his-stomach kind of look, he forced out a, "Yes it is." I put an arm around his shoulders and walked out the door with my pal Bill.

"After you," I said, allowing Fitts to board first. The bus was empty. He moved all the way to the back. I followed him. When he sat down, I sat down next to him. Then I looked him in the eyes and spoke.

"What you did to me was totally wrong," I said. "I found out the whole story, the true story, days later. It wasn't just your firing me that hurt. It's how you screamed at me and what you said that caused extra pain. Do you want me screaming at you, now? Do you?" I said in a soft voice.

Then I added, "I don't remember the last time I wanted to hit someone so badly. Come on, don't you want to hit me? Don't you? Please, throw a punch at me. Please." He sat there as the bus headed to the terminal.

"I am so sorry, Randy. I really am. I don't blame you for wanting to hit me. You were a fine boxing analyst," he answered. "The pressure came down. We were going to take you off the fights for just a short time but give you studio work to replace it. Who knows, you may have loved the studio work. I just didn't have answers for your questions. I totally lost my cool, and I apologize with all my heart."

The fight, anger, hostility, and rage I had bottled up for 13 years left my body. Wild Bill reached out to shake my hand. I accepted. Then we hugged as the bus stopped at my terminal.

"Thank you, Bill," I said. I was thanking him for freeing me from the ugly feelings I had been carrying around for 13 years.

"Thank you, Randy," he said. Perhaps he was thanking me for not hitting him, but I'd like to think it was for freeing him from the same feelings from which he freed me.

I got off the bus and walked to the terminal door. I looked back at the bus and toward Bill. He was looking out the window at me. He waved and gave me a thumbs up. I waved back and did the same.

I never saw Bill again. But those few minutes with him changed my life forever.

In 1982, "Unswerving Irving" told me, "Don't doubt anything," when he mentioned that "maybe you and Teddy can one day patch things up." I responded with, "I doubt it." As you get older (I was 33 back then), you see more things, experience more things, and learn more things. "Unswerving Irving" was right.

Following my dismissal from ESPN, I ran into both Brenner and Arum at many of their events. Nothing nicer than "Get out of my way, asshole!" "Drop dead!" and "Fuck off" was ever exchanged between us.

When I became commissioner in 1988, *Newsday*'s Wallace Matthews asked numerous boxing insiders their opinion on me becoming commissioner.

"Commissioner of what?" asked the CEO of Top Rank in typical Bob Arum style. "What's he commissioner of? New York doesn't have big fights anymore. What's he commissioner of?"

The comments of "Terrible Teddy" were so vile that no newspaper could print them.

But Top Rank did promote shows in New York state while I was commissioner. Lots of them. When there was work to be done, we all played nice.

In 1992, I attended a press conference in New York City. The press conference was to announce a fight between Bobby Czyz, called the "Matinee Idol," and Donny Lalonde, the former light heavyweight champ.

As the fight was to be held in Atlantic City, New Jersey, I had nothing to do with the bout; however, as both fighters were friends of mine, I wanted to say hello to them, so I attended the press conference.

At the press conference, Bob Arum was at the podium talking to the assembled media about the fight. He introduced a few of his fighters who were there, as well as a few other boxing luminaries. Standing with a few members of the media in the back of the room, I was surprised when he said, "Also in attendance, and doing such a great job as head of the New York State Athletic Commission, is Randy Gordon." I waved to him and mouthed, "Thank you." Bob Arum said something nice about me? Huh?

A moment later, I was approached by Teddy Brenner. He was in his late 70s but looked much older. I hadn't seen—or spoken—with him (aside from the vitriolic moments mentioned earlier) since 1982. I felt my adrenaline kicking in and prepared myself for a verbal battle. Then came another surprise, the same as when Arum had so politely introduced me seconds earlier.

"Commissioner, may I talk with you?" asked Brenner.

"Get away from me, Teddy," I sneered at him. "Get the hell away from me!" The fact that he had just called me commissioner did not get lost through the anger I still felt toward him.

"Commissioner, I'm very sick," Brenner told me. "I'm dying. I need to speak with you."

I froze in my tracks.

Brenner had reached out for my sensitive and emotional side. He found it.

"Teddy, I'm really sorry," I said. "What do you have?"

"Among other things, I have Parkinson's disease. Full-blown Parkinson's. It's coming on fast," he told me.

"Oh, Teddy, I am so sorry," I said sadly. Then I stepped forward and gave him a hug. He hugged me back. When I stepped back to look at him, he was crying. That made two of us.

"Commissioner, I need to talk to you for a few minutes. Do you have a few minutes for me?" he asked. "I understand if you don't. I really understand. You have all the reason in the world to hate me. But I really need to say some things to you, and I'm hoping you may want to hear what they are."

I looked around.

"Over here," I said. I pointed to a remote corner of the room.

As we walked, Teddy said, "Thank you for doing this, commissioner."
I looked at him and smiled.

"It's my pleasure, Teddy," I said. I then added, "And my name is Randy. You've known me long enough to call me Randy."

He stopped walking and turned to face me.

"I have always respected your position and the men who held it previously," Brenner told me. He rattled off names. "Torres. Branca. Prenderville. Farley. Dooley. Egan. Krulewich. I didn't like all of them, but I respected all of them."

"Then there's me," I said.

"Then there's you," replied Brenner. "No chairman or head of any boxing commission has ever been as prepared and deserving of the job as you."

I looked Brenner in the eyes. Was this Terrible Teddy, the man who told me to say nothing of the suspended fighter he was putting on ESPN 10 years earlier? I shook my head in confusion.

"I don't understand, Teddy," I said. "What's going on here? For 10 years we haven't spoken. Now this. What's going on? Talk to me."

"As I told you, I'm dying," he said. "Parkinson's disease."

He held out his hands. They were shaking.

"I always liked you," he continued.

You angered me with your honesty on the air years ago. But that was my problem, not yours. I should have had lunch with you and talked things over. I'm sure that would have helped a lot. Instead, all that happened was that I continually called you and ripped into you. But you were right. I was wrong. Everything about the way I treated you was wrong. You should have never left ESPN. Never! I want you to know that I apologize with everything inside of me. Please, Commissioner. Please accept my heartfelt apology.

I took a deep breath. Then I said, "I'll accept, but only if you do one thing."

"Anything, Commissioner. I'll do anything," he replied.

Still looking him in the eyes, I said, "You have to call me 'Randy.'"

We both smiled.

"You got it, Randy," he replied. "Please accept my apology for all the hurt I caused you in the past, Randy. I am deeply, deeply sorry."

"I wholeheartedly accept your apology," I told him. Another emotional hug followed.

During the next few months, I'd meet Teddy for lunch at or near his office, which was then located in midtown Manhattan. We'd talk about current fighters, then the conversation would switch to the old-timers.

One day, he came in with the boxing book he wrote, coauthored by sportswriter Barney Nagler in 1981, entitled *Only the Ring Was Square*. I thanked him but told him I already had a copy.

"Not like this one, you don't," he replied. He opened the book and handed it to me. On the inside cover he had written this:

To Randy,
A man who loves boxing . . . and boxing loves him.
With love and respect always,
Teddy Brenner

"Damn, you love getting me teary, don't you, Teddy," I said. It was another one of those hug-each-other moments.

As the Parkinson's continued to ravage his body, he began to take off from work more and more.

Later that year, Brenner was chosen as a member of the class of 1993 to be inducted into the International Boxing Hall of Fame.

Shortly before the induction in June 1993, Unswerving Irving called my office to tell me that Brenner would be coming to the fights that week at Madison Square Garden's Felt Forum. Rudd wanted to make sure I would be there, either in my capacity as chairman or as a spectator. He said Brenner told him, "If the commissioner is not going to be there, I'm not going."

"Tell him I wouldn't miss seeing him," I told Rudd.

"Just prepare yourself, Randy," he replied. "Teddy is in a wheelchair."

I headed into the Licensing Department of my commission. I walked over to the lopsided and bent file cabinets that housed thousands of applications going back 40, 50, and, in some cases, 60 years.

I looked at the "B" section of the files, then headed to the section labeled "Bra–Bru."

I searched for "Brenner." I found what I was looking for in seconds. I took the file out and put it on my desk. A few days later, I brought it with me to the Felt Forum.

Seeing Teddy was sad. He sat in a wheelchair at ringside. His hands shook uncontrollably, as did his legs. He was only 73, but he looked so much older. Boxing luminaries and celebrities surrounded him, kneeling down to give him a hug. There were former champions Jake LaMotta, Jose Torres, and Alexis Arguello. CBS's boxing analyst, Gil Clancy. Managers, trainers, booking agents, advisors, and matchmakers. Journalists from throughout the country. They all lined up to say hello to Teddy. He acknowledged each of them with a small smile and a nod of his head. Finally, it was time to bring out the first bout. The commission timekeeper rang the bell. The crowd around Teddy dissipated. All the while, I stood off to the side. Then, he motioned for his aide to come close. She did. So did I. I was within earshot to hear him ask, "Where's the commissioner? Please get me the commissioner."

"I'm right here," I said from his right side. He looked up and saw me. He smiled. It was that big, happy, glad-to-be-at-the-fights smile of Teddy Brenner. I leaned down and gave him a hug. What probably took much of his energy, he threw his shaky arms around me and hugged me back.

"Thanks, Commissioner. . . ." he said. I gave him a look. He corrected his mistake. "I mean, Randy."

"Thanks for what?" I asked him. I thought he was going to say, "For being here." But he didn't. He responded with, "For being my friend." More misty eyes.

I regrouped and handed him the folder I took from the New York State Athletic Commission. It was his original application for a matchmaker's license. I congratulated him for his induction into the International Boxing Hall of Fame. I told him the license should be presented to the IBHOF as part of the Teddy Brenner exhibit.

I saw Brenner a few more times during the next few years. Parkinson's sapped him like body shots of so many great fighters we often talked about. But body shots take only a few rounds. Parkinson's takes years. The fight Teddy waged against the dreaded disease was greater and more valiant than that of any fighter Teddy had ever made a match for. Game? Tough? They didn't come any gamer or tougher than Teddy Brenner.

He passed away on January 7, 2000. He was 82. Six months later, Unswerving Irving passed away after a long illness. He, too, was 82. I found irony in the age they were when they both left us. It was 18 years earlier that I had to dig deep inside myself to find what I believed was the right choice to a boxing problem. Terrible Teddy made me reach down inside myself to find that choice. Unswerving Irving confirmed what I believed. The year was '82.

A few months after seeing Wild Bill, a call from Bristol, Connecticut, came into my office. Michele answered the phone, then buzzed me.

"Commissioner, you have ESPN on the line," she informed me. "It's the Programming Department."

Hmm. Maybe they want me as a guest on SportsCenter, I thought. It was from Bill Fitts's office. The lady from ESPN told me that on March 5, 1995, ESPN would be televising a back-to-back boxing doubleheader. One of the fights would be coming from Mexico, the other from Muskogee, Oklahoma. I was asked if I'd like to provide color commentary alongside my old pal, future Hall of Famer Al Bernstein. About the best way I can describe the feeling I had right then is through a texting abbreviation: OMG! The feeling was amazing. This would be my return to ESPN, even if for only one night. I would be flying to Muskogee, Oklahoma, meeting up with Bernstein, and calling a fight card from the Civic Assembly Center. The main event matched Oklahoma's Tommy "The Duke" Morrison against a seven-footer from Louisville, Kentucky, Marcellus Brown. The card that marked my return to ESPN was quite unforgettable, as Morrison stopped Brown in the third round after pounding on the big man for the first two rounds. For me, the highlight was simply being there, doing the card with Bernstein and our fun opening, which featured Merle Haggard singing his hit "Okie from Muskogee."

As I flew home after the show, I looked out the window and smiled. Teddy Brenner told me he'd be watching. Even though I knocked the Oklahoma State Athletic Commission for passing just about any fight, then doubted Brown's ability to stand up under Morrison's firepower, I knew Brenner would like it. I knew that, the following day, there would be no calls from guys I once called "Terrible Teddy" and "Wild Bill."

If there was any reason ESPN gave me the assignment other than as a way to say they were sorry for what had happened 13 years earlier, I don't want to know it. Doing that one show was so therapeutic, so energizing, that only one story will work for me.

For me, getting that call from ESPN was the closure I had been looking for. It was the closure to the wildest chapter of my professional life.

To Teddy, Bill, and Irving, thank you for being such a big part of my life, and ending it in the most perfect way possible.

7

"MURDER, PLAIN AND SIMPLE"

It was Thursday, June 16, 1983. The venue was Madison Square Garden's main arena. A crowd of 20,019—the largest at Madison Square Garden in almost 10 years and a majority of them Hispanic—roared in unity and with delight as their local hero, a 28-year-old journeyman Luis Resto, landed another stiff shot to the face of unbeaten out-of-towner "Irish" Billy Collins Jr. The junior middleweight fight was scheduled for 10 rounds, and this was only the third round; however, the 21-year-old Irishman's face was already sunburn red.

Billy Collins Jr. was 14-0. He was carefully being nurtured by Top Rank Boxing and built into a star on ESPN against an array of handpicked opponents (one of whom was Eddie Flanning, who you read about two chapters ago). On this night, the handpicked opponent for Collins was Luis Resto. Unlike Flanning, however, Resto was not falling down.

Still, Resto was to be another opponent for Collins to learn against, sharpen up against, and fatten his record against. It was hoped by Top Rank that Collins would look so good against the tough, rugged Resto, that it was not unreasonable to think Collins's next fight would be against the winner of the night's main event, a 15-round fight for the WBA junior middleweight championship of the world. The defending champion was unbeaten New Yorker Davey Moore. Facing Moore and his perfect 15–0 record was former two-division titleholder and vastly popular future Hall of Famer Roberto Duran. A Moore–Collins fight at Madison Square Garden would have been huge. A Duran–Collins title fight at Madison Square Garden would have been even bigger. The thought of it was a promoter's dream. Alas, we would never get to see either one of those fights.

Since losing to Sugar Ray Leonard in the "No Mas" fight 19 months earlier, Duran had fought two times. He won on both occasions. His return to boxing after his embarrassing showing in New Orleans against Leonard took place in August 1981. In that bout, fighting for the first time as a junior middleweight, Duran won a 10-round unanimous decision against Nino Gonzales. His next outing, the following month, saw Duran pound out a 10-round decision against rugged Luigi Minchillo.

By the time Moore climbed into the Madison Square Garden ring to take a man-sized beating and lose his title to Duran—who was celebrating his 32nd birthday that night—young Collins's career had come crashing down only minutes earlier, along with the life he knew. What happened that night has stayed with me like a tattoo. The thing is, tattoos can be removed and eradicated. The Collins–Resto fight cannot.

I wasn't in The Garden to see the fight. It was the only boxing card I missed at the famed arena in the 1980s. Early that evening, I left on a flight to Los Angeles, where I would be calling a fight card the following night on the USA Network. The flight would get me into Los Angeles around 10:00 p.m. (PT), about 90 minutes after the show ended at Madison Square Garden. I told my associate editor, Ben Sharav, that I'd be calling him when I landed so I could hear the night's results.

For much of the flight, I edited stories for the current issue of *The Ring* and wrote story ideas for the next one. On several occasions, my mind drifted to what might possibly be happening at Madison Square Garden. I thought about Moore and Duran. I thought about Collins and Resto. If Moore was to win, I believed it would have to be by decision. A knockout or TKO victory would most likely belong to Duran. As for Collins–Resto, there was only one possible winner: Billy Collins. The young Irishman was a rising star. Resto was a 28-year-old opponent. He was there, as I pointed out earlier, to give Collins some work, test him a little, push him a bit, and serve as a barometer as to where Collins was in his career. Resto was there to do all those things and one thing more—lose to Collins.

Soon after boarding the plane, I reset my watch, changing it from Eastern Time to Pacific Time. As we landed, I glanced at it. It was 10:05 local time. In New York, it was 1:05 a.m. The fights were certainly over, and Sharav, never a late-night party animal, would surely be home.

After disembarking in Los Angeles, I rushed straight to the nearest pay phone to call Ben. I needed to get to the phone before dozens of other passengers on my flight beat me to it. I won. Ben answered with a question on the first ring.

"Randy?" was his one-word question.

"Yep, it's me, Ben," I responded. "My flight just got in. I've been dying to see how the card went tonight. I've got tons of people behind me waiting for the phone, so I only have a few seconds. How'd Duran do?"

"Duran won . . . stopped Moore in round five. It was a total blowout!" he told me. Then, before I could even react, he added, "But that wasn't the night's major story."

"It wasn't?" I asked. "What was?"

"Billy Collins lost to Luis Resto," he told me.

"WHAT?" I responded in shock.

"Well, Collins lost a decision," Ben told me, then said, "but immediately after the fight ended, it was found that Resto's gloves had been tampered with. Apparently, there was no padding of any kind in them. Collins's face was beaten to a pulp. The gloves were impounded by the New York State Athletic Commission."

I wanted to ask Ben a slew of questions, but the line behind me was growing and getting impatient.

"C'mon, pal, don't tie up the phone," grumbled one tired traveler.

"I'll be at my hotel in a few minutes. I'll call you back," I told him. "Don't go to sleep."

I headed out to a cab, which took me to my hotel. During the ride, I wondered a little about Duran–Moore, but mostly about Collins losing to an opponent whose gloves had apparently been tampered with.

I sat on my hotel room bed as I called Ben, who again answered on the first ring.

"Yeh, Randy, it was the most vicious beating I have ever seen," was the way Ben answered the phone.

"Was it both of Resto's gloves?" I asked.

"Apparently so," said my right-hand man at *The Ring*.

"You said Collins lost a decision, is that correct?" I asked him.

"That's correct. It was a unanimous decision."

"And you said Collins's face was all busted up, right?" I inquired.

"That's right," was Sharav's answer.

"How did anybody find out about the gloves?" I asked.

"Well, at the end of the fight, Resto walked across the ring to shake the hands of both Billy Sr. and Billy Jr.," Sharav explained.

When he shook Senior's hand, Senior grabbed onto Resto's right glove and held it tight, squeezing it. All he felt was knuckle. He started yelling for a commission rep. The commission then sent an inspector into the ring to impound the gloves.

Nobody knows for sure, but apparently, both gloves had the padding around the knuckles removed. Every time Collins got hit, he was getting hit with taped knuckles. His face was worse than any I've seen after a fight.

"Ben, the Collins's are staying across the street from The Garden, at the Southgate Towers," I said.

I hate to do this to you, but I believe they have a flight back to Nashville around 10:00 a.m. They'll be leaving somewhere around 8:00. I know they'll be up early. Get there at 6:00 a.m. and wait in the lobby. If you don't see them by 7:00, call their room. They will be up. I guarantee it. Get some shots of the kid's face.

There was no argument or griping from Ben. He knew it was something that had to be done. Perhaps he sensed how important his photos would become in this dark moment in boxing's long and storied history.

Sharav walked into the lobby of the Southgate Towers a few minutes before 6:00 a.m. He asked the front desk clerk if fighter Billy Collins had checked out yet. Ben was told he hadn't. So he sat down, read the morning's papers, and waited. The back page of the *New York Daily News* blared out the headline, "DURAN KO'S MOORE." Ben read the coverage of the main event, along with the coverage of the undercard. Included in the undercard coverage was Resto's "victory"—his tainted "victory"—which Commissioner Jack Prenderville quickly changed to a "no contest." He also promised an investigation would get under way immediately.

When it did, the investigation found Resto, along with cornermen Carlos "Panama" Lewis and Pedro Alvarado, guilty of removing the padding from Resto's gloves. One of them kept the two New York State Athletic Commission inspectors busy and distracted. One of them was Patsy Giovanelli, a veteran NYSAC inspector. The other was Richard Hering, who would go on to become my right-hand man and executive director at the NYSAC five years later. On this night, however, Hering was on the job as an inspector for the first time. As Giovanelli and Hering were distracted, one of Resto's cornermen made a slit on the inside of Resto's Everlast gloves and quickly pulled out the horsehair padding from the knuckle area of the gloves. You read that correctly: "Quickly pulled out the horsehair padding." How quickly? I did a test on two pair of the same style/weight Everlast gloves. On my first try, I succeeded in a total of 41 seconds. On my second try, I did it in 33 seconds. My guess is Resto's corner did it even quicker than 33 seconds. They had practice. I didn't.

When the gloves were put on Resto's hands, they still looked out-of-the-box brand new. Cornerman Panama Lewis then tied them and put tape around the wrist area of each glove. Inspector Giovanelli then signed the tape as inspectors do and gave his okay for Resto to leave his dressing room and enter the ring to face Billy Collins Jr. The young, unbeaten, unsuspecting Collins was about to take 10 rounds—30 minutes' worth—of hits from weapons, not padded boxing gloves. The gauzed, taped knuckles of a professional prizefighter were minutes away from slamming repeatedly and sickeningly into Collins's boyishly handsome face.

From the first of Resto's jabs that found Collins's face, to every hook, cross, and uppercut that landed, Collins winced. Collins Sr., himself an ex-pro who had compiled a 38-17-1, 25-KO record from 1958 to 1965, thought his son had a case of nerves in front of the packed crowd at Madison Square Garden and told him to relax after the first round ended. He told him the same thing after each of the next succeeding five rounds.

"Relax and fight your fight," young Collins was told as blood was wiped from his nose before the start of the seventh round.

"I thought maybe Billy Ray [the name the fighter was called by his dad] was sick," the senior Collins told me a few weeks after the fight. "He wasn't looking like the fighter I knew, like the son I knew. This kid could fight, and he wasn't showing it, not at all."

"Open up! Let your hands go!" admonished Collins Sr. as a cut under his son's left eye was worked on before the start of the ninth.

"That's where I started to realize something was terribly wrong," said Collins Sr. in that interview with me. "That's when I realized my son wasn't sick. Nobody who was sick could have ever stood up to the kind of hits my boy was taking. My boy's great condition and heart were holding him up."

Collins Jr. took more of the same punishment in the ninth round but was fighting back. The big difference is, Collins was landing with padded gloves. Resto was landing with taped fists. They may as well have been brass knuckles.

When the 10th round ended, both fighters returned to their respective corners to the cheers of the huge crowd. Then, Resto turned from his corner and headed to the corner of his unmercifully hammered opponent. He extended his right hand to Billy Sr. The elder Collins took Resto's hand as if to congratulate him. When he had a hold of Resto's right hand, he held it in a vice-like grip. He squeezed. He moved his thumb around the knuckle area of the gloves as Resto desperately tried to pull away. Collins Sr. knew immediately what he was feeling. It wasn't padding. It was wet, soaked, rock-hard taped knuckles. He screamed for a commission inspector as he held on to Resto's right glove. Resto kept trying to pry himself free but could not do it. It wasn't until commission inspectors arrived that Collins released his grip. What the commission found were two eight-ounce gloves that had been tampered with.

"THESE ARE THE GLOVES THEY GAVE ME!" shouted Panama Lewis to commission officials. "THESE ARE THE GLOVES THEY GAVE ME! THESE ARE THE GLOVES THEY GAVE ME!"

Although Resto left the ring wearing the gloves, he left with commission officials right behind him. In his dressing room, Resto had his gloves removed by members of the NYSAC. The gloves were then impounded by the state agency.

Collins didn't stay for the postfight press conference. He was taken to a local hospital for overnight observation, but his dad checked him out in the middle of the night, electing to return home the following morning.

Before he left for the hospital, Billy Ray called his wife, Andrea, to tell her the news.

"I lost," he said. "I took a pretty bad beating." He cried. She cried.

At 7:00 a.m., without seeing the Collins family in the lobby, Sharav called their room. Collins Sr. answered. When he heard it was *Ring Magazine*, which he and his son had read religiously from cover to cover, he invited Ben to their room.

The elder Collins opened the door for Ben.

"He's on the bed," Collins Sr. told Ben.

Ben walked into the small room. In it were two beds. There, lying on his back, wearing sweatpants and no shirt, with his head propped on pillows, was Billy Jr. He was holding ice packs to the swelling lumps, bumps, and bruises that covered his face.

"Hi Billy," said Ben.

The fighter removed the ice packs to greet Sharav. As he took the ice packs off his beaten, purplish, misshapen face, Ben felt his knees sag.

"I was aghast," said Sharav. "I never expected to see Billy this badly beaten."

However, I did. I knew what Sharav would see. That's why I sent him there at such an ungodly hour. Boxing can never thank him enough for documenting the tragic scene in front of him.

Sharav asked if he could take a few photos. Both Junior and Senior agreed. As Sharav snapped several photos, Billy Sr. stood against a wall and sobbed.

"Look at my boy," he cried. "Look at what they did to my boy. Look at what they did to him." His words were like those of Vito Corleone as he peered at the bullet-ridden body of his oldest son, Sonny, executed by machine-gun-toting hitmen from the Barzini family in the Academy Award–winning film *The Godfather*.

"Look what they did to my boy," Collins Sr. continued to say, sobbing almost uncontrollably.

The commission's response was swift. And permanent. Resto would never throw a punch again as a pro. Panama Lewis would never work a corner again. Neither would Pedro Alvarado. They were banned from ever holding any form of professional boxing license.

To his family and friends watching at home in Antioch, Tennessee, Billy Ray Collins Jr. was a hero for the gallant fight he waged in Madison Square Garden. A large crowd awaited both Junior and Senior as they stepped off the flight from New York the next morning.

"Bill-Lee! Bill-Lee! Bill-Lee!" they chanted as the men walked toward them. As they got closer, and Billy Ray's pulverized face could be seen clearly, the chanting quickly became less and less. Then it stopped. The silence caused by Collins's battered, swollen, purple face was deafening.

Collins Jr. went to eye specialists, who all concurred that the massive hematomas (swelling) around his eyes would have to subside before an accurate assessment could be made as to any ocular injuries. Ice and time took the hematomas away, but they couldn't take away the tear in the iris of one of his eyes. The injury was permanent, he was told. He'd never fight again.

In the next two months after the assault on Collins—it certainly wasn't a boxing match!—I called the Collins home in Antioch two or three times. Each time I spoke to Billy Sr., he sounded both angry and sad. I couldn't blame him. His son, who lived just up the road, had trouble holding on to a job because of vision problems. Young Collins had his promising boxing career yanked out from under him, and now he couldn't hold on to any job back at home. He became argumentative, especially toward those around him the most—his wife, his parents, and his four siblings.

Billy Jr. went into a depression, a deep dark hole from which no one could pull him out. He began drinking and using drugs. On September 21, 1983—his 22nd birthday—I called to wish him happy birthday. It was the middle of the day. He answered the phone and said he had been napping. This was not the mature and focused Billy Collins Jr. I had known just three months earlier.

I spoke to his father the following month. I wanted to see how Billy Jr. was doing.

"They couldn't beat my boy fair and square so they cheated, they downright cheated," he said over and over. I was the one who called, and I didn't know what to say. Perhaps I was hoping to hear news that young Collins's eyes had miraculously healed and he was back in training. It was not to be.

On March 7, 1984, while riding the Long Island Railroad from my home on Long Island to my office at *Ring Magazine* in New York City, I was reading the sports pages of the local paper, *Newsday*, when a caption among assorted sports stories hit me harder than any punch: "BILLY COLLINS JR., 22, DIES IN CRASH."

I virtually lost my breath, gasping as I saw the headline. After I read it, I sat stunned for the remainder of the almost one-hour ride into New York City.

I thought of the glove tampering, the brutal beating Collins stood up to, the ghastly photos taken by Sharav. We were closing that day on the June 1984 issue of *The Ring*, and I needed to turn in my editorial. It was already written, with each of the three sanctioning bodies in boxing—the World Boxing Council, the World Boxing Association, and the International Boxing Federation—drawing my wrath.

My wrath toward them would have to wait. My wrath was now focused on the men who conspired to remove—and indeed did remove—the padding from Luis Resto's gloves almost nine months earlier.

At that moment, I didn't know the circumstances behind Collins's death, but I did know it was a car accident and I did know of his drinking and drug abuse. I suspected he died while impaired and behind the wheel. His death was ruled a drowning after his car flipped and went into a culvert/pond in Tennessee. I will always believe his death was directly related to the depression, the eye injuries, and his career-ending loss to Resto and company.

When I got to the office, I bolted into the office that had previously been occupied by Bert Sugar and, 15 years earlier, Nat Fleischer.

"Jenny, can you come in here a second, please?" I yelled to my secretary in the adjoining office. When she came in, I told her of Collins's death. She, along with the rest of my staff, had met young Collins before and really liked him.

She began to cry when I told her of the news.

"Please hold all my calls," I said. "I am going to call Billy Sr. Then, I am going to write my editorial on his death." Little did I know it would become one of the strongest pieces I would ever write and perhaps the most effective, talked-about editorial in the long history of *The Ring*.

First, I called the home of Billy Collins Sr. Our call lasted perhaps 20 minutes. He sobbed and wailed his way through all of it.

"Those animals killed Billy Ray," he said. "They killed him!"

"I'm so sorry, Billy," is what I said, over and over. It's all I could possibly say. It's all I could think of saying. He tried to be composed.

But when Collins told me the story of he and his son by the fishing hole shortly before his death, he cried in a wail that was heard over my phone by Jenny in the outer office. Tears fell steadily from my face upon my desk.

"No calls, Jenny," I said. "No calls. I have an editorial to write."

She walked into my office. She stared at me as I sat there and cried. She cried, too.

She walked over to me and gave me a hug.

"Go get 'em, boss," she said.

She knew what I was going to write. She felt it.

Here are a few excerpts from my editorial, which appeared in the June 1984 issue of *The Ring*:

> "The night it happened [the night of the fight], he thought he was gonna die," the elder Collins told me on the phone. "Afterwards, he tried to pretend he didn't care. He tried to be strong around me. But inside, he was dying. One day, Billy told me he was going fishing. A little while later, I decided to join him. When I got down to the stream, I saw him lying . . ." His voice cracked. He swallowed hard, took a deep breath, then continued.
>
> "He was laying face down in the grass, his head in his arms, and he was crying. I laid right down next to him, put my arms around him, and cried with him. Why did that animal [the person who removed the padding] do that to him? Why? He killed my son!"

And this:

> Alcohol became a friend to Collins. . . . Alcohol, which had always been a distant stranger to Billy, was responsible for Collins's death. Alcohol, as well as the person who removed the padding from Resto's gloves.

Along with my final paragraph, which screamed for justice:

> If indeed there is a heaven, Billy Collins Jr. will spend eternity in paradise. As for his killer, the man I think to be his killer, "The Grim Reaper" will come calling one day and send him to burn in the fires of hell for the same amount of time.

I entitled the editorial "MURDER: PLAIN AND SIMPLE."

When the magazine came out in April, I was contacted by FBI special agent Joe Spinelli. I was also contacted by *New York Times* boxing writer and future Hall-of-Famer Michael Katz. My column had touched a nerve. Katz's follow-up story exposed that nerve. Law enforcement officials put a case together against Panama Lewis and Luis Resto. In 1986, both men stood trial in New York City. They were found guilty of assault, criminal possession of deadly weapons (Resto's fists), and conspiracy. In addition, Lewis was found guilty of tampering with a professional sports contest. Prosecutors in the case also charged Lewis, who deliberately removed padding from Resto's gloves, with illegal assault.

Lewis was sentenced to six years behind bars; Resto was sentenced to three. Resto was released in 1989, while Lewis was released in 1990.

Shortly after Resto's release from prison, he walked into 270 Broadway and headed up to the offices of the New York State Athletic Commission. He was 33. His intention: To have his boxing license reinstated, a license that had been permanently revoked by Commissioner Jack Prenderville soon after Resto's bout with Collins. Resto went by himself and without an appointment. He asked to see the commissioner.

I was the commissioner

My intercom buzzed.

"Commissioner, Luis Resto is here and would like to see you," said Michele. When I asked her what he wanted, she said, "He doesn't speak English very well. He just said he wants to see you."

I asked her to send in my bilingual athletic assistant, Emma Elizondo. She'd explain to Resto what I was saying and interpret for me what it was he was trying to convey.

My secretary showed Resto in. Ms. Elizondo was right behind him. When he walked in, I was sitting behind my oversized wooden desk. I stood up and walked in front of my desk to greet him.

"Good morning, Luis," I said.

"Good morning, Commissioner," he said. He reached out to shake my hand. I obliged.

"What is it you are here for?" I asked. Ms. Elizondo repeated my words in Spanish.

"I have come to ask you if I could please have my boxing license back?" he replied through Ms. Elizondo.

I motioned to a chair.

"Please sit," I said, pointing to a chair. He didn't need an interpreter for that.

He looked up at me with the saddest eyes I have ever been looked at with.

"So?" he questioned. Then he spoke Spanish and Ms. Elizondo interpreted. "So, I have come here in the hopes of having my boxing license returned. I was in jail because of what I did and now I come here to you, hoping I can be, uh . . ."

Ms. Elizondo helped Resto find the word he was looking for.

The word was *reinstated.*

He nodded his head. Resto was looking to be reinstated. He wanted to resume his boxing career.

As he spoke, I was in front of him, leaning back on my desk, supporting myself with both hands.

"Luis, I am going to ask you a question, and I want you to answer honestly." The words were repeated to Resto in Spanish.

"Did you know that the padding was being removed from your gloves?"

He took a moment, then looked at the floor. He shook his head.

"No," he said, in a voice that was barely audible.

"Look me in the eyes and tell me that, Luis. Look me in the eyes." As Ms. Elizondo repeated my words, he looked at me. With my index fingers, I pointed to my eyes.

"Right here," I said. "Right here."

"Now, did you know that the padding was removed from your gloves?" I asked again. Ms. Elizondo translated.

He looked me in the eyes and said, "No." Then he immediately looked away.

I took a deep breath. I looked at Ms. Elizondo.

"Luis, please tell me the truth," I said. "You have already been in jail for this crime. You cannot go back to jail again, no matter what you say. So, please be honest. I need you to be honest with me."

Then I asked him again, "Did you know the padding was being removed from your gloves?"

He looked toward me but not at me. In fact, he looked up at the ceiling above my head.

"No," he said.

I looked at Ms. Elizondo once more. I shook my head.

"I'm sorry, Luis," I said. "I cannot reinstate your license."

He did not need Ms. Elizondo's translation.

"Please, Commissioner. Please!" he begged.

"I am sorry, Luis. I cannot do it." I extended my hand.

He stood up and hesitatingly extended his.

"When can I come back and ask you again?" he said in Spanish. Ms. Elizondo interpreted.

"In one year, Luis. In one year. But, to be honest, I don't see your license being returned. Ever!" He lowered his head when he heard my words spoken back to him by my athletic assistant, who then put her arm around him and walked him toward the door.

Resto came back to me the next year and the year after that, looking to have his boxer's license reinstated. Each time came a rejection. He then began coming in for a cornerman's license. For that, I turned him down, as well. I also turned down Panama Lewis's written request for the reinstatement of his cornerman's license.

Throughout the years, I have asked many friends and colleagues in the business if they believed—even a little bit—that Panama Lewis and Luis Resto should ever be relicensed.

One man who echoed the sentiments of almost everyone I spoke to was Showtime boxing analyst Steve Farhood, who, like me, is also a former editor in chief of *The Ring*, and a 2014 inductee into the New York Boxing Hall of Fame.

"I have to say no to any relicensing of either Luis Resto or Panama Lewis," said Farhood. "Despite the fact that both have paid their dues by serving time in jail is irrelevant to the licensing argument. The crime was so heinous that relicensing him is unjustifiable and plain wrong."

In 2009, Eric Drath, of Livestar Entertainment, wrote, produced, and directed a documentary entitled *Assault in the Ring*, which aired that summer on HBO. It is a story that simply had to be told and documented, and Drath did an excellent job in making the pitiful Resto his central character. The documentary, which won a well-deserved Emmy Award, has Resto trying to make amends with the Collins family in Tennessee and with his grown sons, who hadn't seen their father in years. In the documentary, Resto comes across as a likable poor soul who is intellectually deficient and easily steered. An attempted confrontation with Panama Lewis at a gym in Coconut Creek, Florida, gives a perfect example of this, as Lewis quickly diffuses Resto's anger with hypnotic double-talk, sweet talk, and promises that things would get better for him.

While both have been permanently banned from ever being relicensed as professionals in any manner, Lewis still does quite nicely as a trainer in Florida, although unable to work corners at a fight. Resto lives in the basement of a gym in the Bronx, doing menial tasks around the gym to pay his rent. At best, it is a sad existence.

From time to time, I see Resto at boxing cards in New York. Our greetings are short and cordial.

"Hello, Luis," is usually what I say.

"Hello, Commissioner," is usually what he says.

At a boxing card in December 2014, I saw Resto as he was walking into the men's room as I was walking out. We exchanged our usual hellos.

Then he said, in his heavy Spanish accent, "You know, Commissioner, you ruined my life."

At first, I was stunned, surprised, shocked he would say that. In an instant, however, I processed where his life was and where it had come from. He was nowhere, and he had come from nowhere. Panama Lewis had, at one time, convinced Resto that he was good enough to one day fight for—and win—a world boxing title. The smooth, sharp-talking Lewis had Resto convinced years earlier that untold riches would soon be his. Resto liked the way that sounded. He liked the promises. All he had to do was fight. Lewis would do the rest. Then they were caught. And punished.

Now, as he approaches his 64th birthday, he spends much of his time in his drab basement apartment in the Bronx. Perhaps he thinks about what could have been or, at least, what Panama Lewis once told him could have been. Perhaps he replays the night of June 16, 1983, over and over. Perhaps he replays his jail time for the crime he committed.

Luis Resto remains in jail—his basement apartment is his jail cell. Unlike jail, he is allowed to go out into the world. Only, Luis Resto has no place to go, other than to a boxing card with the owner of the gym. Then, it's back to his jail cell. Sleep must be his only solace, but only if he doesn't dream. For Resto, dreams must all turn into nightmares.

No wonder Luis Resto thinks I ruined his life. Resto has never been able to comprehend or realize the lives he derailed and truly ruined: from Billy Collins's parents to his wife, daughter, relatives, and close friends, to Billy Collins himself, who was a shining contender one day, while the next day he was a beaten-up pug, headed into a world of depression, alcohol, drugs, and suicide.

To Panama Lewis, yes, those were the gloves given to you, as you told commission officials right after the fight. But they were given to you in pristine condition. You turned them into deadly weapons and placed them on the hands of Luis Resto, who delivered them repeatedly upon the face of Billy Collins Jr.

Call the actions of Lewis, Resto, and company whatever you feel like. No, they weren't near Collins when he took his drinks and swallowed his pills. Nor were they with him when he drove excessively and dangerously fast, crashing and submerging his car into a culvert. Their plan wasn't for him to die. It was just for him to lose. Maybe a cut eye early and the fight would have been stopped on a TKO. Maybe a hard punch would stagger him and the referee would stop it. Top Rank's plan was for Collins to win. Lewis, Resto, and company's plan was for Collins to lose.

Lewis was too consumed with winning to care. Resto was too easily persuaded to do anything different. So, when Luis Resto looked at me and said, "You know, Commissioner, you ruined my life," I wanted to scream at him. I wanted to look him in the eyes and scream, "You cheated, Luis! You downright cheated! How dare you stand there and tell me I ruined your life! *You* ruined your own life! Panama Lewis ruined your life! I did not ruin your life! Don't blame me! Blame yourself!" But I didn't. I just thought those words. Then, I looked directly at Resto. I stared right through this sad, broken, dejected, pathetic ex-fighter. He lowered his head, just like he had in my office more than

25 years earlier. I stared at him for a moment, then spun around and headed for the door. As I did, he spoke.

"I never thought the fight would turn out the way it did," Resto said. "Panama said they used to do this all the time in the olden days. I didn't mean to hurt him. I just wanted to win. Panama said a big fight would be next, probably a title fight. I'd get paid lots of money. My life would have been different."

My back was to Resto. I didn't turn to face him again. I didn't want to. I didn't want to scream. I didn't want to see those terribly sad eyes one more time. I just shook my head, took a deep breath, and walked out.

I actually believe Luis Resto—I even believe Panama Lewis—when he says they never meant for Billy Collins Jr.'s life to spiral out of control because of their actions. But it did. I know that what happened to Billy Collins on March 7, 1984, happened at his own hands. I didn't need to read through the toxicology report to know that.

But chances are, all this never would have happened had Luis Resto fought Billy Collins with boxing gloves that had not been tampered with.

In the legal sense, Panama Lewis and Luis Resto did not murder Billy Collins Jr.

Yet, as a longtime boxing journalist and state regulator, I know what to call it. After looking at that ghastly postfight photo of Billy Ray perhaps more than anyone, and after hearing Billy Sr. wailing—screaming in pain—on the phone the morning after his son's death, I know exactly what it was.

Billy Collins Sr. cried to me, "They murdered my boy."

He said it was "murder, plain and simple."

8

HANDBALL JIM
AND DOLLAR BILL

One day, circa 1983, a teacher at the Tryon School for Boys in Catskill, New York, was watching from the back of the gym with interest while 17-year-old Mike Tyson was hitting a heavy bag.

The teacher, Bobby Stewart, was a former professional boxer. In the three years he fought pro (1974–1977), Stewart amassed a 13-3 record. He began teaching at Tryon soon after hanging up his gloves.

Stewart had watched hundreds of Tryon's boys hit the heavy bag. He saw kids with speed, and he saw kids with power. But when it came to Tyson, Stewart knew he had never seen anyone like him. In Tyson, he knew he was looking at a diamond in the rough. He also knew he'd have to call his old trainer, Cus D'Amato. You see, Cus was a "diamond expert."

When the pudgy, bespectacled, 72-year-old saw his "diamond," he was ecstatic. Thirty years earlier, D'Amato had trained and guided Floyd Patterson to the heavyweight title but had split with Patterson due to Patterson's insistence on fighting Sonny Liston in 1962. D'Amato lived in a Victorian house in Catskill, New York, along with his longtime friend, Camille Ewald. It was there that Tyson lived, trained, and fought almost two dozen amateur fights in 1983 and 1984, before turning professional in March 1985.

D'Amato's two wealthy friends from New York City—Jim Jacobs and Bill Cayton—helped D'Amato pay his mortgage on the home. He, in turn, housed, fed, cared for, and trained the businessmen's array of fighters. Included among that group was welterweight Kevin Rooney, whom both Jacobs and Cayton had high expectations for, and world champion Wilfred Benitez. But when Rooney was knocked out by Davey Moore in 1981, and then suffered back-to-back stoppage losses to Alexis Arguello and Terry Crawley in 1982, the D'Amato–Jacobs–Cayton triumvirate began looking at Rooney, along with another young fighter—Teddy Atlas—as their understudies to D'Amato; however, when Atlas bolted from the house after a run-in with Tyson in the mid-1980s and before Tyson turned pro, the D'Amato understudy role was left to Rooney.

Under the guidance, teaching, scrutiny, and my-way-or-the-highway rule of D'Amato, Rooney became the physical side of D'Amato. When Cus talked, everyone listened. When Cus barked orders, everyone sprang into action. D'Amato was Jacobs and Cayton's "director of boxing operations," so to speak. Jacobs and Cayton were the business side.

In addition to managing fighters, Jacobs and Cayton owned Big Fights, Inc., a film company that had the most elaborate collection of fight films in the world. Many of those films were found by Jacobs in his travels throughout the world as the world handball champion. He also played racquetball at an elite level.

I know firsthand how good of a racquetball player he was. During the 1980s, in my days as editor of *The Ring*, I played in a racquetball league. Although nowhere near the player Jacobs was, I could hold my own against just about anyone else who wasn't an elite or world-class player.

In those days, Jacobs and I would go to breakfast every Wednesday at the restaurant next to *The Ring* offices at 120 W. 31st Street in New York City—the Cosmic Coffee Shop. We always talked boxing, boxing, and more boxing. One morning at breakfast in the winter of 1984, I asked Jacobs about his handball playing. During his talk of handball, he said, "I also play racquetball at a very high level." I told him I, too, played racquetball and dubbed myself as being "better than most." I added, "I'll make you run!"

Wrong thing to say!

Jacobs smiled. I could see he was holding back a laugh. I wondered why he had that reaction. I soon found out. He challenged me.

Jacobs met me at the racquetball club I belonged to on Long Island the following night. We bet on the game. The loser would buy breakfast the following Wednesday at the Cosmic Coffee Shop.

I was more than surprised when Jacobs said, "20 points wins—and you can start with 19." Until that moment, I didn't realize what I was in for. But, when he said, "You can start with 19," I knew.

Right from the start, balls whizzed by me at speeds I never knew racquetballs were capable of traveling. I was ahead 19–1. Before I knew it, the score was 19–6, then 19–11, and then 19–15. I was running all over the court, while Jacobs was barely moving. He stood in the center of the court and never moved more than six inches in any direction. Sometimes, as I was about to hit the ball, he'd say something like, "Lower right corner." He'd then proceed to return my shot exactly to the spot he said.

It was 19–17, 19–18, and then it was tied at 19.

There's no Cinderella story here. I lost, 20–19. In reality, I lost 20–0. I scored not a single point off Jacobs. I was exhausted from chasing that stupid little rubber ball all over the court. I had just gone 15 rounds against the champion who toyed with me. It was then I realized why he had smiled at my challenge the day before when I said, "I'll make you run!"

I was like a young and cocky, but vastly inexperienced and hopelessly outgunned, fighter, saying to the champion of my weight division, "I'd like to spar with you, and I promise to go easy." I dared him. I pushed his competitive button. You don't ever do that to a competitive athlete. *Ever!* He took me up on my challenge, and I got spanked. I got whupped!

The Wednesday following my drubbing, breakfast was on me. It was at that breakfast that Jacobs told me about a young heavyweight he and Bill Cayton were working with in Catskill. He told me about the young heavyweight, about his troubled background, about being sent to reform school, and about teaming up with Cus D'Amato. Once D'Amato told Jacobs and Cayton about his young protégé, they didn't think twice about funding what Jacobs called the "Cus D'Amato Project."

Only days after I left *The Ring* in October 1984 to replace Angelo Dundee as the USA Network's boxing analyst, I was called by Jim Jacobs, telling me he and Bill Cayton would like to meet with me for lunch. He said they had something to offer me that they thought "will be beneficial to all of us." When I asked him to expound on that, he said, "Please join us for lunch. You'll find out then."

My initial guess was that it had something to do with either their company, Big Fights, Inc., or the teenage heavyweight Jacobs had been telling me about and whom I had seen flatten an opponent in the first round in the Empire Games (a New York state amateur tournament) a few months earlier. I quickly realized that Jacobs and Cayton had a bright, hardworking young man about my age—Steve Lott—working for them, handling their large and growing collection of fight films, so I next figured the meeting had to do with their heavyweight.

I met the duo in a New York City diner near their office on 40th Street. The two were different physically and in age but similar in a business sense. Jacobs, who was 54, stood no more than 5-foot-8, but he was a lean-muscled, all-around athlete. Cayton, at 66, stood at about 5-foot-10, and although a sports fan, he was anything but an athlete. While their partnership had made both men extremely wealthy, each was frugal with their money.

CHAPTER 8

During my frequent breakfasts with him to the Cosmic Diner between 1980 and 1984, Jacobs insisted on picking up the tab ("I know what Bert pays you," he joked). Our eggs, with toast and coffee, or French toast or pancakes, usually cost about $2.99 per person. I used to cringe when I'd see Jacobs leave the waitress a 50-cent tip on the $6 bill. As we stood up to walk to the register, I would discreetly leave another 50 cents on the table or take the quarters off the table and leave a dollar bill. One day, as Jacobs was paying the bill, he forgot that he had already left his tip and walked back to the table. He saw four quarters together on the table and realized he had indeed left a tip and it was two quarters—not four. He scooped up two of the quarters and handed them back to me a bit perturbed.

"Why did you double the tip?" he asked. "She deserves her 50 cents, nothing more. She is slow to bring us our coffee and just as slow to give us refills. And how about when the kitchen rings for her to pick up our orders? She just about crawls to get them! Why would you give her another 50 cents? And how long have you been doing that?"

"I've been doing it for a long time, Jimmy," I told him. "I believe in tipping at least 15 percent. At that rate, my meal alone is 45 cents. You usually leave 50 cents. So, I throw in a little bit more."

He shook his head as if I had plunked down a $50 bill for a tip instead of 50 cents.

"Please don't do that again," he said. "Tips are bonuses for good work. Additional tipping is for exceptional work. She does not do exceptional work. She does not even do good work. The tip I give her is plenty!" He gave me a wink and, just like that, changed the subject.

When Jacobs and Cayton formed their partnership in 1960, they began to buy the rights to fight films. Many were found by Jacobs as he traveled the world in his capacity as world handball champion.

Bill Cayton made his fortune throughout the years by creating sports programming for the early days of television. The sport he gave to the networks was boxing, and it immediately caught on. Later on, he gave them billiards.

While Jacobs loved making and having money, Cayton was worse. He was obsessed with it. He loved it in the same way Jacobs did. But he also loved talking about it to the point of being almost obnoxious.

Just moments after I was seated in the diner at a table with Jacobs and Cayton, the handball legend excused himself and headed off to the men's room. Cayton watched as Jacobs rose from the table and walked down the hall, then disappeared into the men's room. Then Cayton leaned over and looked down the hall. I wondered what or who he was watching. I found out a moment later. He was making sure Jacobs was gone from sight, at least for a minute or so. Then he did something that left me shocked, embarrassed, angry, and numb.

He reached into the inside pocket of his suit and pulled out a wad of money. A thick wad. With one hand, he held it in front of him. With the other hand, he fanned through it. All I saw were big bills—hundreds and fifties. It looked like the brick of bills you so often see Floyd "Money" Mayweather playing with.

I stared at Cayton and wondered what he was doing.

"See these bills, Randy?" asked Cayton.

I nodded my head curiously.

"Well, this is just a piece—a small piece—of what I have earned by working hard."

Is he about to offer me a job? I wondered. *Is that my bonus? Where is he going with this?*

Cayton continued.

"Jim and I know that you're now unemployed. But, when Jim comes back, we are about to make you an offer that will put some money back in your pocket. Remember, if you work hard, you, too, can have this kind of money in your pocket."

I kept hearing, "We are about to make you an offer . . ." over and over in my head.

Then, Cayton patted my left hand, which rested on the table. In a style unto himself, he said, "Oh, and you can order whatever you want. Anything. Don't worry. Jim and I have the bill." Then he again fanned what had to be several thousand dollars, smiled, and put it back in his inside pocket. That entire scene left me bewildered and angry at Cayton, not thankful for the lunch he was about to buy for me or the job he was about to offer me.

A few moments later, Jacobs returned and sat back down. Cayton looked at him and said, "I just told Randy about an offer we are about to make to him. Would you like to tell him, Jim?" Jacobs smiled, nodded, and pushed the glasses that always seemed to be slipping down his nose back up.

"Most certainly, Bill," he replied. Then he began.

"Randy, I've told you about a most extraordinary young heavyweight Bill and I are managing from up in Catskill, New York. He is only 18, but I can tell you, from everything I know about boxing, that he's going to be not only the heavyweight champion of the world, but the youngest heavyweight champion ever. His name is Mike Tyson."

I didn't have to think when I replied, "Younger than Muhammad Ali was when he won the title? He was 21. That means Tyson will have to become champion in the next three years."

"It will happen *before* three years," said Cayton.

"Our plan is to turn him pro before the end of this winter," added Jacobs. "We intend to keep him very busy. Remember at breakfast the other day . . . we were talking about the old-time fighters and how they used to fight at least once a month?"

I nodded.

"Well, Bill and I want to do the same thing with Tyson. We want to get him as many fights as we can in his first year, year and a half, then make a move up in the ratings."

"So where do I come in?" I inquired.

"You can help us get sparring partners," replied Jacobs.

Mike is tearing through his sparring partners faster than we can get them. Many of them leave after just one time in the ring with him. With your connections, we thought you'd be able to help get sparring partners for Mike. For every one you get to work with Mike, Bill and I will pay you $100. You can tell the fighter we will pay all his expenses to come to camp, we will pay him $50 for every round he spars with Mike, and we will pay him $50 for every day he stays in camp.

"Is that $50 for every round he lasts?" I asked.

"Very good question," replied Jacobs.

That's $50 for any part of a round. He may start a round and get pummeled a few seconds into it. That's $50. He may be asked to quickly jump in the ring and finish a round for a sparring partner who could not continue. That's $50. If he spars any part of a round with Mike, he will earn $50. So, if a guy spars three rounds with Mike and stays in camp for the night, he will have just earned $200. A few days of that and he will have earned a nice piece of change. You will earn $100 just for getting him to show up. Now that you're out of *The Ring*, we're sure you can use the money.

I nodded as my mind raced, thinking about the heavyweights I would call as soon as I got home.

Then, Cayton reached across the table and patted my hand yet again.

"If you don't want to use your home phone to make the calls, you can come into our office any time you'd like and use our phones." Then he repeated his words from a few minutes earlier.

"Remember, Jim and I have the check."

His words made me cringe and feel beholden to the wealthy business partners. When I returned home, I called my friend, boxing manager Shelly Finkel, who had accumulated his own fortune as a rock 'n' roll promoter and was friendly with the duo. When I told Finkel about the meeting, he wasn't surprised—either about the meeting or the choosing of some of their words and phrases.

"As you know, Randy, both are extremely wealthy men," said Finkel. "Their actions can sometimes be construed as obnoxious and disingenuous."

"Like Cayton pulling out a wad of money and waving it in front of me?" I asked.

He laughed it off, saying, "Yeh, like that. But he does stuff like that all the time."

"He's done that to you?" I inquired.

"No, but he's asked me, flat out, on several occasions, 'Shelly, how much are you worth?' He does that as a power trip," Finkel related. "He wants to know if he has more money than me. Know what I tell him?"

"No, tell me," I said.

"I tell him, 'Bill, I'm gonna make your day. You're worth more than me,'" said Finkel.

It drives him crazy! He then asks, "How much more? How much more am I worth? A little more? A lot more? How much more?" I never give him even a hint. He asks me the same question every time he sees me, and I always give him the same answer. It's who he is. It doesn't make him a bad person, but it's just who he is.

I understood. Then I asked Finkel, "What do you know about the young heavyweight Jacobs and Cayton are working with?"

"According to Jim, he's the future heavyweight champion of the world," Finkel said. "I'll tell you this—I have never heard Jim talk more glowingly about a fighter than he does about this Mike Tyson kid. He just might be everything that Jim says he is."

Almost immediately, I began sending sparring partners to the Catskills. Some lasted a fraction of a round, some lasted a few weeks. They always got their money. So did I. As for Tyson, he certainly was everything Jacobs told me he was going to be.

Unfortunately, Cus D'Amato passed away one year before seeing the "Cus D'Amato Project" become the youngest heavyweight champion ever.

It was just as unfortunate that Jacobs and Cayton never got to enjoy their champion, either. Within months of Tyson becoming champion, Jacobs fell ill. He was gone within 16 months after Tyson's coronation.

As for Bill Cayton, he was still Tyson's manager, but only on paper. Once Jim Jacobs passed away, the young champion's career was in the hands of Robin Givens and Don King.

At Jacobs's funeral on a cold March morning, Cayton tried to break the ice with Tyson. As usual, he wound up saying the wrong thing.

Instead of "My deepest condolences, Mike," Cayton said to Tyson, "I see you're wearing the coat I bought you."

Tyson glared at him.

"Want it back?" Tyson scoffed. Then he turned away from the man who was still, technically, his manager.

Jim Jacobs's death, in effect, spelled the death blow to Cayton's contract with Mike Tyson.

9

CATSKILL THUNDER

You're gonna eat lightning! You're gonna crap thunder!

—Mickey Goldmill to Rocky Balboa in *Rocky*

He wasn't the greatest world heavyweight champion ever. But he was quite possibly the most exciting. He was also the youngest.

Michael Gerard Tyson was born to James Kirkpatrick and Lorna Smith Tyson on June 30, 1966, in the heart of one of New York's most downtrodden neighborhoods—Bedford-Stuyvesant, Brooklyn. His father bolted from the household before Mike was two, leaving his mother—who began using her maiden name Tyson—to care for and raise Mike and his two siblings, a brother and a sister. Unable to pay the rent, Lorna moved the family a short time later to Brownsville, an even more impoverished area in Brooklyn, where the per capita income is among the lowest in the country.

In such an environment you grow up fast and hard and without many rules, other than the rules of survival. Young Mike fought to eat. He learned early how to use his fists. He fought for everything. He also mugged—and stole. He found solace, comfort, and serenity on the roof of his apartment building, where he raised pigeons.

One day, while Tyson was in his early teens, an older neighborhood tough confronted Tyson as the future heavyweight champion of the world walked down his street holding, stroking, and fatherly kissing one of his pigeons. The older youth asked Tyson if he could hold the pigeon. Tyson gently handed the pigeon over. What happened next would leave, as Tyson told me years later, "an indelible mark on my psyche." The older youth grabbed the pigeon around the neck with one hand and around the head with the other. With one mighty, vicious, violent, sadistic twist, he broke the pigeon's neck, killing it. Tyson screamed, "NOOOOOOOOOOO!" his shout reverberating through the ghetto. The demented bird-killer then handed the dead pigeon back to Tyson, laughing as he did so. He didn't laugh for long. A crying Tyson gently placed the dead bird on the ground. The pigeons were all Tyson had. Now, all he could hear was the laughter from the bird's killer. Anger flared his nostrils. Rage engulfed him. The bird-killer should have turned and run as fast as he could. But he never expected little Mike, the kid with the squeaky voice and the lisp, to be the brutal fighting machine that was about to strike.

Tyson coiled, then exploded a punch on the bigger, heavier, older boy's jaw. A second punch was right behind it. The bigger kid buckled and headed for the pavement. It didn't matter. Tyson continued his fusillade of blows on the teen who had purposefully and laughingly just killed his bird. Head shots and body shots crashed into him. Bones snapped like pretzels. When Tyson was through, he leaned over his bleeding, semiconscious victim and said, "You're gonna probably die here. But if you don't, if you do survive, you'd better make sure I never see your face again. Because if I do, just know I *will* kill you." Tyson told me he never saw the guy again.

That incident took place at the tail end of the 1970s, when Tyson had just begun his teen years. No one—certainly not Tyson—could have imagined the life of fame and riches that were headed his way before the next decade would be even half over.

Boxing was meant for Mike Tyson, especially the 1985–1988 version of Mike Tyson. He had an angry youth and took that honed anger into the ring. In his first year as a pro, opponents were lined up and knocked over at a pace unseen in decades. Before his professional career was one year old, Tyson was already 18–0. No one had lasted the distance.

He certainly was everything his comanager, Jim Jacobs, told me he was going to be. From the time he exploded his heavy fists on the chin of opponent Hector Mercedes for pro victory number one in March 1985 until he fulfilled the prophecy of his managers by becoming the youngest heavyweight champion 20 months later, Tyson was the talk of the entire sports world. No athlete—in any sport—drew as much attention, notoriety, and exposure as the man most of the world called "Iron Mike" but who I nicknamed "Catskill Thunder" right after his pro debut. It was a name Tyson told me he loved from the first time he heard me call him that on television.

I met Tyson shortly before his debut. I was called by Jim Jacobs and his partner, Bill Cayton, to "meet the man you get sparring partners for" (detailed in the previous chapter) in the offices of Big Fights, Inc. At the time, I was announcing for the USA Network's weekly fights—they weren't yet the *Tuesday Night Fights*—and I had the day to myself, so I headed into New York City.

Tyson had just taken a seat in a darkened projection room, where he was watching films of the all the heavyweight champions. Both Jacobs and Cayton walked me into the room. I could sense that each of them wanted to be the one to introduce me. I could also sense that each of them didn't want the other to make the introduction. As I came to learn, it was something they did in an attempt to formulate people's opinion as to which of them was the more powerful partner. In fact, the following year, while interviewing Tyson on camera for the Madison Square Garden Network, I said, "Tyson's managers, Jim Jacobs and Bill Cayton, are swiftly moving their young heavyweight into title contention." After the interview, Cayton, who had been listening on headset, asked me why I said "Jim Jacobs and Bill Cayton," as opposed to "Bill Cayton and Jim Jacobs." I told him I didn't know and it didn't really matter.

"To me, it matters," said Cayton. "Please, next time you mention us, can you put me first?" I told him I would. Whether I ever did I can't remember. I simply gave it no thought one way or the other from that moment onward.

I do remember it was Jacobs who introduced me to Tyson. I was introduced as former editor in chief of *Ring Magazine*. The word *former* hurt to hear. Cayton was quick to jump right in and say, "But you know Randy as the color analyst on the USA Network's weekly fights. Jim and I think he does such a great job on them."

Tyson stood up and shook my hand. It was a firm handshake, although not one of those overly macho, I-can-crush-your-puny-little-hand handshakes.

"Do you like watching the old-time fighters?" Tyson asked.

"I love watching them!" I exclaimed. "Mind if I watch with you?"

"Not at all," said Tyson.

As we watched the heavyweight champions in action, Tyson said, "I have fought each one of them in my mind. I think about the strategy I would need to beat each one."

I found it interesting that this young heavyweight, who had not yet thrown a punch as a pro, was already "fighting" history's top heavyweights.

"Do you beat them?" I asked him with interest. "Some of them? All of them?"

His answer surprised me.

"I win all of them except one," Tyson told me, as, on the screen, Floyd Patterson knocked out Ingemar Johansson in their 1960 rematch and as the announcer was saying, "Making Patterson the first man to ever regain the heavyweight championship."

"You beat all of the heavyweight champs except one? Who didn't you beat?" I asked.

Tyson's face dropped.

"I don't beat Sonny Liston," he responded.

The timing could not have been better. As Tyson mentioned Sonny Liston, the announcer on the film was saying,

> The date is April 15, 1959, and the place is the Miami Beach Auditorium. The fighters are the world's top two heavyweights and quite possibly the two hardest punchers the division had seen since Rocky Marciano. Cleveland Williams, out of Houston, Texas, has a record of 43–2 with 35 knockouts, while Liston, out of St. Louis, Missouri, brings a record of 23–1 into the fight with 19 by way of knockout. Williams weighed in at 210¼ pounds, while Liston weighed in at 212½ pounds.

Almost from Liston's first punch—a ramrod of a left jab to Williams's head—Tyson began to get upset.

"Look at that jab," he moaned. "I can't get through it. There's nothing I can do to get past it. Nothing!" He sat there and groaned every time Liston landed a punch on the lean, muscular man called "Big Cat."

As we watched, Tyson became more upset.

In the second round, Liston dropped Williams with a right cross followed by a left hook. As Williams went down, Tyson became very upset.

"See that! See that! See that!" Tyson moaned. "The man is just brutal!"

When he got up, Liston pummeled Williams in a corner, dropping him with a barrage of blows. When Williams arose again on spaghetti-like legs, the referee waved the fight off, prompting another moan from Tyson.

"I could never beat that man. Never! There is nothing I could do to beat him."

Seeing how upset Tyson was getting, I said, "There's nothing to get upset about, Mike. I guarantee that you'll never have to fight Sonny Liston [who died 14 years earlier]. I guarantee it."

"But I do fight him," Tyson told me. "I fight him in here." He pointed to his head. "And when I fight him, it's very real. And I never, ever, win."

We continued to watch other heavyweights, and Tyson told me of his fight plan for each of them. Included was a plan to use against the man who currently held the heavyweight title, a man Tyson would indeed beat in 1988—Larry Holmes.

Although we continued to view and discuss other heavyweights, it was Liston who stayed on Tyson's mind throughout the entire session. After watching another heavyweight champion in action, Tyson wondered aloud, "How would he [the fighter we just watched] have done against Liston?"

When the film was done, Tyson took a deep breath and said, "One day, I'm gonna be on that film. One day, I'm gonna be champion."

I had heard those words from probably every fighter I ever met. And from just about every one, those words were not even close to being realistic. With Tyson, I knew they were. He was born to be a prizefighter. He was being trained full-time, both mentally and physically, to knock men out. He was a machine who was being groomed and turned into perhaps the greatest fighting machine ever assembled. He had the team and the money behind him. During the next five years, he was every great fighter rolled into one. It took the death of two of his mentors, along with the efforts of a tireless, relentless, intimidating, convincing, powerful promoter—as well as the affections of a beautiful woman— to destroy the mental edge and, inevitably, the invincibility of the fighting machine named Mike Tyson.

Because I had been so close to the scene, I realized everything I had been hearing about Tyson and his fighting prowess was true. From a ringside working press seat, I saw him in each of his first 20 professional bouts. I am the only journalist who can say that. After each fight, Cus D'Amato reminded me I was watching the development of the future heavyweight champion of the world. For him, to see this young, former Brooklyn street thug become heavyweight champion of the world would be, as D'Amato told me, his "greatest dream come true." Unfortunately, D'Amato never got to realize his dream. He contracted pneumonia in October 1985, and passed away on November 4. His death came only a few days before Tyson KO'd Sam Scaff in 1:19 of the first round in the Felt Forum at Madison Square Garden.

On July 11, 1986, Tyson fought Lorenzo Boyd in the Catskills region of Swan Lake, New York. The fight was shown live on the Madison Square Garden Network. The MSG Network's Sam Rosen was the blow-by-blow announcer for the fight. I handled the color.

Going into the bout, Tyson was 22–0. With the exception of one-sided decisions against James "Quick" Tillis and Mitch "Blood" Green earlier in the year, Tyson had knocked everyone else out. Fourteen of them were in the first round. Many of them were quick knockouts. Very quick. There was a 37-second knockout of Robert Colay, 39-second knockouts of Michael Johnson and Ricardo Spain, a 50-second knockout of Mark Young, a 52-second knockout of Trent Singleton, and a 54-second stoppage of Sterling Benjamin. Six other opponents failed to make it to the midpoint of round one. His fastest career knockout would come just 15 days after the Boyd fight, which I was announcing. In that one, it took Tyson just 30 seconds to put an end to Marvis Frazier's night. The fight was seen on ABC-TV with a young Jim Lampley at the microphone.

As Tyson prepared for Boyd and as I prepared to announce the show with Rosen, I took a long, deep look into Tyson's impressive record. I added up the minutes and seconds Tyson had spent in the ring in his 22-bout career. His total in-ring time was 127 minutes, 58 seconds. That included his two 10-round distance fights. Take them out of the equation and his 20 other fights totaled 67 minutes, 58 seconds. That's an average of just 203.9 (let's say 204) seconds per fight. Keeping in mind every round has 180 seconds, those stats show Tyson's average knockout win coming 24 seconds into round two. Going by those stats, Lorenzo Boyd acquitted himself very well. He hung in until a brutal double right, first to the body and followed by an uppercut to the chin, ended Boyd's evening at 1:43 of the second round.

At this point, Tyson's wealthy brain trust had all but locked up a title bout against WBC heavyweight champ Trevor Berbick. In the postfight interview (which is viewable on YouTube), I asked Tyson the question that was on the mind of every boxing fan and boxing journalist.

"Is a title shot looming in 1986, can you tell us that?"

He replied, "I can't tell you that, because, as you know, Jim Jacobs and Bill Cayton keep a close eye on that. But I feel a big, big success plan happening very soon."

After I threw it back to Sam and was off camera, Tyson put an arm around my shoulder and whispered, "Don't say nothing, but I got two more fights lined up in the next month. After that, I'll get at [WBC champion] Trevor Berbick later this year."

In the next five weeks, Tyson stopped Frazier in 30 seconds and followed with a 10th-round TKO of Jose Ribalta. Unbeknownst to Tyson when he fought Lorenzo Boyd, he would also be booked to fight veteran Alfonzo Ratliff on September 6. Ratliff was stopped in 1:41 of the second round.

Eleven weeks later, Mike Tyson fulfilled the prophecy of Jim Jacobs by becoming the youngest heavyweight champion of all time, stopping titleholder Trevor Berbick in the second round in Las Vegas. At 20 years, 4 months, and 22 days old, he was 27–0, with 25 knockouts, and was already being touted as one of the great heavyweights of all time.

In 1987, Tyson defended his title four times. The last time a heavyweight titleholder had made as many as four title defenses in one year was 21 years earlier, when Muhammad Ali made an astounding five defenses in 1966. Since Tyson's four, no heavyweight champion has made as many as four defenses in a single year.

Tyson quickly became a media star. Jacobs and Cayton lined him up for interviews, photo shoots, commercials, news programs, talk shows, radio shows, appearances, and more interviews. All this was happening sandwiched in between his training and fighting.

As 1987 unfolded, two people entered Tyson's life and began to take over. One was promoter Don King. The other was actress Robin Givens.

Although Tyson had made it through the Tryon School for Boys, went to live with disciplinarian Cus D'Amato, and was being managed by two wealthy businessmen, he was still distrusting of most people. King and Givens were not *most* people.

It was late 1997. Tyson had just come off defending his heavyweight titles with a seventh-round destruction of 1984 Olympic heavyweight champion Tyrell Biggs. I was doing an interview with Tyson for the MSG Network in a restaurant in The Garden. Jacobs, Cayton, and Givens, along with a few sportswriters, stood off to the side, watching. The moment I was done, Givens walked over, smiled at me, and said hello, then gave Tyson a kiss on the lips. I heard her say, "Mike, I need you privately for a moment." Tyson nodded, then got up and followed Robin across the room. As he departed, Jacobs and Cayton walked over to me.

"She is up to no good," said Cayton. Jacobs, doing his best to hide his anger, shook his head slowly. He agreed with Cayton.

"Ah, love is in the air," I said, more waiting for a reaction from the two than actually meaning those words.

I got the reaction I expected. From both of them.

"Love, my ass!" Jacobs growled.

"Yeh, she loves him all right," said Cayton in a deprecating tone. "She loves his bank account."

"You got that right, Bill," replied Jacobs.

"This is all about the money," said Cayton, a man who knew more than a little about money and loved it a lot.

We watched as Tyson put his right arm around Robin and walked with her toward the writers and photographers.

I remained with Cayton and Jacobs for a few moments, watching the unbeaten heavyweight champion and his girlfriend entertain the media.

In a voice just loud enough for Jacobs and Cayton to hear me I said, "Well, until now, you've had Don King hanging all over him. Now you've got a king and a queen."

Both men looked at me. Both of them wore a look of anger and frustration.

"King we can handle," said Jacobs. "This," he said, motioning with an index finger toward Givens, "is something I don't think we can do anything about."

He was right.

From there, it got worse.

Jacobs had not been feeling well. He had been suffering from lymphocytic leukemia through the 1980s but hid his condition from everyone but a select few people. By late 1987, however, I knew something was wrong. It showed in his once-athletic body. It showed in his face.

During the first week of 1988, I went to Atlantic City with sportscaster Bruce Beck, with whom I cohosted a show on the MSG Network called *Boxing: The Sweet Science*. We took the trip to interview Mike Tyson, who would be defending his title against former champ Larry Holmes on January 21.

Following the interview, Tyson put an arm around my shoulders and whispered, "Randy, Jimmy is sick. He's very sick. I don't think he's going to make it."

"What?" I blurted out, loud enough for those nearby to hear me.

"He's in Texas right now for some tests," said Tyson. His eyes were watering.

"What does he have, Mike?" I asked the champ.

"I don't really know. I think it's some kind of leukemia. He's been there for a few days. He told me not to worry. He said he was going to Texas for a few days of tests. He said he was coming to the fight and that he'd be okay. I'm really worried about him."

I thanked Tyson for telling me, to which he replied, "I know you and Jim are close. But he hasn't talked to anybody about this, except maybe Lorraine [Jim's wife], Bill, and one or two others. He told me it's nothing. He told me not to even think about it. But I do think about it. I'm worried. I think it's serious. I think he's dying."

Although I knew Jacobs had been sick, that was the first I had heard anything of him being terminally ill.

On the drive home with Beck, we talked as much about the condition of Jacobs as we did about our interview with Tyson, which we were thrilled with.

Jim Jacobs was a favorite of everyone in the business. To think he could be terminally ill was not acceptable.

I returned to Atlantic City on January 20, the day before the fight. I was going to be doing the radio broadcast of the fight, alongside former heavyweight champion James "Bonecrusher" Smith. That afternoon, I saw Jacobs in the hotel's stationery store.

"Hi, Jimmy, how're you feeling?" I asked.

He became defensive.

"I'm feeling fine, Randy," he responded. Then he added, "Why would you ask me that?"

He saw through my very basic, everyday question.

"It's just an expression, Jim," I replied. "You know. How ya doin'?"

He didn't buy it.

"That's not why you asked me, is it?" he questioned.

"No, Jim, it's not," I said. "I know you. I've known you for years. We had breakfast every week for years while I was at *The Ring*. You've always been the picture of health. You just look . . ."

"Look what?" he snapped. "I look what?"

My thought was to say, "You look sick," because he did. He looked very sick. Instead, I said, "Well, you just look tired. You look drained. You know how I feel about you and I just have been concerned, that's all."

"Well, unconcern yourself, okay!" he shot back. "I'm fine. I'm just fine." He turned and walked away, leaving me feeling awful for asking. But I knew something was going on.

The next night, I got to the arena about an hour before the start of the undercard. While Bonecrusher and I were doing microphone checks with the control truck about an hour before going on the air, Jacobs approached me. When I saw him, I held up an index finger to let him know I'd only be a moment. He nodded his head.

When I finished giving the truck the levels they needed, I removed my headset and turned to Jacobs. I wondered why he had stopped by. I decided to keep it as simple as simple can be.

"Hi, Jimmy," I said. I stood up to greet him and extended my hand. He reached out, shook my hand, and then embraced me.

"Randy, I'm sorry for going off on you the way I did yesterday. I came over to apologize. You're a good friend and . . ."

I cut him off.

"Jim, you don't have to apologize for anything," I said. I stopped there and looked him in the eyes. I wanted to say more but didn't. I waited for his response. He knew I understood.

"Thank you, Randy," he said. "Thank you for everything. You're a true friend." He gave me another hug, said "Have a great broadcast," then turned and walked away. Those were the last words he ever said to me. It was the last time I ever saw him. It was the last fight of Mike Tyson's career he ever attended. While he watched from ringside as Tyson stopped Holmes in the fourth round, he watched from his bed two months later as Tyson KO'd Tony Tubbs in round two in Tokyo. Following the right uppercut that ended Tubbs's night, Jim Jacobs closed his eyes for the last time. The words Tyson spoke to me about Jacobs—"I think he's dying"—a few days before his KO of Larry Holmes became prophetic. Two days after Tyson beat Tubbs, Jacobs died from complications of his leukemia.

From here, Tyson's life began to fall apart. Rapidly.

Even though Tyson and the world knew his managers were Jim Jacobs and Bill Cayton, it was just Jacobs's name that appeared on the managerial contract filed with the New York State Athletic Commission. Knowing he was dying, Jacobs realized his death would leave Tyson without a manager of record. So, after discussing the situation with Cayton, the two then decided they'd void the current contract and have Tyson sign a new one, naming Bill Cayton as his manager. At about the time of the Holmes fight, Jacobs and Cayton met with the chairman of NYSAC, former world light heavyweight champion Jose Torres. They told Torres of their plan. Commissioner Torres gave his approval.

The duo had to act fast, as Jacobs was about to leave for Texas for another round of medical treatments, and they were not optimistic about his chances of survival for much longer. In addition, they felt promoter Don King closing in, smelling money the way a shark smells blood. They also felt Robin Givens closing in from another side—the marital side. If she latched onto Tyson before a contractual change could be made, she'd marry him and wind up as his manager for sure. In such a position, she would be in total control of the vast fortune Tyson would be capable of earning.

Tyson liked and respected both men, but he related more to the athletic, fun-loving, and easy-to-talk-to Jacobs than the older, more businesslike, and money-oriented Cayton. On top of it all, he trusted both men. He had no reason not to, as they had supported and helped him from the moment Cus D'Amato notified them of having just watched the "next great heavyweight."

So as not to cause any commotion and talk at the commission, as well as to prevent any leaks to the media, Jacobs, Cayton, and Tyson met at the diner where I had been taken to lunch by the wealthy managers a little more than three years earlier. They brought with them a new, blank manager's contract. Chairman Jose Torres had already signed it.

There, Jacobs and Cayton discussed Jacobs's health issues and explained to Tyson that it would be in his best interest to resign the contract, naming both Jacobs and Cayton as his managers of record. An emotional Tyson, concerned for Jacobs's health, willingly signed his name to the document. So did Cayton. It was then brought back to the commission and filed. Bill Cayton was now Mike Tyson's manager of record.

The quiet transition from Jacobs to Cayton as Tyson's manager was now complete. On February 7, 1988, Robin Givens became Robin Givens-Tyson. She was quick to the altar but too late to the gate to become her husband's manager. By this time, Jacobs was fighting for his life, not for the managerial control of Tyson. He and his partner had already taken care of that. Cayton beat Givens—along with Don King—in the race to the managerial reins of the best heavyweight on the planet.

The move infuriated both Givens and King, for obvious reasons. Each of them had Tyson's attention but not his managerial reins. While King and Givens kept an eye on Cayton, they also kept an insanely jealous eye on one another. They told Tyson stories of love, friendship, loyalty, and trust. They pulled at him from both directions.

His career unraveled rapidly. He and Robin divorced on Valentine's Day a year after they got married. In 1990, he lost his title and undefeated record when he was stopped in the 10th round. The following July, he was arrested in Indiana for the rape of beauty pageant contestant Desiree Washington.

Shortly before his trial began later that year, I spoke to Tyson by telephone. We talked for perhaps 20 minutes. He gave me his version of what happened the night Ms. Washington claims Tyson raped her. He claims what happened was consensual.

"Randy, Commissioner, I did not rape her," he told me.

In January 1999, I was working with South African heavyweight Francois Botha against Tyson in Las Vegas. A few days before the fight, I saw Tyson at a prefight press conference. We actually bumped into one another while turning a corner backstage at the MGM Grand about five minutes before the start of the press conference. I was pacing in the darkness because Botha was late arriving, and Tyson was pacing because he was deep in thought about his life. As we bumped into one another in the dim light, we each were quick to say, "I'm sorry" and "Excuse me." Then, through the darkness, we recognized one another.

We quickly embraced.

"Hi, Randy," said Tyson. "I heard you were working with Botha for this fight."

I nodded my head, saying, "Yeah, I'm handling his PR for this fight. I can't believe, in almost a month out here, this is the first time we have been able to speak with each other. How are you?"

Usually, that question draws an answer of "I'm fine, thank you," and a return response of "How are you?"

Not this time. After I asked Tyson that question, he said, "Not good, Randy. I'm really messed up."

I stared at him. My look said to him, "Please explain." He went on.

"Years ago, King told me he was my best friend, that I should trust only him. He said I shouldn't trust Robin, because she was after my money."

I listened intently. Tyson went on.

He told me, "She don't really love you. It's the money she loves." But Robin would then say to me, "Sweetheart, I'm your best friend." She told me I shouldn't trust Don [King], because all he wanted was my money. It really drove me into a dark place what they did to me. Each one was basically telling me the truth about the other's intentions, while at the same time, trying to put themselves off as my best friend. Can you believe that?

Then, standing in front of me, he put his hands on my shoulders and said, "I'm going to ask you a question, Randy. Please give me an honest answer. I need honesty right now."

I had no idea what kind of question Tyson was going to ask me, but I looked him in the eyes and told him, "Whatever it is, Mike, I promise to be 100 percent honest."

He nodded and said, "Fair enough."

Then he asked me, "Are you my friend?"

"Am I your friend?" I repeated.

"Yes, are you my friend?" he repeated. "Don King told me a long time ago that you were not my friend, that all the people I thought were my friends really weren't my friends at all. So, are you my friend?"

For a moment I stood there, taking in the magnitude and scope of Tyson's question, and the thoughts that must have been in his head. Then I replied to his question.

"Of course I'm your friend, Mike. I have always been your friend and supporter. I was your friend when I was a sportscaster, I was your friend when I was commissioner, and I am still very much your friend now. I will always be your friend. That is 100 percent the truth."

He smiled and gave me a hug.

"I'm glad to hear that, Randy," Tyson said, almost in a whisper. "I am in so much pain. My head hurts from the pain I've gone through."

He put his hands on the sides of his head. I could really see he was in anguish and pain. The years of being betrayed by those he thought were closest to him had worn him down.

"I'm fucked up, Randy! I'm really fucked up!" said the self-professed "Baddest Man."

I heard his pain. I felt his pain. I gave him a hug. Then, the voice of the fight's promoter—Dan Goossen—ended our brief "love-in."

"Come on, Mike, we're about to start."

"Thank you, Randy, for being my friend," said Tyson. "Thank you."

Just then, my walkie-talkie crackled with the voice of Frans Botha.

"It's Buffalo. I'm outside. I'll be right in."

"Copy, Buffalo," I said. "The PC is about to get under way! Step on it!"

"Buffalo copy. Be right there."

Within a minute, Botha walked in. He took his place on one side of the podium, while Tyson sat on the other side.

The press conference went off smoothly. Afterward, both fighters spoke with the media. Then Botha; his father; his manager, Sterling McPherson; his cutman, Jacob Duran; and I headed back to Botha's suite to watch video of Tyson's last few fights. A few hours later, we headed to the tent set up outside the hotel that housed Botha's makeshift training center. There he jumped rope; hit the speed bag; did some floor exercises; and hit the mitts, held by Jacob Duran, one of the best cornermen boxing has ever seen.

That night, after dinner, the phone in my room rang. It was my wife, Roni. She was home in New York. I looked at the clock. It was just after 8:30 p.m., which meant it was just after 11:30 p.m. in New York.

As I answered the phone, her first words to me were, "What happened between you and Mike Tyson today?"

I was confused.

"Huh? What happened?" I asked her. "Nothing happened. We saw each other backstage before the start of today's press conference. We had a nice little chat. Actually, he was a bit emotional."

Before I could explain, Roni said, "A nice little chat? He thinks you hate him. What did you say to him?"

"What???" I said in a surprised, shocked voice. "How could he think I hate him? He asked me if I was his friend. He told me he has no friends from his past.

I told him I *was* his friend and always would be. He hugged me. I hugged him. What do you mean he thinks I hate him?"

Roni explained.

"Just a few minutes ago, I was watching the news on NBC," she said. "When the sports report came on, they mentioned the press conference for Saturday's fight between Tyson and Botha. There was a sound bite from Tyson. He was asked if he's ready for the fight."

"What was his answer?" I asked my wife.

"He said he's ready physically, but mentally he is bummed out, because he believes so many people from his past, people he thought were his friends, have turned on him. He mentioned Don King and Robin Givens. He also mentioned you."

"WHAT!" I blurted.

"He said, 'Even my longtime friend Randy Gordon, the former boxing commissioner in New York, has turned against me. I don't know who to trust anymore.'"

"I can't believe it," I told Roni. I explained our chance meeting backstage and what was said. I told her Tyson seemed very happy to hear me say I am very much his friend.

"After all that emotion, this is what he said to a reporter only minutes after we spoke. Go figure!" I said to her. Then I added, "The poor guy has been used by so many people, he no longer knows who his friends are or who he can really trust."

In the summer of 2012, Tyson teamed with director Spike Lee to star in a one-man show on Broadway entitled *Mike Tyson: Undisputed Truth*. It is the best one-man show I have ever seen, and I have seen plenty. Tyson's honesty and passion are what make the show so incredible. I have seen it live twice and several more times on television.

From the ghetto to world fame; from destitution to untold riches; from a world championship to a jail cell; from rooftops in Brownsville, Brooklyn, to studio sets in Hollywood and on Broadway, Mike Tyson has been through more in his life than the wildest script any movie could have ever come up with.

Of every fighter I've ever interviewed, covered, spent time with, talked to as a friend, and watched from afar, none have ever been more captivating, more exciting, more head-shaking, more unbelievable, and more complex than Mike Tyson.

Most remember him as Iron Mike.

To me, he will always be Catskill Thunder.

The building that housed the offices of *Ring Magazine*. Count up four floors above the green awning. The corner office was occupied throughout the years by Nat Fleischer, Bert Sugar, and me! *Courtesy of the author*

Muhammad Ali graced the cover of the October 1979 issue of *The Ring*, the first issue of the magazine put out by Bert Sugar and me. We were on our way! *File photo of* The Ring

It was at O'Reilly's where I first met Bert Sugar in 1979. He hired me at that meeting, then bought drinks for the bar's patrons. *Courtesy of the author*

With my mentor and the man who turned me loose on the sport, Hall of Famer Bert Randolph Sugar. *Courtesy of the author*

With fashion model Christie Brinkley in New Orleans in 1980, where Brinkley photographed the "No Mas" fight for me at *Ring Magazine. Courtesy of the author*

In 1960, I watched my first fight. It was announced by Don Dunphy. Twenty years later, here I am, announcing alongside this legend. *Courtesy of the author*

With one of history's greatest champions—Alexis Arguello—in this 1982 photo. *Courtesy of the author*

I put Gerry Cooney on the cover of the January 1981 issue of *The Ring*. The cane Gerry is holding belonged to John L. Sullivan decades earlier. *File photo of* The Ring

A sketch of "Basement Bertha," done for me by *New York Daily News* cartoonist/columnist Bill Gallo in 1982. Note what Gallo wrote ("Get me Gerry Cooney"). *Courtesy of the author*

Interviewing Mike Tyson in 1986, after another victory. Four months later, Tyson would win the heavyweight championship of the world. *Courtesy of the author*

I am relaxed and joking with fans at ringside in Atlantic City in 1988, as my MSG Network partner, Bruce Beck, rehearses minutes before we went on the air. *Courtesy of the author*

With then-heavyweight champ Mike Tyson, one week before his title defense against former champ Larry Holmes. *Courtesy of the author*

Between two legends in 1992: Aaron Pryor, left, and Rubin "Hurricane" Carter, right. *Courtesy of the author*

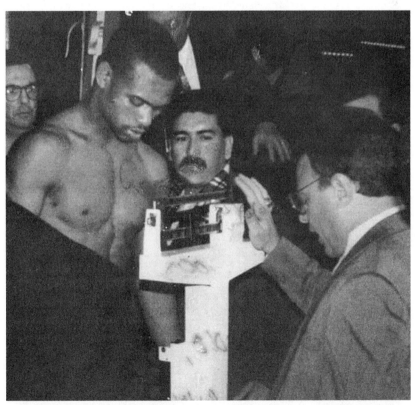

As commissioner, here I am weighing in Roy Jones before his fight against Jorge Vaca in New York in 1992. After sizing up Vaca, Jones walked over to me and said, "I will knock him out in the first round!" He did! *Courtesy of the author*

Commissioner Gordon chats with his boss, New York governor Mario Cuomo, following one of the governor's amazing speeches. *Courtesy of the author*

Listening to the most brilliant man I ever met—Governor Mario M. Cuomo. *Courtesy of the author*

Here I am with my pal of almost 35 years, "Irish" Wayne Kelly. This is the last known photo taken of the great referee and U.S. war hero. A massive stroke took the man the boxing world knew as "IWK" in 2012. *Courtesy of the author*

Christie Brinkley and I strike the same pose in 2013 as we struck in 1980. The only similarity between the two shots is that she's just as beautiful in both! *Courtesy of the author*

I met actor/comedian Robin Williams in 2014, and we really hit it off. It broke my heart when, only a few days later, he took his life. *Courtesy of the author*

Cooney and "The Commish," the real-life *Twins. Courtesy of the author*

With one of the greatest fighters in history, "Manos de Piedra," Roberto Duran, in 2016. *Courtesy of the author*

Getting blasted (playfully) by Marvelous Marvin Hagler and Gerry Cooney in this 2016 photo. *Courtesy of the author*

Actress Rosie Perez is one of my favorite guests. She has a terrific sense of humor and also a wealth of knowledge about and a passion for boxing. *Courtesy of the author*

Feeling relaxed in the studio at SiriusXM moments before the "On the Air" light went on. *Courtesy of the author*

Our show on SiriusXM Radio is called *At the Fights*, and here's Cooney and me at the fights. *Courtesy of the author*

With one of boxing's brightest stars, Ireland's Michael Conlan, in 2018. *Courtesy of the author*

Ringside with Irish female superstar Katie Taylor. *Courtesy of the author*

As Tracy Morgan and I were talking, my wife said, "Smile, guys." We did. Tracy is *always* smiling. *Courtesy of the author*

10

COMMISSIONER
GORDON

The summer of 1988 was only days old and that Friday was already a scorcher. I was on the sun-drenched deck of my house on Long Island, sipping on a homemade lemonade while writing a segment for the next version of *Boxing: The Sweet Science* on the MSG Network. Then the phone rang. I wondered if it was some annoying salesperson or one of a thousand charities about to ask for money. I playfully answered the call, the one that would put my life on a different track.

"Gordon residence," I began.

A professional, serious-sounding female was on the other end.

"Good afternoon. Is this the home of Randy Gordon?" she inquired.

"Yes it is." I responded, and thought, *Yep, salesperson.*

"Is Mr. Gordon available?" asked the lady.

I was about to tell her, "No, he's working right now. This is his underage son and I can't buy anything," but I didn't and said, "You're speaking to him. How may I help you?"

"Do you have a moment to speak with Governor Mario Cuomo?"

Did I just hear what I thought I just heard? Nah. She was probably a volunteer from the "Re-elect Mario Cuomo for Governor" campaign. But then I realized the gubernatorial elections were not for another two years. There was also *no question*. She had just asked, "Do you have a moment to speak with Governor Mario Cuomo?"

I said "Sure," and she asked me to "please hold for just one moment."

I wondered which one of my friends was playing around. A moment later I heard, "Hello, Randy, this is Governor Cuomo." I was silent. It was like the scene from *The American President*, starring Michael Douglas and Annette Bening, when President Andrew Shepard phoned lobbyist Sydney Ellen Wade for the first time, only to have her doubting it was really him. That's what I did.

After the man's introduction and my momentary silence, he said inquisitively, "Hello, Randy, are you there?"

I was desperately trying to think who this could be on the phone, other than the governor of New York.

"Bruce?" I asked, thinking it was one of my MSG on-air colleagues, Bruce Beck, playing a joke on me.

"No, this is Governor Cuomo," the voice said.

"Al?" I inquired, then thinking it might be my USA Network sidekick, Al Albert. Both Bruce and Al had called me many times with brilliant impersonations of celebrities. I figured this was another of those times.

"No, this is really Governor Cuomo," said the voice.

More silence from me.

"Hello? Randy? Are you still with me?" asked the voice, which sounded so much like the brilliant orator and popular chief executive of New York.

"Uh, yes I, uh, am," I answered, sounding anything but brilliant.

The voice at the other end laughed and said, "I guess you're having trouble figuring why I might be calling."

"Sam?" I questioned, still thinking it was one of my friends. This time I went with another MSG on-air colleague, Sam Rosen.

"Not Sam," said the voice. "Mario. Mario Cuomo."

I still didn't believe it was one of America's top politicians—and my future boss—on the line. Knowing Bruce Beck, Al Albert, and Sam Rosen didn't speak Italian, I said, "Okay, you got me. But I do know that Mario Cuomo can speak Italian. What can you say to me in Italian?"

Thank goodness Mario Cuomo has a great sense of humor, is quick-witted, and understood where I was coming from.

"*Credimi. Questo e davvero* Mario Cuomo," he said in fluent, crisp Italian. His words meant, "Believe me. This is really Mario Cuomo." I was blown away. This could not have been any of my playful, talented, voice-impersonating colleagues. None of them spoke Italian like that.

"Ah! Joe!" I said. I thought it was one of my best friends from high school. "How's it going, big man?"

"Not Joe," said the voice. "Mario."

Stymied, I squinted.

"Okay, if this is not Bruce, Al, Sam, or Joe, just what would the most brilliant politician in America be doing calling me, a boxing announcer?" I asked. "Let's hear your answer to that . . . Governor!"

Without stopping to think of a clever answer, the voice gave me one immediately.

"Yes, Randy. I would like to appoint you to be chairman of the New York State Athletic Commission," he told me.

Now, I totally didn't believe it was Governor Mario Cuomo, even though it did sound exactly like him.

"Well, I'd like to, Governor," I said. "But I can't."

"You can't?" he inquired. "Why not, if I may ask?"

"Well, I am about to launch my campaign for president," I told him. "The election is in five months and I need to get ready."

He played along. Again, thank goodness for his sense of humor.

"Isn't it kind of late to be launching a run for the White House now?" he asked.

"Not at all," I responded. "My campaign will be fast and furious. Just wait until I get to all those primaries."

Still playing along, the voice asked, "But let's just say things don't work out in your campaign for president. Would you still be interested in becoming chairman of the New York State Athletic Commission?"

"I sure would!" I responded. Then I asked again, "Who is this? Really, who is this? I give up."

"Well, this is *really* Governor Mario Cuomo," he said, accentuating *really*. "Being that you still don't believe it's me, I will be in my office in the World Trade Center all next week. Does Tuesday work for you to come in and meet with me?"

I laughed and said, "Sure, Tuesday is fine." He asked if 1:00 would work, and I said that was fine, too. Then he told me what floor he was on and what to do when I got there. Then, we hung up. The call left me wondering what friend had just pulled what I thought was one of the greatest impersonations I had ever heard. I planned on going to the World Trade Center the following Tuesday. I figured as I walked in and headed to the elevators, he (whoever "he" was) would meet me there, say "Surprise!" then we'd go out to lunch. I went back to my writing and didn't give the interesting call another thought.

On Tuesday, I arrived in the city almost an hour before my scheduled meeting. I walked around the grounds of both World Trade Center buildings and gazed up at their majestic height. That wasn't my first visit to the Twin Towers, but it was the only time I ever was able to take my time on the promenade and admire their beauty. Although I took no photos that day, the images of what I saw are burned into my memory. When I think of the World Trade Center, when I talk about the World Trade Center, those images are what flash in front of me.

As I walked around, I constantly kept looking for a familiar face, one who may have been behind the voice of Governor Mario Cuomo. Nothing. No one. I entered Tower One and headed to the ground floor elevator. I continued to look for the friend I was sure would come walking over and say, "Fooled you, didn't I?" Still no one!

I took the elevator to the 40th floor, just as the "voice" had told me to. It was then over to another elevator bank and on to the 57th floor. When I stepped off the elevator on the 40th floor, I took one final look around. Still no one.

This isn't right, I thought, *that somebody would actually send me on a trip into Manhattan and up to Governor Cuomo's office as a joke.* I figured for sure he'd be there as I stepped off the elevator and reveal himself, then we'd go to a nice lunch at Windows on the World on the 97th floor. I figured wrong. The joke was being played out in full, and I was mad.

Even though I really wanted to turn around and head home, I decided to take the final leg of the journey and head to the governor's office 17 floors farther up. I stepped on the vacant elevator and pressed "57."

These elevators moved at high speed, unlike the antique we had at *Ring Magazine*, which seemingly took forever to travel a mere five floors. In a heart-beat, I arrived at the 57th floor.

When the door opened, I was staring at a wall with the seal of New York State. It said:

Office of the Governor of New York State
Mario M. Cuomo, Governor

I swallowed hard.

Then, an armed, uniformed officer, who was standing next to the elevator door holding a clipboard, said, "Good afternoon, sir. Can I help you?"

I was thinking that a huge prank had been pulled on me. I looked at him in embarrassment. Of course he could help me. He could listen to my story of how a caller to my home four days ago tricked me into believing he was the governor of New York and wanted to meet with me for the purpose of making me New York State's boxing commissioner.

As he looked at me and awaited my answer, I frantically searched for one. I realized a short version of the truth was my only explanation why I was there.

"No, Officer, I doubt you can help me," I said to him. "Someone is playing a joke on me and led me to believe I had a meeting with the governor. I believed him and came up here, thinking he'd reveal himself, we'd laugh, and then have lunch."

"Well, let's just see if someone is playing a joke on you," said the officer. "May I have your name?"

"My name is Randy Gordon," I said, as he looked down at his clipboard and I continued. "But there's no way it's on your list. I'll just head back down and . . ."

"The governor is expecting you," he said. "Please have a seat. I will let the governor know you are here, Mr. Gordon."

I froze in my spot and stared at the officer. He pointed to a waiting area with a couch and a few chairs, then said, "You may sit here if you wish while I contact the governor. He is expecting you, so you won't be waiting out here very long."

My thoughts raced back four days, to the phone call I received at home. It wasn't from any of my announcing colleagues or personal friends, as I had suspected. It was indeed from Governor Mario Cuomo himself. I was in a panic. Suddenly, I couldn't remember a thing we had spoken about, other than the fact he wanted me to be the state boxing commissioner. I did remember joking around about that. Then I wondered, *Did I say anything off color to the governor?*

I was too nervous to sit, so I walked around the empty reception room. What would the governor ask me? What would I say? How long would the interview take? Would there be an "interrogation team" in the room with us? I had been so certain that the call was from one of my practical-joker friends that I gave only a fleeting thought as to the prospect of becoming chairman of the New York State Athletic Commission, the oldest athletic commission in the country and a position previously held by some very wealthy, powerful, and influential men. Included in that small group of perhaps 15, dating back to 1920, were men like William Muldoon, James A. Farley, and General Melvin Krulewich.

It didn't take two minutes before the officer walked into the room and said, "The governor will see you now, Mr. Gordon." Was I dreaming? Or would this turn into a nightmare?

Together, we stepped through the doorway of a rectangular glass enclosure that was perhaps 10 feet long and several inches thick. I later found out the enclosure was bulletproof. Then we waited for the door to close behind us. When it did, the officer tapped a code box on the door in front of us. You could hear the click of it unlocking. Then he pushed it open.

The officer stood at attention, pointed to the end of the hall, and said, "Walk to the end of the hall and look to your right. You will see another uniformed officer sitting at a desk at the end of the hallway. Walk to him and he will show you into the governor's office."

My heart rate must have been close to 200. I was seconds away from having a one-on-one interview with the governor of New York, and I was totally unprepared. I remember thinking, "Maybe he'll get called by President Reagan and will have to postpone our meeting, which will give me time to really think about this." Then reality set in and I realized I was moments away from meeting Governor Mario Cuomo. I had nothing prepared, nothing rehearsed, nothing thought about. I would have to ad lib my way through the interview.

I did as the officer instructed and walked to the end of the wide hallway. Then, I looked right. At the end of another wide hallway sat a state trooper at a desk. He hung up a phone and stood as I walked toward him.

"Good afternoon, Mr. Gordon," he said. "I will show you into the governor's office." He knocked on the door. Then he opened it, held it for me, and motioned for me to enter. When I walked in, I quickly looked around the largest private office I had ever seen. Then, from behind a large desk, perhaps 10 yards away, Governor Mario Cuomo walked toward me.

His muscular, 6-foot-1, 200-pound frame looked much bigger as he approached me.

"Still think it's not me?" he said with a laugh. My heart rate was now in the "Red Zone."

I extended my hand. He shook his head.

"Real men hug," said the governor. "You guys in the boxing world are always hugging."

We embraced and he said, "Now, *that's* the proper greeting for my new commissioner of boxing." I smiled a huge smile, but the thought of what was going on was overwhelming.

Governor Cuomo then pointed to a leather armchair in front of his desk and invited me to "have a seat and relax." He walked to the other side of the desk and sat down in a plush leather chair.

"Care for any tea or coffee?" he asked. I respectfully declined.

Then he placed both hands on his desk, took a deep breath, and leaned forward.

The questions I was not prepared for were about to begin.

"So, why do you want to become chairman of the New York State Athletic Commission?" he asked.

My mind raced as I searched for an answer. Quickly, I decided there was only one thing to do: be as honest as possible. Being unprepared was one thing. But being unprepared and BSing the governor would never go over. So, I decided to take the only route I was comfortable with: speak the truth. It had gotten me fired from ESPN six years earlier, and I figured it may get me tossed out of Governor Cuomo's office, but the truth is what I intended to—and needed to—tell Governor Mario Cuomo.

"Sir," I began. "I really need to tell you something."

"Go right ahead, Randy," he said.

I took a deep breath.

"Sir, last week, when you called me at home, I was totally sure it was a joke . . . that it wasn't you on the phone, but one of my friends, playing a joke on me." I continued, "I was certain that whoever it was would meet me here at the World Trade Center and we'd have a good laugh over lunch. I never thought for a moment you'd really be calling to ask me to head the State Athletic Commission. Because of that, I never gave any . . ."

Governor Cuomo cut me off.

"You never gave any real thought as to accepting the position?"

"Exactly, sir," I said, nodding my head.

"Well, there are two things I like about that," he said.

I looked at him quizzically. He smiled. Then he continued.

"By not thinking about my proposal to you, your answer will not be thought out and rehearsed. Also, what you just did shows me your honesty. I like that."

As I smiled and thanked him, he continued.

And, speaking of your honesty, I know the story of you losing your job at ESPN for telling the truth. That is one of the most impressive stories I have ever heard. That, along with your well-known love affair with boxing, is the reason I called you and the reason I want you to be my new chairman of the New York State Athletic Commission. Now, being that you've given this no deep thought, tell me why you would like to be chairman.

I didn't have to think of an answer. While I really didn't want to give up my career as a sportscaster, I found the thought of holding the reins of boxing in New York State incredibly appealing.

"Sir [I kept calling him that], the Athletic Commission needs a take-charge boxing guy at the top. I don't remember the last time such a person headed the commission."

"What about former light heavyweight champion Jose Torres [the man I was replacing]?" asked the governor. "Certainly, he was a boxing guy."

"Yes, he was, sir," I replied.

But, let's be honest. While Jose has a lot of great qualities, none of them is as a commissioner. He openly roots for certain fighters, he is out of the office more than he's in it, and, for the last year, everyone knows he's been writing a book on heavyweight champ Mike Tyson. Jose Torres is a great boxing guy, but he's not a great boxing commissioner.

"Fair enough," replied Governor Cuomo, who then asked, "What about me? I was the interim chairman when I was secretary of state. I was in the office. I didn't root for fighters. Are you going to sit there and tell me I wasn't fit to be the chairman of the New York State Athletic Commission?"

When I didn't answer him immediately, I could see the astonished look on his face. He pointed at me and started to speak.

"Are you really going to sit there and . . ."

An intercom buzz from his secretary interrupted the governor's remarks.

"I'm sorry for the interruption, Governor, but Reverend Sharpton is on the line."

She was referring to the African American civic leader in New York City, Reverend Al Sharpton, who never missed an opportunity to seize a photo op or a TV or radio interview when a racial issue or news item was involved. On this occasion, a major racial item was making front-page news. Sharpton was all over it, looking for headlines.

Governor Cuomo's face went from cheerfully combative to a scowling anger. He slammed his right fist on his desk. Then he slammed it again.

"I'm sorry, Governor," said his secretary, hearing New York's political leader's anger and displeasure at the phone call.

"That's okay," Governor Cuomo said. "Tell him I will be with him in a moment."

At that point, I looked at the governor and said, "I'll go wait in the hall. This sounds important."

Governor Cuomo held up his hands.

"No, stay there. I want you to hear this," he said. Then he asked me, "Are you familiar with this ongoing Tawana Brawley case?"

"I am very familiar with it, sir. She's the teenage African American who has claimed she was raped by several white police officers, smeared with feces, and left for dead in a garbage bag."

"That's right," replied Governor Cuomo. "But her whole story was made up. There were no police officers and there was no rape. She placed herself in the plastic bags. Her whole story is one big lie. I have told Reverend Sharpton that and he continues to fuel the fire. Stay right there. I want you to hear this." With his hands, he gestured for me to stay put.

With that, Governor Cuomo picked up the receiver to the phone on his desk.

"What, Al?" began the governor. He listened for a moment to what Rev. Sharpton had to say. Then he jumped in, with verbal guns blazing.

"Al, I don't want to hear any more of this. None of it is true and you know it! End this now, Al! I will waste no more time on this!"

Then Governor Cuomo told Reverend Sharpton, "Don't call me again unless you have something truthful and meaningful you want to talk about."

He slammed the receiver down. For a few minutes, we discussed the case, which was making national headlines and ended soon thereafter when Ms. Brawley's case was shown to be untrue.

Governor Cuomo took a deep breath.

"Maybe I should come back another day, sir," I suggested. "There's a lot more important things going on for you than talking about boxing."

With his right index finger, he pointed at me and said, "On the contrary. *This* is what I want to be doing. I want to talk to the man who I believe is going to be the next chairman of the New York State Athletic Commission. Now, let's see, where was I?"

I swallowed hard, remembering exactly where he was. Then I told him.

"I was telling you that I thought the commission had been made up of political hacks, especially at the top, most who didn't know the difference between a left hook and a fish hook, for years, and you had just commented, 'Are you really going to sit there and . . .' Then your secretary buzzed that Reverend Sharpton was on the line."

"Oh, yes!" exclaimed Governor Cuomo with a sly smile. I knew exactly where he was going with his next question. He continued where he left off.

"Are you going to sit there and tell me, the man who holds the key to give you this position, that I am a political hack? That I don't know the difference between a fish hook and a left hook? Are you really going to say that?"

There was no room to tap dance. Only the truth would work. But it had to be the truth delivered correctly.

"Sir, you were certainly not a political hack. But when I look at the boxing knowledge each of the past chairmen possessed, their knowledge paled when compared to mine."

Governor Cuomo glared at me, pointed at me, and said, "Careful, Randy, careful. You're treading on thin ice." Then he sat back in his chair, folded his arms across his chest, and waited to see if I could escape the thin ice.

"Sir, if it came to a debate between you and me in politics, world issues, economics, the environment, or just about anything else, you'd win," I said. "But in a debate about boxing-related material, I'd win, Governor!"

He smiled and leaned forward on his desk.

"You've got balls, Mr. Gordon," said Governor Cuomo. "Chutzpah. I like that."

Then came the first of Governor Cuomo's three big questions.

"Okay, tell me why you would like to be the head of the New York State Athletic Commission."

"Unlike all the other chairmen, I live for this, sir. I live it every second of my life. I have a passion for it. I love the sport of boxing. I feel I can make a difference because of my love and passion," I told him.

"Fair enough," he said. Then he asked me, "Looking into your political records, I see you have never voted in an election. Why is that?"

"Because of the events of November 22, 1963, sir," I replied.

Governor Cuomo did not have to think about what happened on that day 25 years earlier.

"What does President Kennedy's assassination have to do with you not voting in a presidential election?" he asked.

"Sir, I have always believed that Lee Harvey Oswald did not act alone. I believe there were other shooters, and I believe those shooters were commissioned by our government. I believe President Kennedy was assassinated by the U.S. government."

I was sure my answer was going to signal the end of the interview. What followed came as a complete shock.

"I don't disagree with you, Randy," said the governor. "But what does President Kennedy's assassination have to do with you not voting?"

"When that happened," I told him, "I became skeptical of politicians and the entire political system."

"Do you think politicians are corrupt?" Governor Cuomo asked me.

"Since that time, I've been skeptical of politicians," I said. "Yes, I think a large number of them are corrupt."

"I'm a politician," said Governor Cuomo. "Do you think I'm corrupt?"

"Not at all, sir," I replied. "But I think you're one of the rare ones." I then added, "I have heard it said so many times over the years that boxing is full of piranha. I think your business is worse. I think you and I are two of the real good guys, swimming with a lot of piranha."

He didn't disagree. He just smiled. Then he asked his third—and final—question.

"How would you describe your loyalty?"

I gave him a puzzled look, and he expounded on his question.

"Your loyalty," he said. "Are you a loyal worker, a loyal colleague, a loyal friend? One day, my ship—the ship you will be riding on—may go down. If that happens, will you stay aboard with me or will you do like most people do—jump ship? Are you a loyal person?"

"I am going to say this in words which will make you cringe, sir," I told him. I paused, saying, "I have a Mafia-like loyalty. I am fiercely loyal."

Governor Cuomo winced.

"You're right, I am cringing," he said. "But I get your point. I guess I will just have to see if you mean what you say. Do you have any questions for me?"

"Just one," I said.

"Just one?" he asked. "You can ask more. Feel free." He sat back in his chair and we locked eyes. You could see he was wondering, *What one question?* and *Why one question?*

"You asked about my loyalty. What about yours? This is a very political position . . . always has been. What if some senator's relative or constituent needed a job? Do I get tossed from your ship to make room for that person?"

He smiled.

"Not a chance!" he replied. "I have the same kind of loyalty as you claim to have." Then, he quickly added, "Though, I would describe my loyalty in a different way than you did." We both laughed.

Then, he stood up and extended his right hand.

"Commissioner Gordon," he said. "Congratulations! You are now an employee of the people of the state of New York. I know you are going to be a great commissioner and do a real service to the people of the Empire State."

I shook his hand and thanked him. I told him I would inform the president of Madison Square Garden, Bob Gutkowski, with whose network I had just signed a lucrative announcing deal.

"Keep me posted," said the governor. "I will give you several names, along with telephone numbers to call in case you have questions."

Then he broke into a wide grin.

"What?" I asked, giving him a puzzled look.

"You're going to be Commissioner Gordon. Will I be Batman?"

"Sure!" I joked. "You're the one always helping the people. You're the superhero."

He put his arm around my shoulder.

"I know you're going to make us all proud of you. Commissioner Gordon, enjoy the ride."

Then he repeated my new title a couple more times.

"Commissioner Gordon . . . Commissioner Gordon. I like the way that sounds."

For the first time, I didn't call him "Sir."

"So do I, boss. Thank you."

I only have one regret after meeting Mario Cuomo, working for him for the next seven years, and getting to know him as well as I did: the man should have held not the highest office in New York State, but the highest office in America.

He should have been president of the United States.

11

IT'S ABOUT TIME

As I discussed in chapter 2, one of the three young men I trained with in my competitive boxing days was Wayne Kelly. We met in 1968, only days after he had returned from a nightmarish year of service in the U.S. Army. I have never met a more likable and loyal, funny and friendly, lovable and loving, sensitive and caring, yet tough and rugged—and totally screwed up—individual.

In 1966, Kelly was barely out of high school when he was called for military induction. Unlike so many others, he answered America's call and stepped forward. During the next several years he fought an unwinnable war in a place he described as "Hell on Earth": the jungles of Vietnam. It was there he smelled, tasted, heard, saw, and even caused death.

I met Wayne the week he returned home from his tour of duty, honorably discharged from the U.S. Army. We met when our paths converged at a boxing gym on the North Shore of Long Island.

Shortly before the days of 1968 ran out, I drove to one of the few boxing gyms I knew of on Long Island, a P.A.L. Center in Port Washington. It was a hole-in-the-wall gym, with no locker rooms, no shower, a toilet that was broken more often than not, and a sink that supplied only cold water. But it had a ring, a heavy bag, and a speed bag, which is all two 19-year-olds like me and Wayne needed to break into boxing.

As Wayne and I became close due to our mutual love of boxing and from training together, we enjoyed downing a beer or three while sitting on the sand dunes at Jones Beach on Long Island's South Shore. We talked about boxing and our dreams of a bright future for both of us.

It was there I first heard his favorite expression: "We're not here for a long time, so we may as well have a good time." It was his favorite saying, one that became his life's mantra. It was there he began calling me his "Hebrew brother from another mother," eventually shortening it, calling me his "Main He-bro." He became "I.W.K.," short for "Irish Wayne Kelly."

It was also on those sand dunes that he opened up about his time in Vietnam. It was on those sand dunes I learned—not in college, but right there—about the horrors and unthinkable things humans are capable of doing to one another.

There was never a time he told me a story about Vietnam where I didn't cry. He cried, too. Sometimes he cried uncontrollably.

"Things were done over there that no humans should ever do to one another," Kelly cried to me one night. "I wish I never saw what I saw. I wish I never heard what I heard. I wish I never did what I did. I have nightmares all the time about what happened over there. I wake up screaming many nights and drenched in sweat. I wish I could put an end to the nightmares, but I can't. They won't stop."

I suggested a therapist, but Wayne would say, "They'll judge me crazy."

"But you are," I'd say, laughing.

"I know that and you know that," he'd say, "but nobody else knows. I'd prefer keeping it that way. Maybe in time, my nightmares will go away."

They didn't. They just got worse.

It was early in the summer of 1969 that I first saw how bad Wayne's nightmares were. After a run along the Jones Beach shore, we took an easy stroll back on the same route. I remember talking about Joe Frazier's upcoming title defense against Jerry Quarry at Madison Square Garden and saying that we should get tickets, when the unmistakable sound of a low-flying helicopter sent Wayne into a glassy-eyed trance. It was the first of many times I would see this reaction in Wayne.

He looked over his shoulder and out over the water. Perhaps a mile down the beach, a Coast Guard helicopter was on patrol over the crowded waters.

"Get down!" Wayne screamed at me. "Get down!" Not knowing what Wayne had just seen, but reacting to his warning, I ducked. He then ran to the people nearest us on the beach, screaming, "Get down! Get down!" and pushing as many as he could onto the sand. As the helicopter "whop-whop-whopped" its way past us, I watched in stunned disbelief as Wayne went into a fetal position in the sand, covering his head with his arms. As the helicopter passed, beachgoers yelled and cursed at him.

"What are you, a nut job?" screamed one guy.

"Are you crazy, man?" bellowed another.

I held my hands up as a shocked crowd began to gather. From our one-on-one talks on the sand dunes I immediately realized what was happening.

"He just got home from Vietnam," I explained. "The helicopter scared him. I'm so sorry."

No one knew much about post-traumatic stress disorder (PTSD) then, and they didn't understand, care, or feel Wayne's pain.

"Get your nutty friend some help, pal. He needs it!" one upset man said as he pointed to Wayne, who was still in the fetal position in the sand as the angry throng of people continued to gather around.

I helped Wayne to his feet. He shook his head a few times, trying to refocus. His eyes were clear again, free from the zombie-like look he had worn only seconds earlier. He had no idea what had just happened.

"What the hell was that all about?" I asked him as we quickly walked away from the scene.

"I don't know," said Wayne. "Why were people yelling? Did I do something?"

I gave him a puzzled look.

"You don't know? You don't remember?" I questioned.

He shook his head slowly. It was a Vietnam flashback. It was what he had told me he had in his sleep and what he was afraid of when he even thought of Vietnam during his waking hours. Now I, along with dozens of others, had seen it firsthand. Unfortunately, it would get worse, not better.

In the mid-1970s, Wayne got married. When he was single and sleeping alone, only his pillow had to deal with whatever nightmares tore through his mind. Unfortunately, that was no longer true once he was married. Wayne would wake up screaming and more than once inadvertently hit his wife during one of his nightmares. It finally became too much for her, and she left.

A few weeks later, Wayne hit rock bottom.

With my wife working late, Wayne and I went to a Chinese restaurant for dinner. We sat in a booth against the wall. Across the aisle from us, perhaps seven or eight feet away, was a Plexiglas partition. A waiter walked over to us and placed dishes and tea cups in front of us, along with Chinese noodles and duck sauce. Then he walked away to get silverware. When he returned a moment later, Wayne and I were both downing the Chinese noodles as if we hadn't eaten in a week. Wayne glanced to his left and saw the waiter about to put the silverware down. His face changed expression. I looked right at Wayne. Then I looked at the waiter and back at Wayne again. He was wearing the zombie look I had seen before. I knew something was about to happen. Something awful.

"Wayne, no!" I shouted at him. It was too late. Wayne sprung from his seat. He drove his left shoulder into the waiter's stomach and slammed him into—and through—the Plexiglas partition. The stunned waiter was on his back on the other side of the partition as patrons began screaming. Wayne was on top of him but quickly and athletically jumped off and began raining punches off the waiter's face, like you would see in an MMA fight.

"Stop it, Wayne!" I shouted as I pounced on Wayne's back, trying to pull him off.

Wayne threw me off of him and struck the waiter once or twice more before I put him in a choke hold from behind. As I did, other patrons came to my assistance. My scared, sick, and enraged buddy got in a few more punches to those in front of him before we were able to bring him to the floor and subdue him. At first, he struggled violently. Then, as fast as it started, he calmed down. His facial expression changed. He was once again Wayne Kelly.

Male patrons held on to his arms and legs, but there was no more need to subdue him. Another nightmarish flashback had come and gone.

Wayne looked at me and asked, "What happened?"

I just looked at him and said, "Wayne, you lost it, buddy, you lost it. We are in a Chinese restaurant and you had a flashback. You just hurt somebody bad."

We glanced at the assaulted waiter, who was being attended to by coworkers.

"He just got home from Vietnam," I said loud enough for everyone in the restaurant to hear. "He has flashbacks."

"He should be in a loony bin," said one of the men who helped subdue Wayne. "He should be in a straitjacket, not in a restaurant."

Just then, the local police arrived. Several of them ran in, weapons drawn. The owner pointed to us. We were told to lie on our stomachs, then were handcuffed with our hands behind us.

After the police sat us up, witnesses told them that it was Wayne who had instigated the assault. They were told that although I was with him, I tried to stop him. They undid my cuffs.

"What happened here?" an officer asked me.

Wayne was seated on the floor. His head was lowered. It was a scene I had become all too familiar with.

"He's a Vietnam veteran," I told the police. "He has been having flashbacks." Although so little was known about PTSD then, one of the officers was very familiar with it.

"My younger brother has the same thing," he said. "He got back from 'Nam just a few months ago. He goes in and out of sanity."

"Listen," I pleaded. "My friend's dad is a lieutenant in the Garden City [Long Island] police department. Please call him."

A call was placed to him, and he came minutes later. He drove Wayne home. Amazingly, no charges were pressed by the waiter. As it turns out, his younger brother, just like the police officer's younger brother, had fought in Vietnam. He, too, was having issues with flashbacks. The waiter understood the demons ravaging Wayne's existence.

The next day, a doctor was found who specialized in PTSD. Wayne began visiting him several times a week. Many times, I drove him there and waited for him. I saw the change. Through hypnosis, the doctor was able to talk to Wayne and explain things to him. He would have Wayne say things he was holding in. In the span of a few months the demons—most of them, anyway—were exorcised. The doctor explained to Wayne that he could not erase the things Wayne had seen and done. He helped Wayne understand them and put those awful memories in the recesses of his mind. In those sessions, he found that one of the things Wayne enjoyed talking about most and being around was boxing. He told Wayne to concentrate on what made him happiest and most content. The cure was simple: boxing.

By mid-1975, the flashbacks had ended and Wayne was a different man. While only remnants of it remained for him, the Vietnam War—and his inner war—was finally over.

I had become a boxing writer, hired by G. C. London Publishing Co. They put out monthly boxing magazines called *World Boxing*, *International Boxing*, and *Big Book of Boxing*. Wayne went to work for the Town of Hempstead on Long Island in their Division of Services for the Aging. He kept himself busy after work by going to the gym with me and to many of the local boxing matches—both amateur and pro—in the New York City, Queens, Brooklyn, and Long Island areas.

Eventually we both started refereeing amateur bouts. While I enjoyed refereeing and felt I could be a good ref, I wanted to be involved in boxing as a writer and an announcer. So I actively pursued those avenues. Wayne loved climbing in the ring—as both a ref and a fighter—and actively pursued both.

Refereeing was something Wayne and I had discussed a few times before. After hours, both of us were volunteers in the Town of Hempstead's Boxing Fitness Program. The man in charge of it was a full-time employee of the town and a noted referee in boxing circles: Arthur Mercante.

Mercante was a no-nonsense instructor with the attitude of a military drill sergeant. He was also in Jack LaLanne shape, looking much younger than his 55 years.

After a few months of training youngsters and businessmen (and after "refereeing" several of their sparring sessions), Wayne and I started refereeing on the amateur circuit in the New York City area under the watchful eyes of the two men who ran the amateur program in that area: Vic Zimet and Dick McGuire. They watched us ref a few amateur fights, had us attend a seminar or two, and then made us referees. We both loved being the "third man in the ring."

Although I loved being a ref, I didn't like having to be out so many nights, especially after the birth of my daughter, Ali, in early 1977. Being a boxing writer kept me out enough. I decided I'd leave the refereeing to Wayne.

It didn't take long before both Zimet and McGuire saw enormous talent in Wayne as a referee.

"You're wasting your time as an amateur ref," Zimet told him. Wayne, however, was hesitant. Zimet told me to "convince your friend to take out his referee's license. He is as good as anybody out there."

"Anybody?" I questioned.

"Anybody," he said.

After an amateur show in April 1977, with Wayne refereeing perhaps half of the bouts that night and handling every knockdown and stoppage flawlessly, I picked up on Vic Zimet's suggestion.

"Wayne, it's time to become a professional referee," I told him. I could see he was about to object. I jumped in. "I don't want to hear it!" I said, holding up one hand. "Zimet knows you can ref. So does Dick McGuire. I've always known it. So have you. It's time to take out your license. Wadda'ya say?"

"You're right," Wayne said, smiling. "What will I have to do?"

"You go to the New York State Athletic Commission," I told him. "You ask for an application to be a referee. You fill it out. You pay a fee. They may ask for references. Put Vic Zimet and Dick McGuire down. Put me down."

"How about Arthur Mercante?" Wayne asked.

"Why not?" I responded. "He knows you can ref. Who's better than Mercante as a reference?"

"I'll do it!" Wayne said, excitedly. "I'll do it tomorrow. I'll go into the city." Then, with pleading eyes, he asked, "Will you go with me? I can't go alone."

I forgot. Part of Wayne's emotional scars from his hell in Vietnam was his inability to travel alone. Heading into crowded Manhattan and to the downtown office of the NYSAC on a crowded subway may well have triggered a relapse in the 28-year-old Vietnam vet.

"Sure, I'll go," I said. "I'll tell my boss I lost a filling, but I'll be in a little late."

"Great!" said Wayne. "We can leave early."

We were at 270 Broadway, the offices of NYSAC, before they opened at 9:00 a.m. We had breakfast at Ellen's restaurant on the main floor of the building. There we ran into the chairman, James Farley, and his athletic assistant, Marvin Kohn, who were dining together.

"You're not coming in to take out another license, are you, 'fighter-writer'?" asked the chairman.

"No, I'm here with Wayne Kelly, who will be applying for a referee's license," I told him.

"A referee's license?" asked the chairman. "What experience do you have?"

"I have reffed for the last year in the amateurs, sir," Wayne told him.

"He's really good, Mr. Chairman," I added. "Really good!"

"What references will you be able to put down?" the chairman asked.

"Oh, a lot, sir," Wayne stated. He began to tick off a few names. "Vic Zimet. Dick McGuire. Bobby Cassidy. Arthur Mercante."

The last name is all the chairman had to hear.

"Arthur Mercante?" he asked.

"That's right," said Wayne. "He has seen me ref plenty of times."

"Can I call him?" asked the boss of boxing in New York State.

"You absolutely can," said Wayne excitedly.

"Then, let's go upstairs," said Chairman Farley. "I'll call Arthur while you fill out the papers."

When we arrived on the fifth floor, the home of the powerful New York State Athletic Commission, Chairman Farley had his secretary give Wayne the paperwork. He then disappeared into his office to call Arthur Mercante.

Wayne was finished filling out the one-page form when the chairman walked out. He wasn't smiling.

"I'm sorry, Wayne," the chairman began. "Mr. Mercante said you're good but need a lot of work before you can become a professional referee. He suggested another few years in the amateurs."

"But, sir, if you call Vic Zimet . . ." Wayne was cut off.

"I'm sorry," said Farley.

"Or Dick McGuire, he'll tell you . . ." Again, Farley stopped him.

"I'm sorry, Wayne. Like Mr. Mercante said, maybe in a few years you can try again."

I was the only one who talked on the way home. Finally, Wayne said, "I'm gonna fight again."

"What?" I responded.

"I'm gonna fight again," Wayne said in a low voice, almost whispering. "Tomorrow I am going back into training."

I understood his feelings. I didn't want Wayne to fight again, but I understood. I really understood. All it took was one phone call to local matchmaker Gene Moore for Wayne to resume his boxing career.

Gene and his friend, Jimmy Winters, were putting on a show a few weeks later at the Commack Arena on Long Island, and they needed another fight. To them, Wayne was more than just another body in another fight. He was a ticket seller. Promoters love ticket sellers. Also on the card was our training partner, Tony Danza.

The fight took place on May 7, 1977. Wayne's opponent was tough localite Tom Healy. Although Wayne trained, the fire he had shown before was absent. He was thinking more about his rejection from being a referee, something he wanted to do so much, and how Arthur Mercante—who heaped praise upon him in the two or three times a week they saw one another—could have him rejected from becoming one. It deeply bothered Wayne. It deeply bothered me too.

As for the fight, Wayne dropped a hard-fought four-round decision to Healy. Danza won his bout on a third-round knockout. The young man he beat—Tom Molloy—would become the Florida state boxing commissioner some 30 years later.

In his dressing room after the loss to Healy, Wayne took his anger out on the chairs . . . and the garbage pail . . . and the walls. Those holes in the wall weren't there when we walked into the arena.

After his loss to Healy, I convinced Wayne to forget about competing and concentrate on refereeing. Together we had studied the nuances of being a referee, and we knew every rule in the book. He was 28 years old, 6 feet even, and 185 shredded pounds. He was more equipped—physically and mentally—to become a referee than any person who has ever stepped through the ropes to become the "third man in the ring." I knew it and Wayne knew it.

As Wayne continued in his job as a social worker for the Town of Hempstead, he supplemented his income by moving furniture with his childhood friend. He also continued to ref amateur fights and exhibitions. Everyone involved in the boxing world told him he should take out his professional license. He just smiled and said, "Thank you."

Although Wayne said he wasn't going to fight again, I could sense the anger about not becoming a professional ref was making him want to. He stayed in heavy training. Finally, in October 1978, almost a year and a half after dropping the decision to Healy, Wayne was back in the Commack Arena ring, this time against Willie Turner, who brought an 0–1–1 record into the ring against Wayne's 2–2 record. In a four-round slugfest, Turner outpointed Wayne. It was Wayne's third loss in a row.

He was quite dejected following the loss; however, he told me, "I can't hang up my gloves after three-straight losses," and he vowed to come back with a win. That win came seven months later in Commack, when Wayne KO'd Tony Sparks in the first round. The following month, in the same arena, Wayne faced Alvin Bracy and notched another first-round stoppage. Afterward, his words surprised me.

"That's it," he told me. "That was my last fight. I'm 30, and I want to get back to working on getting my referee's license. Whatever it takes, I am going for it."

I smiled, seeing an inner peace in my friend. He was the happiest I had ever seen him.

A few days after Wayne's final fight and his decision to pursue a professional ref's license, my professional career also took off. I was called by Bert Sugar to join him at *Ring Magazine*. The following year, I was hired by ESPN. My boxing career had taken off for the stars. Wayne could not have been happier for me.

In February 1982, Wayne came over to watch a championship fight on television with me. It was light heavyweight titleholder Michael Spinks versus Mustafa Wasajja. Spinks won the match on a sixth-round TKO. The fight was stopped horrifically late by referee Tony Perez, who allowed Wasajja to take punches after he was obviously out on his feet. At the end, Wayne and I leaped up simultaneously, screaming at the TV, "Stop the fight, Tony, stop the fight!" When he did, Wasajja slumped in a corner, unconscious. After the match, I looked at Wayne and said, "It's time."

He gave me a puzzled look.

"Time for what?" he asked.

"Time for you to head into the New York State Athletic Commission for your ref's license," I responded.

He smiled. He nodded. He agreed. He knew it was indeed time. I told him I knew the chairman, Jack Prenderville. He told me he'd go in "first thing Monday morning." Before he could ask, I told him, "Sure, I'll go with you." He smiled and breathed a sigh of relief. He still didn't like taking trips into the city by himself and was happy when I told him I'd go along.

As we had done five years earlier, we arrived prior to the 9:00 opening of the athletic commission. Again, we went to Ellen's for breakfast. From there, it was up to the Licensing Department of the NYSAC.

Wayne requested—and received—the paperwork to fill out. When he came to the line that asked for references (five were requested), I said, "Use me. There's one." Former light heavyweight contender Bobby Cassidy, who sparred with Wayne quite often, was another one. So was Gil Clancy, and so was Vic Zimet. For his fifth reference, Wayne put Arthur Mercante.

We both smiled, because Mercante not only worked in the Town of Hempstead with Wayne, but also he had seen Wayne referee on many occasions—he even used Wayne for his amateur shows—and had nothing but praise for his work.

Then came Wayne's license application.

The morning after Wayne filled out his application, he received a message from a secretary in the Town of Hempstead's Department of Services for the Aging. She said the New York State Athletic Commission had called, asking to speak with him. Wayne was excited. He had the right to be. He was expecting to hear that his application had been approved and that he needed to bring in a completed medical report, along with a recent EEG and EKG. He called the commission as soon as he hung up with his office. It was not the news he expected. He spoke personally with Chairman Jack Prenderville.

"I'm sorry, Wayne," Prenderville said to him. "Your application to be a referee has been rejected."

"What? How? Why?" Wayne said, fumbling his words. He couldn't believe it. "I have the credentials. I have the skills. Please take a look at me in action."

"I'm sorry, Wayne," Prenderville repeated. Then came the crusher.

"Your references were impressive. Being that one of them works for the commission in the same capacity you applied for, we called him. We called Arthur Mercante. He said you're good but that you're not ready. He said you will be ready one day, but that day isn't now. I have to go on what Arthur tells me."

Wayne tried to change Prenderville's mind.

"But if you call . . ." Wayne started.

Prenderville cut him off.

"I'm sorry, Wayne. Perhaps next time." Click.

Wayne was numb. He was rejected again. Again, Arthur Mercante was behind the rejection.

A secretary at *Ring Magazine* buzzed my office. She told me Wayne Kelly was on the line. I reached for the phone excitedly, expecting to hear good news.

"So, when's the first show you'll be reffing at?" I asked as soon as I picked up the phone.

"Mercante did it again!" Wayne said.

"Are you kidding?" I responded. "Please tell me you're kidding, Wayne."

"No," he said softly, his voice cracking. "He told Prenderville I'm not ready. He said I'm good but that I'm not ready."

"Not ready?" I said, loud enough that my staff in the outer office stopped what they were doing and turned their heads to look into my office. "Not ready? Wayne, I'm sorry," I told him. "I'm really sorry. I'll figure this out. I'll speak to Prenderville."

"Thanks, Randy," replied Wayne, "but I'm not even going to appeal to Mercante when I see him in his office at the Town of Hempstead."

"You're not? Why not?" I wanted to know.

"That political juice," Wayne replied. "I don't want to piss him off. Forget it!"

When we hung up, I slammed my fist on my desk.

I was worried about Wayne and what the bad news might do to him—or lead him to do to others; however, he handled the news well. We continued to work out together and went to lots of boxing matches together. When he refereed, I was ringside. No one was better.

Wayne handled his disappointment well. He went about his life and only talked about it when I brought it up—which was quite often.

Soon after his second license rejection, he met a young, attractive brunette named Sheila McKay. She was almost 10 years younger than Wayne, but they were in love almost at first sight. They were married in August 1983. In 1984, their daughter Jackie was born. In 1986, they had a son, Ryan.

In June 1988, I received the phone call from New York State governor Mario Cuomo, during which he said he wanted to appoint me as Jose Torres's replacement as chairman of the New York State Athletic Commission. Until it was made official, I told no one, except my family. That included Wayne.

I made Wayne my first order of business, my first act as Commissioner-elect (so to speak) Gordon. I called him after leaving my first meeting with Governor Cuomo. When he answered the phone, I said, "IWK, I have a question for you."

"Hey, my main He-bro," he responded. "What's your question?"

"How'd you like to fill out your application and become a professional boxing referee?"

There was silence on the end of the phone.

"Wayne? Are you there?" I asked.

"Uh, I'm here, but I don't get the joke," he responded.

"What joke?" I asked. "This is no joke. You are finally going to become a professional referee."

"Randy, have you lost it?" Wayne inquired. "Don't you remember what happened twice before?"

I played dumb.

"No, refresh me," I said.

"How can you not remember?" asked Wayne in a puzzled voice. "Are you okay?"

"I'm fine," I told him. "I just don't remember what happened twice before. Refresh me."

"You're scaring me, Randy," said Wayne. "How can you not remember? Arthur Mercante, remember? Twice before he had me shot down."

"Why, what did he do?"

"Randy, please stop," Wayne begged. "You are really scaring me. Mercante told the chairman I wasn't ready."

"Ah, yes, Mercante," I said. "But I wouldn't worry about Mercante anymore. I can promise he won't go to the chairman this time. I know that for a fact."

"How do you know that?" he pressed.

"I just do. I know he will absolutely not go to the chairman."

"How do you know? I am not going in unless you tell me how you know!" he continued.

It was time to stop teasing. It was time to tell him.

"I know that, Wayne, because . . ."

I paused.

". . . because I'm the new chairman."

"What?" was Wayne's first response. "Are you fucking kidding me?" was his second.

I told him the story about getting called by Governor Cuomo. I then told him this was my first act as commissioner and that he should come in the following week with medicals and a money order for $25 in hand.

"IWK . . . this may be the best phone call I have ever made."

"And this may be the best phone call I have ever received," he said.

When I hung up, I wiped my misty eyes. Incredibly, Wayne said he did the same thing after our conversation.

During my first week in office, Wayne came in. We joked about the fact he had traveled into the city by himself.

After his medicals were turned in, along with his license fee, my secretary brought the application to me. I signed it, making it the first document I signed as chairman of the New York State Athletic Commission.

I stood and walked out from behind my desk. I extended my hand. Wayne extended his.

"Congratulations, Wayne, on becoming a professional boxing referee," I said. "We have both believed, for a long time, that you can be not just a professional referee, but a professional referee at the highest level. I have no question you will become the best. Now go out there and prove it." I then added, "It's about time."

Then we embraced. And, yeah, we both got a bit emotional.

Why not? It had been a long road to this point.

It really was about time.

In the next 24 years, Wayne went from being the rookie referee on the staff to the senior referee. Naturally, he was my first choice for a big fight. But that's not because we were so close. That's because he was so good.

From the first title fight he refereed until his last one, for the IBF flyweight title in Italy in October 2011, Wayne was the epitome of everything a boxing referee should be in the ring. He was the boss. He was in control. The fighters respected him.

He was the ref who disqualified Andrew Golota in July 1996, in his fight against Riddick Bowe in Madison Square Garden. The DQ precipitated one of the largest riots boxing has ever seen; however, he was totally correct in his DQ, a decision most other referees may not have had the courage or confidence to make. I drove Wayne into Madison Square Garden that day, and I drove him home. It took a police escort to get us out of the building that night.

As we pulled out of the parking garage and with my wife still in tears from the ultra-terrifying riot, I broke the silence by saying, "So, Wayne, you always wanted to be a referee, huh? This is one for the books!"

He also was the third man for Arturo Gatti's phenomenal war against Wilson Rodriguez in March 1996, as well as the ref for dozens of other title fights.

Larry Hazzard, who tops my list as the greatest referee of all time, was watching Wayne in action with me one night and said, "You had this Wayne Kelly pegged all along as a great referee." Then he added, "He really is."

In 2006, Wayne met noted author Nelson DeMille, himself a Vietnam vet. He and Wayne spoke for hours about the horrors they saw. DeMille told Wayne a trip to Vietnam would put to rest any ghosts and demons that still remained in the recesses of his mind. DeMille promised Wayne he'd find the trip "therapeutic." On his advice, Wayne went to South Vietnam.

While sitting at a bar, a Vietnamese gentleman asked Wayne if he was an American. Wayne said yes. The gentleman asked Wayne if he had fought in the war. Wayne nodded. The gentleman said he had fought in the war, as well. They even discussed a specific gunfight, the Battle of LZ English in Bongson.

Incredibly, both had fought in that battle. The only thing is, the gentleman fought for the NVA—the North Vietnamese Army. He was a Viet Cong. That day, in battle, he and Wayne were trying to kill one another. Now, they embraced. Wayne said, "We cried until we laughed. Then we drank."

In September 2011, Wayne had been suffering from abdominal pains for a few days. A Russian doctor friend of his, who Wayne had picked up at the airport, diagnosed Wayne's abdominal distress. It was an infected gallbladder that was ready to burst.

Rushed into surgery, his gallbladder was removed. Unfortunately, the surgical procedure had to slice through Wayne's thick stomach muscles. He was stitched and stapled back together. His postsurgery pain was both lengthy and excruciating. The mere acts of sitting, standing, and walking were brutally painful.

My wife and I were with Wayne at a boxing show on Long Island on Saturday, January 29, 2012. At the fight card, Wayne and I ran around, saying hello to seemingly every person in the house. But my wife and I could see he was in pain. We commented that Wayne didn't look well.

On Wednesday, February 2, 2012, I was walking out of a gym on Long Island after training a client. As I approached my car, my phone rang. It was Peter Frutkoff, one of Wayne's and my closest friends for years.

"Where are you?" asked Peter.

"I'm getting into my car outside North Shore Fitness," I responded.

"Get in but don't drive," he said.

"Why, what's going on?" I responded as I climbed behind the wheel.

There was a pause. Then Peter spoke.

"It's Wayne. He had a heart attack this morning."

"What??!!" I screamed. "Where is he? What hospital? I'm going there now!"

There was another pause. I quickly knew what was coming. My tears were flowing before Peter could get the words out.

"He didn't make it," he said, choking up. "He's gone."

That was the saddest moment of my life. When my mom passed from cancer in 2007, I was prepared for the end. The same with other close friends and relatives. But not this. Not Wayne.

As it was winter, my windows were up. No one heard my scream of grief.

"I'm sorry I had to be the one to tell you this, Randy," said Peter. "Ryan tried to reach you, but you were in the gym."

I heard him say "shopping" and "Target" and "quickly," but I was overcome by grief and heard little else, other than him pleading with me not to drive right away. I didn't. I couldn't. I was unable to see through the tears. My brother Wayne, the tortured soul I had met 43 years earlier and had been through so much with, the young man I shared dreams and beers with on the sand dunes at Jones Beach, the man I proudly appointed as my first act as chairman of the NYSAC and watched become one of the best referees in the sport, was gone. Gone! He was 63. I pounded on my steering wheel. I screamed. I cried uncontrollably.

When I was done perhaps 15 minutes later, I drove away in silence, having my own flashbacks of Wayne. The sparring sessions, the talks on the sand dunes, watching fights on TV with him, his fantastic Super Bowl parties, his chili, holding and playing with his babies, him doing the same with mine, watching our young daughters play together, being in the dressing room with him on the night of a fight card, giving instructions to the fighters with him, sitting at ringside as commissioner while he reffed a fight and having him smile at me from a neutral corner between rounds, seeing him for the last time four days earlier.

Wayne wanted to be a professional boxing referee. He could have refereed about 100 more title fights had he not been held back for 11 years. As it is, he became, not only a professional boxing ref, but also a great one. One of the greatest I ever saw.

At his wake, packed beyond capacity with relatives, friends, colleagues, fans, clients, and admirers, I was one of his eulogizers. I brought a can of beer with me. With his daughter Jackie and son Ryan sitting in front of me, I spoke.

My eulogy lasted perhaps 10 minutes. That I was able to stand there and not lose it or break down was amazing. It was the same as when I spoke at the funeral of Chuck Minker 22 years earlier.

Near the end of my eulogy, I said,

When I think of Wayne, several words come to mind. One of them is "wonderful." He was as wonderful a person as you'll ever find.

Another is "awesome." He was an awesome father, an awesome colleague, an awesome referee, and an awesome friend.

Another is "youthful." He loved working out, he loved looking good, and he did his best to stay young.

Another is "nice." He was nice to a fault. I never saw him treat anybody badly—unless of course, they deserved it.

That drew a laugh.

"The last one is 'exuberant.' Wayne lived his life with that youthful exuberance that made him so special."

I then said, "When you take the first letter of each word—'Wonderful,' 'Awesome,' 'Youthful,' 'Nice,' and 'Exuberant,' they spell WAYNE."

CHAPTER 11

I then took the beer in my hand as the tearing crowd watched.

"A long time ago, Wayne and I used to sit in the sand dunes at Jones Beach and talk about everything," I told them. "We talked about Vietnam, about our successes and failures, about our hopes and dreams . . . and about life and death. He had made me promise, that if he died before me, I would open a can of beer in front of everyone to celebrate his life."

With that, I popped open the can. I held it up.

"To Wayne!" I toasted.

"To Wayne!" they responded in unison.

Thank you for being in my life. We had a good time.

⑫

THE GREATEST
OF *ALL* TIME

Most of us have had at least one special moment in our lives that we can set aside and look back at with fond memories. I've been extremely fortunate, because I have had so many treasured moments. In fact, I've built a special room for those moments, complete with still photos, portraits, sound bites, and movies. That special room is in my mind.

One of those moments involved Muhammad Ali. Actually, three of those moments involved Ali. All took place when I roamed the New York boxing scene as Commissioner Gordon.

The first of the three moments took place at an exclusive dinner in 1992, at the Hotel Pierre in New York City. Ali was being honored for his humanitarian efforts. As commissioner, I was seated on the dais—next to Ali. It was truly a night to remember, because, on my right was Ali, and on my left was world-renowned artist LeRoy Neiman. From the moment he was seated, Neiman began sketching.

Publicist Murray Goodman, who had helped put this event together, showed me to my seat on the dais. He introduced me to both Neiman and Ali, not realizing I had known them both for a long time. I shook hands with Neiman, and he nodded, saying respectfully, "Nice to see you, Commissioner." Then, when I turned to Ali, the champ said to Goodman, "I know the commissioner. We go back to Deer Lake," referring to his Deer Lake, Pennsylvania, mountaintop training camp, where he prepared for most of his big fights in the mid-1970s, one of which was the "Rumble in the Jungle" against George Foreman. We reached to shake hands. His big right hand engulfed mine, but I remember how gentle his grasp was. I also felt the slight shaking in his body, the result of the Parkinson's disease that was engulfing him like a slow-moving glacier.

The list of politicians, dignitaries, and celebrities who took the podium to praise Ali was long—and, on several occasions, tedious and boring. One politician kept pronouncing Ali's first name as MOO/Hammad. He didn't do much better with his last name, either. He pronounced that as Alley (as in "I'm gonna take him out in the alley and whup him good!"). Each time the politician said MOO/Hammad Alley, I squirmed. After several mispronunciations, Ali knew I was uncomfortable. He tapped my tightly clenched right fist on the table, the one I wanted to slug the politician with, and motioned me to move close to him. When I did, he whispered, "It's okay. He probably doesn't even know who I am." I stifled a laugh, but when I looked up, it seemed as if everyone present, close to 1,000 guests, was looking at Ali and me, wondering what Ali said that was so funny.

Finally, it was my turn to speak. I received a nice round of applause, then turned to see Ali applauding. LeRoy Neiman wasn't applauding. He was still sketching.

The room grew quiet. I placed both hands on the podium and began speaking.

"In 1967, Muhammad Ali was stripped of his heavyweight title by boxing's regulatory bodies," I began.

He was stripped of the title for his failure to step forward when called for induction into the United States military. The first of those regulatory bodies to take Ali's title was the New York State Athletic Commission. At that time, an 18-year-old high school senior out on Long Island, who happened to be a huge boxing fan, was among those who felt it was wrong to strip Ali of the title he won in the ring just because he was exercising his religious and political beliefs. So this high school senior wrote letters to the chairman of the New York State Athletic Commission—Edwin Dooley—and to Nat Fleischer, the editor in chief of *Ring Magazine*, which also declared Ali's title vacant. He told Commissioner Dooley and Mr. Fleischer just how unfair he thought it was to take Ali's title away. He also told Mr. Fleischer that the magazine had not only lost a heavyweight champion, but a loyal reader, as well. He signed his name to both letters and included his phone number. It surprised the high school senior that he received phone calls from both Commissioner Dooley and Editor in Chief Fleischer.

As I looked at the large audience, I could see everyone was listening intently. Then I turned and looked at Ali. He, too, was listening with interest. I continued.

The high school senior thanked each of the well-known men for taking the time to call him. Then they each explained how they had a responsibility to the public to punish Ali for his illegal and anti-U.S. actions.

The teenager then said to each man, "But you're not a court of law." To Commissioner Dooley he said, "You are there to regulate boxing." To Mr. Fleischer he said, "You are there to write about boxing, to report on boxing, and to give us the ratings." To each he said, "What you're doing is unconstitutional. You can't just take his title away from Ali. He won it in the ring. He should be allowed to lose it in the ring." *Ring Magazine*'s boss told the youngster it wasn't unconstitutional. Commissioner Dooley said, "Stop listening to Howard Cosell. Ali broke the law and now must pay for his actions."

I looked out at the crowd. I had everyone's attention. Each of them knew the story of Ali and his three-and-a-half-year exile from boxing because of his failure to be inducted. This story they didn't know, so they watched. And they listened. Eyes shifted and several heads turned, but only to look at Ali. His eyes were transfixed. On me!

Yes, the high school senior did listen to Howard Cosell. He knew Cosell was correct in calling Ali's banishment from boxing "unconstitutional." But there was nothing the high school senior could do but watch with sadness as one of the great boxers of his—or any other generation—was stripped of his ability to make a living in the ring. Of course, in 1970, Cosell's words were proved prophetic, when the Supreme Court overturned Ali's banishment, calling it unconstitutional and ordering the boxing establishment to allow Ali to resume his boxing career.

I then turned to Ali, who was sitting straight up and looking right at me. I said to him,

Muhammad, that high school senior from Long Island now stands before you as the former editor in chief of *Ring Magazine*, the same magazine which stripped you of the title, and as the chairman of the New York State Athletic Commission, the same regulatory body which was the first boxing commission to take your title away. I can't undo what was already done, but I want you to know that if I had been in either position when that situation came up, I would have honored you for standing up for your rights and not vilified you. You are, and always will be, the "People's Champion."

The moment I said that, the entire room not only applauded, but also stood and applauded. Then Ali stood and walked over to me. He embraced me and said in a low voice, "I love you, Commissioner."

"I love you, too, Muhammad," I said.

Incredibly, he then took my left hand and raised it, as if he was the ref and I was a victorious fighter. The audience stayed on their feet, applauding. Then I raised his right hand, and the applause grew even louder. It became thunderous when Ali—all 6-foot-3 of him—tapped me on the shoulder and motioned for me—all 5-foot-6 of me—to raise both my hands in the air. When I did, he did the same. Then he hugged me again.

"Thank you, Commissioner," he said.

"No, thank you, champ," I replied.

When we sat down, LeRoy Neiman pushed two sketches in front of us and told us he wanted us to have them. One was of Ali. The other was of me.

What an afternoon!

My jaw is still hanging in disbelief, and even today, that sketch, now framed, still hangs in my den.

Less than a year later, Ali was a guest at a dinner of the Boxing Writers Association, held at the Marriott Marquis Hotel in Midtown Manhattan. Again, as a perk of being Commissioner Gordon, I was seated next to "The Greatest."

Although I had noticed Ali's trembling from Parkinson's disease when I was with him at the Hotel Pierre, his trembling was much more evident on this night. His hands shook slightly but steadily, and his upper body bounced up and down like a man on a subway car.

Yet, although the Parkinson's chipped away at his motor skills, it did not affect his memory. At this event, Ali amazed me with his patience, for the line of fans waiting for his autograph and photo seemed endless. Even during the dinner portion of the evening, Ali was besieged to sign cards, photos, hats, and boxing gloves. There was even a guy in the line who kept coming back for more, cutting in front of someone each time, bringing with him no less than five items to sign on each trip. It was obvious he was not an autograph collector but an autograph dealer. On his third trip to the dais, I whispered to Ali, "Champ, this guy keeps cutting ahead of people so he can have you sign a bunch of items. He's a dealer who's gonna probably sell all the stuff you're signing for him." The guy saw me whispering to Ali, and when Ali raised his eyes to look at him, the guy knew he had been caught. He began to walk away. Ali held up his right hand, then motioned for the guy to come back. The champ turned to me and leaned close. Then, in a low, barely audible voice, he whispered into my right ear, "Let him have his fun." Then he signed several more items for the guy. After signing them, he turned to look at me. He could see I was fuming at the guy both for cutting into the line and taking advantage of Ali's good nature.

"It's okay," Ali whispered to me. Then he smiled and patted me on my right hand, which was again—like it was as the politician continually mispronounced

Ali's name at the Hotel Pierre—angrily balled into a fist, wanting to slug the creepy dealer. With Ali's reassuring pat, I let go of my anger.

"I'm always talking you out of fights," Ali joked, in reference to my same reaction a year earlier toward the politician. I was amazed he remembered that unimportant incident.

Maybe it wasn't so unimportant, after all.

A few months later, Ali was in New York City for the day, heading overseas on one of his many goodwill trips. He had called my office at the New York State Athletic Commission around 9:00 a.m. and asked if I could stop by to see him at his hotel. I told him I had some work to finish, but I'd be there within two hours.

"The last time I was on the phone with the commission," he joked, "I was about to be suspended," in reference to his 1967 banishment from the sport by Chairman Dooley.

The hotel Ali was staying in was right off busy Times Square, the same area where tens of thousands of revelers and partiers flock on New Year's Eve. But this was not a chilly December 31 night. It was summer and a broiler in New York. The temperature was in the 90s.

I arrived at his hotel just before noon and headed to his room. I knocked. Ali's publicist, Murray Goodman, opened the door.

"Hello, Commissioner," he said. Then he pointed across the room. Ali was rising from the couch.

"Sit there, Muhammad, you don't have to get up," I said.

"I'll stand for you any time, Commissioner," he responded. I went to shake his hand. He reached for it, shook it, then pulled me close and embraced me.

"So nice to see you," he said.

"Likewise," I replied.

"I have a few calls to make," said Goodman. "I'll be back in a little while. Can I get you guys anything?"

We shook our heads and thanked him. Goodman walked out, leaving me with Ali.

"Commissioner, do you like magic?" Ali asked.

"I love magic, Muhammad, but you have to do me one favor."

"What's that?" he asked.

"Call me Randy," I requested. "In my job I'm the commissioner. In here, I'm your friend. I'm Randy."

"I know that," said Ali. "But it's a respect thing, and I do respect you. I will call you Randy, but don't be offended if I call you 'commissioner.'"

Then he took a deck of cards and shuffled them.

"Pick a card, any card," said Ali. "Look at it, remember it, and don't tell me what it is. Then place it back in the deck."

I did.

Then, Ali shuffled the cards. He then said, "Think of your card." Playing along, I thought of it. Ali placed the deck against my forehead and said, "Keep thinking of the card." I kept thinking of it.

Ali then spread the cards out on the coffee table in front of the couch. They were all facedown. All except the card I chose. It was face up. I was amazed

"I got more," said Ali.

He wasn't lying. He performed magic for at least another half hour for me, doing some tricks I had never seen before. In one of them, the card I chose and put back in the deck was not there when Ali spread the cards out. Then he shuffled the deck and told me to tap it twice. I did. When Ali spread the cards out, my card had "magically" returned to the deck.

"I'm gonna save the big trick for later," Ali said. "Right now, let's take a walk."

"A walk?" I responded. "Where to?"

"Let's go outside to Times Square. I feel like being bad."

My brow creased, and I gave Ali a puzzled look.

"You feel like being bad? How so?" I quizzically asked him.

"Take a walk," he said. "You'll see."

He headed toward the door, and I followed him. His suite was down the hall from the elevator, and the walk, which should have taken us 15 seconds, took us closer to 15 minutes, as several hotel guests and even a few of the maids wanted to shake Ali's hand and get his autograph. Being Ali, he needed to oblige each of them. When we got on the elevator, the shocked expressions of the five or six people in the car were priceless. It was the same when the elevator arrived at each floor and another guest or two stepped on.

"Wow! Muhammad Ali!" shrieked a woman who got on after one stop.

"I don't believe it!" exclaimed a man entering on another floor.

The lobby was yet another story, as perhaps a dozen people quickly turned into two and three dozen people who had to see, touch, and talk to Ali.

When we finally made it outside, still being trailed by a few autograph-seekers, we were a block from Times Square.

"What did you mean before when you said you feel like being bad?" I inquired of Ali. He smiled.

"In a minute I'll show you," he said. He wore a mischievous look, like a kid trying to sneak something past a parent.

Heads turned and fingers pointed as Ali and I walked side by side toward the famed tower in Times Square, which sits in the middle of Seventh Avenue and 42nd Street. It is where, on New Year's Eve, a million or so chilled revelers bid farewell to the outgoing year and welcome in the new one.

As we got to the corner of Seventh Avenue and 42nd Street, Ali turned to me and asked, "Are you ready to be bad?"

I just gave him a puzzled looked, shrugged my shoulders, and turned my palms up.

"Watch," he said. He looked up at the light. It was changing from red to green for those heading east on 42nd Street and from green to red for those heading south on Seventh Avenue. He took me by the left arm and began walking. As we got to the middle of the street in the walkway, he stopped. Then he thrust both hands skyward. It was your typical, familiar Muhammad Ali pose.

Instantly, people recognized him. The driver of the car stopped at the light directly in front of Ali recognized him immediately. He threw his car into park, opened the door, and ran out of the car to shake Ali's hand. The guy in a van behind him did the same thing, and so did the two guys in the car behind the van. Within seconds, dozens of people were surrounding Ali, thrusting pens and objects for him to sign. They asked him to autograph everything from the paper bags that held their lunches to business cards, ballcaps, and folded papers that were in their pockets. One lady even took a Sharpie from her purse, handed it to Ali, and asked him to sign the back of her yellow blouse.

Meanwhile, the traffic light had changed in both directions. The cars at the light that was just red were ready to move; however, the drivers of the first five or six cars in that line had abandoned their vehicles to run and meet Ali. The others behind them did not know what was going on, other than there was some kind of excitement up ahead. Horns began blowing and shouts of "C'mon, move!" could be heard. The same thing happened at the light that had just changed from green to red. Cars that had entered the intersection and saw Ali suddenly stopped. Many of those drivers also got out of their cars and made their way to Ali. Traffic was now snarled in both directions. A domino effect began taking place, with traffic backing up for blocks.

Nearby traffic police and foot patrolmen got word on their radios of a "disturbance at the intersection of 42nd Street and Seventh Avenue" and quickly made their way to see what was going on.

When the first patrolman arrived, he saw what the "disturbance" was about and who was causing it. Standing almost next to him, I heard him say into his walkie-talkie, "The ten five at 42nd and Seventh is being caused by boxer

Muhammad Ali. Drivers have recognized him and have abandoned their vehicles. There is no emergency here other than a celebrity causing a temporary traffic problem." He then approached Ali, who was playing with the growing crowd.

"Hey, champ, you're causing a little traffic jam here," said the officer. Then Ali playfully shook his fist at one of New York's finest, and the crowd laughed, as did the patrolman. Then Ali put an arm around the patrolman and said, "I'm just having a little fun."

"Well, have your fun on the sidewalk, champ," said the patrolman. "If I don't get traffic moving, headquarters is gonna have my head." Then he added, "But can I quickly get you to sign this?" He pulled out a small pad.

"To Joe," said the cop.

"Why, absolutely!" said Ali. "To Officer Joe . . ."

Ali signed the paper. Then, as other officers approached, Ali motioned to the dozens of people around him to clear the street. As he walked toward the sidewalk, his admirers followed him. The drivers went back to their respective vehicles. On the sidewalk, Ali signed autograph after autograph. If that had been today, videos would have been taken and hundreds of photos would have been shot with mobile phones. For certain you'd be watching it on YouTube.

The eight or so policemen who had shown up quickly surrounded Ali and asked where he was headed. When he said, "Back to my hotel" and pointed up the road, one of them said, "Follow us," and led him from the lunchtime crowd, which was still getting larger.

I had gotten pushed and nudged into the crowd, and was perhaps 10 feet from Ali. At 5-foot-6, it's easy for me to get lost in a swelling crowd.

"Commissioner?" Ali called. "Commissioner, where are you?"

I heard him and raised my right arm. Ali pointed to me and said to a cop, "That's the boxing commissioner. He's with me." An officer motioned for me to come forward as other officers cleared the way for me. Then they created a phalanx around us and walked us back to the hotel.

In the hotel lobby, they walked us to the elevator, where Ali and I got on and headed back to his room. Once on the quiet elevator, Ali and I looked at one another.

"Is that what you meant by being bad?" I asked him.

He just smiled and nodded his head.

Then he said, "If you remember, I told you before I was saving a big trick for later. Well, it's later."

"I'm looking forward to seeing it," I told him.

We got off the elevator and walked down the hall to his room. Once inside, Ali walked to a cabinet, which housed the room's refrigerator, opened it, and took out two bottles of water. We were both sweating from the blistering heat we had just come in from, and Ali said, "Sit down, Commissioner. Relax for a few minutes. I'll show you my big magic trick in a minute." He pointed to a leather chair on the side of the plush couch in his suite. As I sat down, he sat on the couch.

"Hot out there, huh?" he said. Then he asked me, "Do you like the heat?"

"I love it," I told him. "I'll take the heat over the cold any day."

"Me, too," he said.

Talk of hot weather gave me the perfect opening to ask Ali a question about which I had long been wondering.

"Speaking of heat, Muhammad, where did you feel the heat more—in the ring in Zaire against George Foreman or in Manila against Joe Frazier?"

As I asked Ali the question, he was taking a mouthful of water. He swallowed it, then leaned forward, looked at me, and said, "It wasn't even close. Manila wasn't just hot. Manila was hell!"

He stood up and walked toward me. Then he held his hands on both sides of his face, with his chin tucked on his chest and his arms pulled in against his sides. It was a style he popularized and called it his "Rope-a-Dope." He employed it mainly while resting on the ropes and allowed opponents to flail away and punch themselves out while doing so.

Then he explained why he did that against Foreman, one of the hardest punchers in the long and storied history of the heavyweight division.

"It wasn't just hot that night in Zaire," he said.

It was humid and very sticky. In fact, the humidity was 100 percent. It poured right after the fight ended. It was even a hot rain. Up until that night, I had never felt anything like it. I tried to dance and stick and move in the first round, but I knew I'd never be able to keep that pace up for 15 rounds. After I got a good look at George in the first round, and some more in the second, I saw how wide his punches were. I also knew how much he wanted to knock me out. He was fighting in the same heat and humidity as me, so I quickly figured I'd slow my pace down and conserve energy. I'd let George use all his energy. So I went back to the ropes and let him throw everything he had, hoping I could block everything. Then I began talking to George, saying things like, "George, you hit like a sissy!" and "I thought you were supposed to be such a hard puncher, George!" and "You can't punch!" and "Harder, George! Hit me harder!" The fight got easier as it went on. That's because George got tired and punched himself out.

As he was telling me this, his hands were still up. He was still doing the Rope-a-Dope as he explained his victory plan in the "Rumble in the Jungle."

"But Joe Frazier?" I asked.

Ali lowered his hands, looked down at me in the chair, and, after taking a deep breath, said, "That night was hell! It was pure hell!"

I stared up at Ali. He raised his eyes a bit and paused. You could see he was thinking about the fight, reliving the classic history recalls as the "Thrilla' in Manila." I was in a position few journalists or fans had ever been in. I was in a room, in one-on-one conversation, with arguably the greatest personality the sports world has ever known, and he was recalling and recapturing the night of October 1, 1975. He was taking me back, via his own personal time machine, into the ring with him against Joe Frazier.

"It was over 120 degrees in that ring," said Ali. (I have heard from journalists who were there that the number was closer to 130 under the television lights!)

I thought of Zaire as I came out for round one. I knew that, unlike Big George, Joe Frazier was not going to punch himself out. I knew I would be forced to both move and slug with this guy. I was hoping to catch him early with a hard shot and hopefully stop him. I did not want to be in that ring for one hour. The fight turned into everything I didn't want. The more I hit him flush, the harder he fought back. With Joe, it's not so much one punch you feel, but all of his punches. And he just keeps coming . . . and throwing . . . and throwing. Through all of that heat, through all of that wicked heat, he never stopped. He never let up. I blocked a lot of his shots on my arms, but after a while, even my arms hurt.

As Ali talked, you could see, feel, and sense the faraway place he was in.

"Round after round I went out there and reached down like I had never had to reach down before," Ali recounted.

I can feel the heat right now. I can feel his breath on me. I can hear his grunts when he punches. They became louder and scarier as the fight went on. I tried so hard to end it with one punch, but he never showed me he had taken enough. Oh, I had him puffy and cut and swollen, but he just fought back harder. Going into the 13th round, I remember thinking, "Tonight, I am going to die. I am going to die right here in this ring." I hurt everywhere. My insides felt like they had been pulverized. Every breath I took hurt. It felt like knives were being stuck in my lungs. My face hurt. My ears hurt. My jaw hurt. My hands hurt. Nothing felt good. Nothing felt right. Even when I connected with the right that sent his mouthpiece flying, he came back in for more. He wanted me to kill him. But he was determined he was gonna kill me first. After the 14th round, I couldn't go on anymore. My heart told me to get out there for three more minutes, but my body wouldn't respond. I was spent. I was on empty. There was nothing left. I couldn't even raise my arms. I went back to the corner and told Angie to "cut my gloves off. I'm through." I really believed I was going to die. Then Angie looked at Frazier's corner. He saw Eddie [Futch] waving his hands, not allowing Joe to come out. Angie told me, "You won, Muhammad. Joe's not answering the bell." I fell onto the canvas, not from happiness, but from exhaustion. I can still feel it. I can feel all of it.

As he recounted the story, his eyes still showed him in another time and place.

Despite the fact that I had read quotes after the fight and heard Ali say that he really was going to remain on his stool to start the 15th round had Frazier come out for that final round, and despite the fact that Ali had just told me that same story, I found his words almost surreal.

"Were you really finished that night, Muhammad?" I asked him. "I'm sure Angelo and Bundini would have touched a nerve in your competitive spirit to get you out there for the 15th. Do you really believe you would have stayed on your stool?"

Ali then shook for a brief moment, obviously returning from his trip back in time. He looked directly at me. He took a slow, deep breath and spoke.

"Commissioner . . . Randy . . . I say this to you as your friend and as a man: Had Joe Frazier come out for round 15, he would have been the only one coming out that round. I had nothing left. Nothing! My fight was over that night!"

On countless occasions I had heard Ali tell that same story on television and radio. Magazine articles and reports of the fight also told that same story. But now, I was being told the story by the man himself. I have watched the fight in its entirety dozens of times in the years since that afternoon with Ali. On every viewing, I hear Ali's voice narrating just for me: "The fight turned into everything I didn't want . . . he just keeps coming . . . and throwing . . . and throwing . . . tonight, I am going to die."

Right after Ali said, "My fight was over that night!" he looked at me and smiled. It was a painful smile.

"Okay, are you ready for my big trick?" he asked.

"Yes, I am, Muhammad," I said. "But if you don't mind, I have one more question for you."

"Fire away, Commissioner," he replied.

I took a deep breath. It was a tough question, one I had only heard him answer 28 years earlier.

The question was about his first title defense, on May 25, 1965, against the man he beat for the heavyweight title, Sonny Liston.

"Muhammad, I have long wondered what happened in certain events in history," I began. "I wonder what really happened in Dallas, Texas, on November 22, 1963. I wonder what really happened in Jack Johnson's title-losing fight to Jess Willard in Havana, Cuba, in 1915. And I have long wondered what happened against Sonny Liston that night in Lewiston, Maine."

He looked at me. He was deep in thought.

"You don't have to answer that question, champ. I'm sorry," I said.

He smiled.

"You ask tougher questions than Howard Cosell," he joked, adding, "but I am going to answer that."

He continued.

"I was supposed to fight Liston back in November in Boston, but a few days before the fight, I got hit with appendicitis. It came on fast. It felt like 100 Joe Frazier left hooks. I was rushed into surgery, and the fight was postponed."

The rematch was rescheduled for May 25, but a new venue needed to be found. The fight would now be heading to the St. Dominic's Hall, a 4,000-seat ice-skating arena in Lewiston, Maine; however, with rumors flying of the threat of violence due to the assassination of Malcolm X three months earlier and the possibility of Malcolm's followers retaliating against Ali and the Nation of Islam (whose extremist wing, the Fruit of Islam, had taken responsibility for Malcolm X's murder), the smallest crowd to ever witness a heavyweight title fight (2,434) turned out for the fight.

"Liston seemed a lot slower to me," Muhammad recalled. "He seemed easier to hit than when I first fought him. He also seemed a lot older, even though it had been a little over a year since we had previously fought."

I reminded him that Liston's age was anywhere between 35 and 40 when they fought the rematch.

"I realized that," said Ali, "but I went into my fight thinking he was young and dangerous."

He continued.

"I hit him early in the fight with a good right. I noticed how easy it was to land the punch, so I set him up with a few jabs."

He stood up and pumped his long left in my direction as he explained.

"Then I dropped a quick, chopping right on him. BAM!"

He fired a right that was exactly like the right that dropped Liston.

"He went down. Quite frankly, I was surprised to see him on the floor. I thought to myself, 'What is Sonny doing? Is he taking a dive? He'd better not be! I want to knock him out!' I stood over him and yelled, 'Get up and fight me, sucka!'"

Confusion followed. Former heavyweight champion Jersey Joe Walcott, who should never have been put in the position to referee the fight, did not send Ali to a neutral corner. Walcott also claims he never saw or heard a count from the official timekeeper.

Liston arose, and the fight continued. Then, Walcott walked over to the timekeeper, who was sitting next to *Ring* editor Nat Fleischer. Both of them said Liston had been down for more than 10 seconds. They told Walcott the fight was over.

"I walked back to my corner after Jersey Joe stopped the fight," Ali recalled,

and said to Angelo and Bundini, "What's going on? This guy just laid down!" Angelo said, "You hit him with a helluva right hand, that's what happened!" By the time I was being interviewed, I made up a story that [old-time actor] Stepin Fetchit taught me a chopping punch he learned way back from Jack Johnson, called the "Anchor Punch." The fact is, I threw a right, it landed, and Liston went down.

"Muhammad, I have heard stories about members of the Fruit of Islam taking Sonny's wife and young son hostage before the fight," I told Ali, "and threatening to kill them if he beat you. Have you ever heard that before?"

"I did hear those stories, but not until well after the fight," Ali said.

I also heard stories well after the fight about Liston being shot in the arena, as well as the Mafia being involved. All I know is that when I stepped into that ring, the only guy I was listening to was Angelo, who kept telling me, "Remember to box this guy. Use your jab and use your speed." I know that I hit him, and I know that he went down. All the rest of the stuff I have heard just like you have heard the talk.

One of those who do not buy any of the assassination and kidnap stories is Gene Kilroy, Ali's longtime business manager and longtime friend and confidante.

"That's all bullshit!" Kilroy told me when I asked him about the possibility of Liston being strong-armed into taking a dive.

"The fact is, Liston was a bully," said Kilroy.

Plus, he was an old man. When guys stand up to bullies, the way Ali did against Foreman and the way Buster Douglas did against Tyson, the bullies usually lose. Ali had no trouble hitting Liston from the moment the fight started. He had already caught Liston with a hard right and also landed a left before hitting him with that chopping right hand. A few years later, Leotis Martin beat Liston badly . . .

slapped him around. Liston was finished after the first fight against Ali. You can take all those conspiracy theories and throw them out the window!

After Ali finished talking about the rematch against Liston, he excitedly asked, "Okay, Commissioner, are you ready for my big trick?"

"Let's have it," I said.

"Here we go, Mr. Commissioner, let's have you stand right here." He walked to a spot in the middle of the room and pointed to where he wanted me to stand.

I walked to the spot. Ali then walked in front of me, perhaps eight feet away.

"I am now going to levitate," he told me.

"Levitate?" I questioned.

"That's right," he said. "I am going to levitate. I am going to come off the ground. I am going to fly."

I just looked at him in curious wonderment.

"We just need some deep concentration here," said Ali, "so I'll ask for complete silence while I do this."

I laughed and said, "The floor is yours, Muhammad."

"Thank you, Commissioner," he said softly. "Now, watch my feet."

He turned to his left and placed his left foot in front of his right. Then he took a few deep breaths and lifted both arms straight in front of him.

A moment later, Ali began to rise off the ground. I laughed at the magic Ali was performing. It looked so real as he elevated—levitated—perhaps one inch upward. I stopped laughing a moment later as I leaned over and began looking under Ali's feet. With his right forefinger, he motioned for me to go down lower.

"Look under my feet," said the champ.

I did. My eyes scanned the area under his feet. Nothing was there but air. He wasn't up on one heel, and he wasn't up on his toes. His feet were making no contact with the ground.

Then he came down as softly and gently as he went up.

"Well, how'd you like that?" Ali asked me.

I stared at him for a moment, then asked, "Will you do that again?"

He took a deep breath and rolled his eyes.

"Now you're asking a lot of me," he said with a sheepish grin. "It takes a lot of concentration and energy to do this. I don't know if I have another one in me right now," he said.

"Try," I asked him. He smiled and nodded. Then he said, "You can put your ear to the carpet so you can see better. You ready?"

"I'm ready!" I said.

Ali went through the machinations again. He put one foot in front of the other. He lifted both hands straight out in front. Then he drew in a deep breath and blew it out slowly through his mouth. He stared straight ahead. As he did all this, I laid on the floor with my left ear on the carpet. I watched his feet closely. I was sure I would see this time how he did it.

I understand magic. I enjoy magic. I think most of us do. But I also understand what magic is. It is distraction. It is sleight of hand. It is deception. It is doing something through trickery that really cannot be accomplished—like levitation.

I learned a long time ago that Superman isn't real. I know that humans cannot fly.

Well, all I saw under Ali's feet was an inch of air and space. He was not leaning on anything and his feet were not resting on anything. Nothing was between his feet and the ground. He stayed up for perhaps five seconds. Then he came down.

I know this cannot possibly happen. I know this cannot possibly be done. Then will someone please tell me how he did it? Someone please tell me what I saw—or didn't see. Was I hypnotized?

Muhammad Ali showed me how he did the other card tricks. This was the one trick he said was real.

On my way back to my office, I could think only of that final trick Muhammad Ali demonstrated for me. It frustrates me that I don't know how he was able to "fly."

When I was a child and saw a magician perform a trick on television, I'd ask my father, "How did he do that?"

Not knowing the answer, my father would say, "It's magic. Just enjoy it."

And so, without learning the answer to how Ali did that, I have come to accept what I saw and will always enjoy that memory; however, I will always be curious.

Hmm. Muhammad Ali always said he could "float like a butterfly."

Maybe he can.

When you're "The Greatest," I suppose anything is possible!

13

TWO KING-SIZED
WHITE ENVELOPES

Mexico City, Mexico. It's the capital city of the Hispanic nation. It's where the Aztec, Maya, and Olmec civilizations began in the fourteenth, fifteenth, and sixteenth centuries. It's the cultural, economic, educational, and financial hub of the country.

To us boxing fans, Mexico City is all that, and more. It is home to the World Boxing Council, the sanctioning body that has rated fighters and handed out championship belts since 1963. Since its inception that year, the WBC has had two presidents. The first was Jose Sulaiman, who passed away in 2013. The second was, and continues to be into 2019, Mauricio Sulaiman, Jose's son.

In the fall of 1988, I was invited to the WBC Convention in Mexico City by Jose Sulaiman. It was, in his words, "Boxing's celebration of a new leader in our sport, a celebration of glorious and fabulous things to come in the great state of New York and in our wonderful sport."

I had become chairman of the New York State Athletic Commission only a few weeks earlier amid much fanfare, and now, Señor Sulaiman was inviting me—a known adversary of all of boxing's sanctioning bodies—to be his personal guest in Mexico City.

In a phone call from the WBC's el presidente the week I took office, Sulaiman said,

Mr. Chairman, you are no longer a journalist. You will no longer speak with your typewriter and your voice. You will speak with your leadership and with your actions. You are a regulator in what is, historically, boxing's Mecca. Your leadership will be felt far and wide. Other states, which are not nearly as big and powerful and respected as yours, are members of the WBC. I can only wish and hope you, too, will become a member of the WBC. I hereby extend an invitation for you to join us at our yearly convention, which, this year, will be taking place in Mexico City. My invitation includes airfare for you and a guest, limo pickup upon your arrival and departure, first-class accommodations at a five-star hotel, unlimited food and beverage, as well as use of all the amenities within the hotel, including the spa, health club, and massages.

It was far too incredible an offer to turn down. But, turn it down I did. I learned years ago if a deal sounds too good to be true, it probably is exactly what you're thinking—and then some. This deal had strings and attachments all over it. I thanked Sulaiman for his generosity and friendship, then told him I would indeed attend my first sanctioning body convention, but my agency would pay for my trip to Mexico, along with all my expenses.

When I told my right-hand man—Rich Hering—about the phone call, he saw right through Sulaiman's words.

"Randy, who is Jose Sulaiman's best friend, at least in the boxing business?" asked Hering.

I didn't have to think about the answer.

"Don King," I said. We looked at one another and shook our heads.

Don King was heavyweight champion Mike Tyson's promoter; however, he wanted to be more than Tyson's promoter. He wanted to be Tyson's partner, manager, and sole trustee. He wanted a lion's—make that a king-sized—share of the profits.

With Tyson's beloved Jim Jacobs having passed away earlier in the year, King began to move in. King had a big problem, however: Tyson still had a managerial contract with Bill Cayton. The thing is, Tyson did not have the same relationship with Cayton as he did with Jacobs. With Jacobs, Tyson could talk not only boxing, but also sports. He could talk about girls. He could talk about anything. Jacobs was like Tyson's big brother. With Cayton, Tyson could only talk about business—about his next fight, where it was, when it was, how much he would earn. Tyson wanted more than that. He wanted Cus D'Amato and Jim Jacobs. They were gone. All he had was Bill Cayton. Tyson needed more. Don King knew that.

"Satan is no good for Mike," King would say to the media, then correct himself with, "Did I say Satan? I meant to say Cayton." The media laughed. Mike Tyson laughed. Bill Cayton fumed. On my second day in office, Cayton even paid a visit to see me, warning me that King and Tyson would probably come up soon, trying to get me to break Tyson's contract with Cayton.

"Don King is going to be in Mexico City without question," said Hering, adding, "and I'm willing to bet Tyson will be there, too. Be very aware that they will be all over you and sucking up to you from the moment you arrive."

Hering's words could not have been any more on target.

When my flight landed in Mexico City, an announcement came over the PA system in the cabin: "Will passenger Randy Gordon please ring his flight attendant call button."

I couldn't imagine what that was about but immediately did so. Moments later, a female flight attendant approached me.

"Good afternoon, Señor Gordon," she said. "When you disembark, look for a man holding a sign with your name. He will be wearing a white hat with the letters WBC."

I thanked her and smiled. Rich Hering was right. The "sucking up" had begun.

After walking down a short hallway, I, along with the other passengers, passed through a set of double doors. Written above the doors in big, block letters were the words "Customs and Immigration."

Two security guards pointed the way and kept saying, "Have your passports ready."

As I passed them, I looked to the left and saw a single line of passengers—hundreds of them—waiting to have their luggage checked before being admitted to Mexico. The heat in the admittance area was stifling—perhaps in the mid-80s—and the ventilation—even with overhead fans—was stuffy, at best. Sweat was already beginning to roll down my face.

Then, standing just a few feet from the security guards, I saw a man with a white hat.

Three big letters stood out: "WBC."

I glanced at a sign he was holding: "Commissioner Randy Gordon"

I smiled. I smiled not only because my ride was there, but also because of how the sign was worded. It didn't just have my name on it. It said "Commissioner Randy Gordon." More sucking up!

That sucking up continued after I identified myself. The man said, "Good afternoon, Commissioner. I am Ruben, your driver [I remembered his name, because Ruben Olivares is my all-time favorite Mexican champion]. We are approved to walk through Customs. All you need to do is have your passport stamped."

I followed Ruben to a counter, where an agent opened my passport and, without looking at the photo, stamped it.

"Have a nice stay in Mexico, Commissioner," he said.

I smiled brighter than the Mexican sun. The agent had just called me "commissioner." Obviously, the long-reaching arm of Jose Sulaiman's politics was already at work.

"Muchos gracias," I said to the agent, trying to be cool.

I then walked out to the car—a black, freshly washed, highly polished, brand-new Lincoln Continental. As Ruben held the back door for me, I made my way into the car. With the sun in my eyes, I was startled to see the silhouette of someone in the backseat.

Was this a limo sent by the WBC to pick up arriving boxing personnel and officials, here to attend the convention? I wondered. *Why not send a van instead?* I quickly found out.

The silhouette was that of Jose Sulaiman himself. My eyes opened wide in amazement.

"Jose!" I exclaimed.

"Commissioner Gordon, welcome to my country." We embraced.

"Are you here to pick somebody else up, Mr. President?" I asked.

Sulaiman laughed. He saw that I didn't get it.

"Yes, I am here to pick someone up," said the WBC's president. He paused, then looked at me.

"I am here to pick *you* up."

The blank stare and look of surprise on my face told him I still didn't get it.

"Why do you look so surprised, Commissioner? Your being here gives me massive joy and pride."

As he looked at me, I was still wearing a puzzled expression.

"I see I am going to have to explain this to you," Sulaiman said.

"*Conducir, hasta en hotel, por favor,*" he told the driver. "Drive to the hotel, please."

Then, Sulaiman turned to me.

"Commissioner . . ." he began. "I will always call you 'commissioner.'"

"My name is Randy," I responded. "Please call me 'Randy.'"

"I will do that, because we are friends," he said. "But in public, I will only address you as 'commissioner.'"

"And is it okay if I call you 'Jose' in private and 'Mr. President' in public?" I questioned.

"It sure is, Randy," he said. He reached out and we shook hands.

I sat back in my seat, took a deep breath, and then turned to the left to look at him.

"So, to what do I owe the honor of you being here to greet me, Jose?" I asked.

He smiled. Then he patted my left hand and spoke.

Randy, my friend, the position you have been elevated to is one of the biggest in our sport, whether you realize it or not. You have always been respected, as both a writer and as a broadcaster. You may not know it yet, but there is power in your position. Huge power. You will be heard more than ever, and you will be respected more than ever. In the week here in Mexico, you will come to learn that, to feel that, to understand that. You have made yourself known throughout the business, and now, by being named as commissioner in New York, your name has been elevated to the top of the sport. I am honored to be able to pick you up.

During the ride, which was perhaps a half hour, Sulaiman filled me in on the itinerary for the week.

There were lectures, workshops, seminars, more lectures, more workshops, and more seminars. There were dinners, free time, meet-and-greets, a bus trip to an Aztec shrine, and shopping trips. My American cash was turned into pesos. I don't remember exactly, but I believe I exchanged 200 American dollars for pesos. What I received in return were tens of thousands of pesos (*I like this peso exchange!* I remember thinking).

When we arrived at the hotel, Señor Sulaiman directed a bellman—in Spanish—to take my bags from the car up to my room. He pulled Mexican currency—a lot of it—and handed it to the bellman. I don't know how much it was, but the bellman's eyes nearly popped out of his head when he saw his tip. He began bowing to the WBC's president.

"Muchos gracias!" was all I understood. Sulaiman smiled at him.

"They work hard," he said to me.

Then he added, "You have been upgraded from a standard room to a suite."

"But, Jose, my agency is paying for this," I responded. "They have already approved a standard room. They are not going to approve anything more."

Sulaiman put his arm around my shoulders.

"I know this, my friend," said Sulaiman. "The hotel's owner does business with me. He has approved your upgrade at no additional charge."

"Thank you so much, Jose, but I really can't . . ." He stopped me.

"Randy, please, I wanted to give you so much more, but you wouldn't allow me to," said Sulaiman. "At least take this upgrade as a small token of my friendship."

I took the upgrade but swore there would be no more upgrades, gifts, or presents of any kind.

I hadn't seen anything, yet!

At the evening's convention-opening cocktail party, I saw the immense power Jose Sulaiman wielded in boxing. Officials from throughout the world, especially referees and judges, were all over him, like ants at a picnic. Included were two officials—a referee and a judge—who were both veterans, not only in boxing, but also in the art of "sucking up."

It was almost embarrassing as I watched each of them stay as close to President Sulaiman as they could. When he moved, they moved. When he stopped, they stopped. Me? I had fun mingling with officials I had only known from seeing them on TV and in boxing magazines.

After perhaps a half hour, a gentleman walked over to me and said, "Commissioner Gordon, I work for Jose Sulaiman. Mr. Sulaiman requests the honor of your presence at his table." He then escorted me across the room to a corner table, at which perhaps 12 people were seated. Sulaiman was one. Don King and Mike Tyson were two more. WBC executive Chuck Williams was another. Julio Cesar Chavez was another. Former bantamweight champion and Mexican legend Ruben Olivares was also there, and so was Hector "Macho" Camacho.

As we were seated, Arthur Mercante, the senior referee in New York, came over, hoping to find a place at the table. He stood behind me and put his hands on my shoulders.

"I see you have met my new boss," Mercante said to Sulaiman. I smiled and played along, enjoying the fact I was indeed his boss, at least in New York State. Mercante must have gagged on his words, as he had never been a fan of mine. He must have gagged even more when Sulaiman said, "Yes, Arthur. The commissioner and I have been friends for a long time. But now, instead of being a journalist, he is the man in charge of boxing in the Mecca—New York. You are lucky to have such a man to call your boss." Then, El Presidente Sulaiman stood up. When he did, the entire room grew quiet. To the table and the rest of the room, Sulaiman said, "Commissioner Gordon is exactly what boxing needs right now." He held up his glass and toasted me.

"To New York's new boxing czar," said Sulaiman, loudly. I stood up to acknowledge the WBC's president and the warm applause I was receiving, then nodded to everyone and smiled.

Then, as I was about to sit down, I heard somebody call out "Commissioner Gordon," from several seats down. It was Don King. He looked at me and gave me a thumbs up. I smiled at him and mouthed, "Thank you." He pointed to me, then back to himself, and made a talking gesture with his right hand. I nodded. He nodded back. Mike Tyson, who was sitting next to King, waved at me and said, "Hi, Commissioner." I smiled and said, "Hi, champ."

That night, when I returned to my beautiful suite, I removed my sport jacket and threw it on the bed. As I did, I spotted a large envelope on my pillow.

A welcome letter from the WBC and meal coupons, I thought. I wasn't even close.

When I opened it, there was a short, simple, typewritten letter. Another sealed envelope was underneath the letter, which said:

Commissioner,

Welcome to Mexico City and to your first of many WBC conventions. Please accept this as a small token of our appreciation for you electing to become a member of the worldwide WBC family.

The typewritten signature said, "Your Boxing Family from around the World."

I glanced at the envelope inside the first one I opened. It was thick. It was filled.

What's in here? I thought. *This is too heavy and thick to be coupons or vouchers.* I tore open the envelope. My eyes nearly exploded out of my head.

It was a stack of money. Several stacks. I don't know how much it was, because I didn't count it. I did fan quickly through a stack, however. It was all U.S. currency. They were all hundred-dollar bills.

I gasped and dropped the stack on my bed.

My mouth fell open. For a few moments, I became dizzy. I sat down on the bed and took a few deep breaths.

What should I do? I thought. There had to be tens of thousands of dollars in there.

In my days in TV, I was often given a food per diem by the network. It was in the ballpark of $100 per day. On long events, for example, the Olympics, the food per diem was often paid in advance: so an expected stay in the Olympic Village could range in the neighborhood of $3,000. My first thought was that this was food per diem money for the week in Mexico City. I reached for the envelope again. Maybe it was Mexican currency. Maybe it was pesos. I looked at each stack. It was U.S. currency. That wasn't Abraham Lincoln's picture on each bill. It was Ben Franklin's. This could buy me a lot of onyx chess sets and sombreros!

The thought of keeping the money lasted for a microsecond. Then I got real.

Being that nobody knows what room I am in except Jose Sulaiman, this can only have come from him, I thought. *I am supposed to meet Jose for breakfast at 7:30 tomorrow. I will discreetly hand the envelope back to him.*

I went to sleep, knowing I would be doing the right thing in the morning.

"Be very aware that they will be all over you and sucking up to you from the moment you arrive." Those were the words of my right-hand man, Rich Hering, back in New York after I told him about the phone call I received from Jose Sulaiman. I kept hearing those words as I drifted off to sleep.

I knew Rich would be proud of me.

Most importantly, I was proud of me.

"Jose, this was on my pillow when I walked in from the beautiful dinner last night," I said as I slid into the booth in the breakfast atrium, pushing the envelope toward him.

He looked at the envelope, then at me.

"This is yours, keep it," he said.

"I did nothing to earn this," I replied.

Jose looked at me and patted my left hand.

"Do you really believe you did nothing to earn this?" he asked. He didn't wait for a reply. He began rattling off my accomplishments in boxing, from my days at *World Boxing Magazine*, to rebuilding *Ring Magazine*, to my work as a TV analyst, to my new position as chairman of the New York State Athletic Commission. He had done his homework.

When he was finished, he pushed the envelope back in my direction.

"You have more than earned this," he said, adding,

and in becoming one of the most powerful commissioners in the sport, I would be honored if you allow me to put you on the executive board of the WBC. If you desire, I can make you the WBC's director of commission affairs [a title he quickly pulled out of the air]. You can be a supervisor at many WBC title fights, not just in America, but all over the world.

With a laugh, he added, "While the WBC does much charitable work, we are not a nonprofit organization. You will be paid for work you will do for the WBC." Pointing at the envelope, he said, "Consider this a signing bonus. This is but a small down payment for the respect and admiration the WBC has for you." He pushed the envelope back toward me.

During the next hour, our breakfast and conversation was interrupted several times by WBC members—especially referees and judges—who wanted to make sure El Presidente Sulaiman knew they were in attendance (attendance at these conventions, in particular by referees and judges, often means lucrative assignments to title fights throughout the world). So, they stopped by to say hello and shake his hand. Some even tried to sit down with us, to which Sulaiman said professionally and politely, "If you can just excuse us for a short while. Commissioner Gordon and I are having a breakfast meeting." One New York judge, a known "suck up" in the game of "boxing politics," actually sat down and refused to leave, talking endlessly to Sulaiman about what a great leader he was.

He finally left when I said, "I'm not sure if you heard President Sulaiman say that we are in a breakfast meeting. Please allow us to continue. We'll see you later." The judge heard me clearly and left the table. To that, Sulaiman said, "Commissioner, I love how you handled that. You are such a professional. The WBC is fortunate to have you aboard."

He again slid the envelope back toward me. I smiled at him and thanked him for the kind words. But I didn't touch the envelope.

When our waitress brought our check, I grabbed it. A playful argument between Sulaiman and I began concerning who would pay the check. I won. I—the New York State Athletic Commission—would be paying the check.

After I paid the check (President Sulaiman left a generous tip for the waiter), we slid out of the booth and shook hands. He then said, "Commissioner, er, Randy. Thank you for breakfast. I am so happy you have become part of the WBC family. I will see you later, Commissioner . . . er, Randy." We both smiled, then hugged.

As I turned away, Sulaiman shouted, "Randy, wait!"

I looked back at him. He was pointing to the envelope.

"You forgot this," he said.

I shook my head.

"Leave it for the waiter," I said. "I'm sure he will appreciate the tip!"

"Randy! Randy!" came Sulaiman's voice. I walked away with a smile as ring officials from throughout the world descended upon Sulaiman like ants at a picnic.

As I went from seminar to seminar and workshop to workshop, I couldn't get that white envelope out of my head. Did every new member of the WBC who headed a state boxing commission receive such a gift? Was I the only one who received it? If so, what was behind that? What was it all about? I certainly didn't buy into Sulaiman's statement that it was a down payment for me being a supervisor at upcoming WBC title bouts. Throughout the day I wondered.

My wondering ended the next day. The attendees of the convention were being taken on a bus trip to the site of the ancient Aztec ruins. Several buses were needed to transport this worldwide delegation of members of the WBC boxing fraternity.

As I was walking to one of the buses, I heard a loud, bellowing, unmistakable voice calling my name from perhaps 100 yards away. The voice belonged to Don King.

"Commissioner Randy Gordon! Commissioner Randy Gordon!"

I glanced over my shoulder. Approaching was the bombastic, electric-haired promoter. Thoughts crossed my mind to when he had done something similar with me in Las Vegas a little more than five years earlier.

It was May 19, 1983, the night before the Larry Holmes–Tim Witherspoon heavyweight championship fight. It was around 11:00 p.m., and I was sitting at the casino bar with several boxing writers. The bar was situated in a corner of the casino, and my seat was on the end. It was the closest seat to the casino.

As we were talking, *Sports Illustrated*'s Pat Putnam said, "Randy, somebody is calling you. Listen." We all stopped talking. All we heard for a moment were the ding-ding-dings of the slot machines, the bells of the winning machines, the sounds of coins clanking into the trays, and the shouts of glee from the winners. Then we heard, faintly, "Randy Gordon! Randy Gordon!" We looked around as the call of my name grew louder and louder.

"Randy Gordon! Randy Gordon!"

We all looked around. Then, one of the sportswriters saw the caller through the casino crowd. It was Don King, always looking to be noticed. As I was at the end of the bar, I was the first one King noticed, and so, he called my name over and over as he walked closer. As he was perhaps 30 yards away, he added three more words onto his loud calling of my name:

"Randy Gordon, you're killing me!" He began pointing at me.

"Randy Gordon, you're killing me!" he said over and over. Each time he said it, he continued to point. Each time he said, "Randy Gordon, you're killing me!" he sounded angrier and angrier.

"What did you do, Randy?" asked Putnam.

"Yeh, listen to him!" said another writer. They were right. King was loud. He sounded really angry.

"Randy Gordon, you're killing me!" he roared, now only a few yards away.

"What the hell did you do to piss him off, Randy?" asked another writer.

I shrugged my shoulders.

"You got me," I said. "I can't think of anything I did."

Then, King arrived at the bar. He stopped a few feet from me. His stepson, Carl, was at his side.

"Randy Gordon, you're killing me!" he said again, looking quite angry.

Puzzled, I asked, "How am I killing you, Don? How?"

"You're killing me on the USA Network. Every week you're killing me!" he shouted.

I was more puzzled than ever.

"How can I be killing you?" I asked in wonderment. "I haven't even mentioned you!"

"That's what I mean!" shouted King. "You talk about Bob Arum. You talk about Dan Duva. You talk about Mickey Duff. But you never talk about me! I beg you to talk about me. Say something good. Say something bad. Just say something about me. Anything! Talk about your poor, struggling, hungry Uncle Don for a change. Please! I beg of you!"

We all laughed. So did King. Then he motioned to the bartender, "Drinks are on me for these good gentlemen."

There were about eight of us. Technically, none of us should have allowed the fight's promoter to buy us drinks. In many journalistic circles, accepting a drink or even a cup of coffee from someone we are writing about or whose show we are covering can lead to immediate suspension or even job termination. But we all accepted King's "drinks are on me" offer.

So, when I heard my name being called by King in Mexico, I said to myself, "Here we go, again!" Little did I realize this would be nothing like the scenario in Las Vegas.

As I stepped onto the bus, King was fast approaching but still about 20 yards away. He was accompanied by heavyweight champion Mike Tyson.

"Randy Gordon, save a couple of seats for your pals!" yelled King.

I headed to the center of the bus and then slid into a seat next to a window as other WBC convention attendees filled the bus.

As a WBC member from Japan was about to sit next to me, a voice called out, "Commissioner, hold that seat next to you—and the one behind it." Don King and Mike Tyson were aboard the bus and walking toward me, just a few seats away. King sat next to me. Tyson sat in the aisle seat behind him.

Tyson was just a few months—but dozens of pounds—removed from a devastating 91-second knockout of Michael Spinks. For that one, Tyson weighed 218¼ pounds. The fight had been on June 2. For Tyson, the rest of the summer was spent in overdrive party mode. My guess is he weighed no less than 260. To this day, I have not seen him as heavy as he was in Mexico.

Tyson reached over the seat and patted me on my right shoulder.

"Nice seeing you, Randy," he said.

King turned around, for Tyson—and the bus—to hear, and said, "That's Commissioner. We used to know him as Randy, but now it's Commissioner.

Commissioner Gordon." Then he paused and added, "It's Commissioner Gordon, just like in Batman. Commissioner Gordon battles evil."

I knew exactly where King was going with that.

He turned to me and leaned close.

"Commissioner, our friend, Mike, is being bamboozled, swindled, and hustled by Satan." I didn't correct him and say "Cayton." I didn't need to be the straight man for his tired, long-running attempt at humor.

"Satan is using deceit, fraud, and trickeration to keep Mike bound to a contract which was signed by your predecessor, Jose Torres, also by deceitful and unlawful methods, I might add."

"Mike is going to be calling upon your office soon to help terminate the contract, Commissioner," said King. "Your action and response to this matter is of utmost importance to the career of this young, great champion." As he spoke, Tyson was leaning forward, his hands on the back of King's seat, his head resting on his hands.

"Ya gotta help me, Commissioner," pleaded Tyson. "Please get me out of this contract. I never would have signed it had I known all I do now. Please help me."

King shook his head.

"Those guys really screwed Michael over," replied King, "those guys" being Jim Jacobs, Bill Cayton, and Jose Torres.

Then, as Tyson continued to plead with me to help him, break the contract he kept insisting was illegal, King reached inside his sport coat and said, "See this, Commissioner, it's yours." He held the right side of his pocket open. I saw a white envelope.

"I believe this belongs to you, Commissioner," said King. He reached into his pocket and pulled the envelope out. He handed it to me. My first thought was that the envelope contained legal documents and papers Tyson intended to present to the commission. I thought the envelope had a letter asking, as a licensee of the commission, for a hearing. I took the envelope from King.

"Open it," said King.

"Open it," said Tyson.

The envelope wasn't sealed. The flap was tucked inside the envelope. I pulled the flap out and looked inside the envelope. I gasped.

There, almost jumping right out of the envelope at me, were stacks of money, just like the one that had been on my pillow the night before. This time, there were even more stacks. This time, I didn't fan through any of it.

"It's yours," said King, patting me on my right leg and speaking in an untypical low voice. "Jose Sulaiman said you left his 'executive bonus' on the breakfast table yesterday morning. He wanted to make sure you received this and asked me if I wouldn't mind giving it to you." I dropped it like a hot potato. It fell on the seat between me and King. Tyson and King laughed. I didn't.

"Don't be scared of it," said King. "It's yours. You earned it." I heard the same words from Sulaiman.

"I didn't earn that," I replied, pointing to the envelope between us. "I did nothing at all to earn that."

"Oh, you're so modest, Commissioner," said King. "Of course you earned it." I shook my head.

"I don't know whose money that is, but I do know it's not mine," I insisted.

"Consider it a down payment for everything you've done for your boxing friends," said King. "Keep it!"

Then he said in a low voice, but loud enough for Tyson to hear, "Let's get back to the hearing you'll be called upon soon to give to this young, great champion," King said, motioning to Tyson. "Your predecessor assisted in roping Mike into a contract he should have never signed. We are counting on you to do the right thing and, after a hearing, break the contract." Then he took the envelope, which was still on the seat between us, placed it on my lap, and said, "Don't forget your bonus."

He and Tyson laughed heartily once more. Once more, I didn't.

"I cannot break the contract, gentlemen," I said.

Tyson and King squinted. They were both startled to hear me say that.

"Of course you can," replied King.

I shook my head.

"Only one thing can break the contract," I said, looking first at King, then at Tyson.

"What one thing is that?" asked King.

"The truth," I said.

The facts will speak, and the truth will be told. After I hear the facts, I will know the entire story behind the contract. If the truth says the contract should be broken, it will be broken. If the truth tells a different story, the contract will not be broken. That's the only way this can be done. That's the only way it *will* be done.

"Well, the truth will indeed speak to you, to the commission, and to the world!" King bellowed. "And when you hear the truth, you will free Mike Tyson from the grips of Satan."

Then he picked up the envelope and said, "This still belongs to you." He began to hand it back to me.

"Stop! Just stop!" I said, forcefully, holding up my right hand. "Stop! Enough!"

I turned to Tyson.

"When you come in for the hearing," I said to him, "just speak the truth. You say you were tricked into signing the contract. Tell us all about that. Let the facts speak. Let the truth speak. I'll see you up at 270 Broadway."

Tyson got the picture. So did King.

We had a great time seeing the ancient Aztec ruins. In fact, the rest of my week in Mexico was terrific. I attended seminars and workshops, and met a lot of people in my industry from throughout the world who are still my friends today. Of course, every day it was fun watching officials do their best to suck up to and stay close to Jose Sulaiman, notably the two from New York.

I returned home, proud of how I had handled two situations that have put many politicians and executives on the unemployment line or even in jail. I went to Mexico on a boxing business trip, and I certainly learned about the business of boxing. At that convention, I grew as an executive and learned a lot as a commissioner. I had a real good time.

I didn't need those two king-sized white envelopes to have a good time.

14

TRUTH OR TRICKERATION

It was a few minutes before 6:00 a.m. when I walked into my office at the New York State Athletic Commission. In my left hand I held my black leather attaché. In my right hand I carried a cup of coffee. Black. Large.

I walked into my office and sat in my oversized brown leather chair. I sipped my coffee as I perused a pile of legal papers and notes.

Today was the day Mike Tyson wanted. Today was the day Don King wanted. This was the day both of them had asked me for 10 months earlier in Mexico City. This was the day that meant so much to them that they were willing to buy my vote for a decision in their favor.

As I mentioned in a previous chapter, the two most beloved and trusted men in Tyson's life—Cus D'Amato and Jim Jacobs—had passed away in late 1985 and early 1988, respectively. This left Tyson's boxing business—and principal earnings—in the hands of Bill Cayton.

By the time I was with the two of them in Mexico City, Tyson's marriage to Givens was already on the ropes, as was his fighter/manager relationship with Cayton. In Mexico City, Tyson made it quite clear to me that he was tricked into signing the new contract with Cayton. I was very interested in holding a hearing on the matter but told both Tyson and King that neither I nor the commission could call for a hearing. I told him that a request in writing had to be made to the commission.

"You just want a letter from me, asking you to break the contract?" Tyson questioned.

"Don knows how to do it," I told Tyson. "He has a group of attorneys who work for him. They know how to go about doing this."

When I returned to New York, I sat down with Rich Hering and explained everything that had happened in Mexico City.

"Get ready," said Rich. "We'll be hearing from Tyson very soon."

From the way the two of them were all over me in Mexico City, I assumed Hering to be correct. A certified letter from King's attorneys—who also represented Tyson at this point—would surely be placed on my desk momentarily. The days came. The weeks came. The months came. So did the seasons. I saw Tyson and King in early fall of 1988. The winter of 1988–1989 came and left, and so did the spring of 1989. Still, there was no letter.

Tyson's battles with both his wife and manager were well-documented and discussed ad nauseum in boxing circles. Tyson was happiest and most content—it seemed—when he was back in the gym, doing what he did better than anyone. The extra pounds I had seen in Mexico City melted away quickly, and Cayton and King put together Tyson's next bout. Each knew that the other wanted him out.

On one occasion, Cayton came to see me in my office.

"I want you to know that Mike Tyson is going to formally call a hearing with you and ask you to break the contract we have," Cayton said.

I listened.

"I don't know when it will happen, but it will," he continued.

That contract is iron-clad. Tyson signed it last year. He signed it in front of me, Jim, and Jose Torres. He knew Jim was dying, and he knew it was Jim's name on the contract as manager. Mike has always known that both Jim and me [sic] are his managers. I have video of Mike saying things like, "I don't choose the fights. My managers, Bill Cayton and Jim Jacobs, do. They just line 'em up so I can knock them down." He signed the new contract to protect himself against what is going on now.

"And what exactly is going on?" I asked Cayton.

"Don is what's going on, Commissioner! Don King! He's trying to have this commission break the contract, which will leave Mike a free agent. Then he'll move his son in as manager and take everything Mike has. He's going to act fast, because if he doesn't get there first, Robin will."

"There's been no formal letter requesting a hearing," I said.

"There will be," he replied. "There will be."

There were things for Tyson to do first. On Valentine's Day 1989, Tyson and Givens didn't give each other cards, candy, or jewelry. They exchanged divorce papers, ending their tumultuous one year of marriage. Eleven days later, Tyson was in the ring, knocking out Frank Bruno in the fifth round.

King was at Tyson's side everywhere he went.

On a few occasions, Bill Cayton would call my office to ask, "Has Mike sent any papers yet, requesting a hearing?"

"Not yet, Bill," I told him. "You will be among the very first people I call if and when those papers arrive."

"Not *if*," he'd say. "*When!*"

Several months went by, and still there was no word from Tyson. On July 21, Tyson faced perennial contender Carl "The Truth" Williams. Just 93 seconds after the opening bell, the fight was over. Tyson was 37–0, with 33 knockouts, 17 of them in the first round.

While his boxing record was pristine and perfect, his life was anything but. There were the managerial issues with Cayton; battles with trainer Kevin Rooney, who was pro-Cayton and anti-King; constant pressure from King; and relentless hounding and scrutiny by the media. This wasn't how he envisioned his life the night he made his pro debut against Hector Mercedes.

Days after the victory against Williams, the long-anticipated letter from Tyson and his battery of attorneys arrived at the commission. Tyson was officially requesting a hearing.

Basically, the letter charged that Tyson had re-signed a fighter/manager contract with Bill Cayton to act as his sole manager. The letter charged that Tyson had no knowledge that Jim Jacobs would not be a part of his managerial team.

I called a quick staff meeting. It included my secretary, Michele; my executive director, Rich Hering; and athletic assistants Emma Elizondo, Ruby Tyrell, and Marvin Kohn.

Despite the fact I intended to keep the hearing as low-key and out-of-the-spotlight as possible, the media knew about it instantly. Within minutes after reading the letter and going over it with Rich Hering, my phone rang incessantly. *Newsday. New York Daily News. New York Post. New York Times.* ESPN. ABC. CBS. NBC. *Sports Illustrated.* The letter had been in my hands for less than an hour, yet every media outlet was on it. While I first thought it was Don King's office that had leaked the story, I quickly shook off that theory. King had nothing to gain by involving the media. He wanted the hearing for Tyson, and now he would get one. Involving the media was of no benefit to him. Realizing King's office had nothing to do with the leak, I realized it could only have come from my office. I shook my head. I knew exactly where the leak came from—who it was—but I couldn't prove it. Not yet, anyway (see chapter 15).

I called my two other voting commissioners, then called the commission's legal counsel, Carl DeSantis, who went right to work in preparing a response to Tyson and setting up a hearing date.

A few days before the hearing, the man I replaced as chairman, Jose Torres, the former light heavyweight champion, called me and asked if he could stop in to see me. I told him the doors to his old office were always open to him.

"Don't trust the commission," said Torres. "I don't want to spell it out, but they are not your friends."

I heard him loud and clear. The two other voting commissioners, aside from me, were against Governor Cuomo's appointment of me. They fought my confirmation by the Senate. DeSantis, according to Torres, was "too close" with Don King and suggested I seek his replacement.

It was too late to make changes.

Great, I thought to myself. *I'm in this battle by myself.* Indeed, I was.

The hearing, which was held in our weigh-in room, began at 10:00 a.m. We allowed no cameras, just a room filled with reporters.

Tyson and King showed up around 9:15 and were greeted by an army of fans. Word quickly circulated throughout our building that Mike Tyson was inside, and workers came down from higher floors and up from lower floors to see him, shake his hand, get his autograph, and talk to him.

He and King came into my private office, but we weren't alone. Rich Hering was there to ward off any attempts of either King or Tyson to sway my decision.

"The truth will be told today," bellowed King. "The deceitful practices and trickeration of Satan upon the contract held to be valid by the New York State Athletic Commission will come to light, and Mike Tyson will be free from his bonds of slavery."

"Very nice," said Hering, who then asked the duo to head down to the weigh-in room, as we had some paperwork to discuss.

After they left, Hering said, "Just remember, the most important thing is for Tyson to tell the commission why the contract should be broken. Let him tell it, let him spell it out. Don King is *not* to interject anything. This hearing is about Mike Tyson, not about Don King."

When I walked out of my office a few minutes later, I saw Tyson sitting on the floor in the hallway outside the makeshift hearing room, shaking hands and signing autographs. As I passed Tyson, I said, "Okay, let's have anybody involved in today's hearing move inside." In particular, I was addressing Tyson, who looked content signing anything thrust in front of him and shaking hands as if he were a politician running for election. I had never before—or in my years at the NYSAC after that—seen the hallway so crowded.

I sat at a table set up for four people. The other three there were my two commissioners and the commission's legal counsel. At the end of the table, next to our legal counsel, was a middle-aged stenographer. She wore a dress that was buttoned up to her neck and went down to her heels. She was expressionless, there only to do her job.

I explained the rules to Tyson: We, the commission, would ask the questions. He would provide the answers. For almost a half hour or so we delved into his early beginnings; his tough upbringing; his being sent to the Tryon School for Boys in upstate New York; his being noticed by ex-boxer Bobby Stewart; being taken to meet Cus D'Amato; meeting Jim Jacobs and Bill Cayton; moving into D'Amato's home; discussing a career in boxing; signing a fighter/ manager contract with the understanding that Jacobs and Cayton were to be his managers, while Cus would be his trainer; his meteoric rise to the championship.

I asked him if he was happy with how his career was going. "After all," I said, "you are undefeated, the heavyweight champion of the world, one of the most famous celebrities in the world, a multimillionaire, and just 23 years old."

"I *was* happy," he said. "Until last year. Then something happened which made me realize things weren't right. That's why I am asking you to break my existing contract."

"What kind of things weren't right?" I questioned. "Tell this commission *why* we should break your contract. *Why?*"

He looked me in the eyes. He paused for a few moments. Then he spoke.

"My contract should be declared null and void because I was getting fucked in the ass," he said.

Don King, sitting behind Tyson, exploded in laughter, his goose-like cackle being heard by my staffers down the hall. Members of the media chuckled. The matronly stenographer took her hands off her keyboard and glared at me. Her eyes asked me to say something, which I intended on doing even without her baleful look.

"Mr. Tyson," I said calmly, doing my best to remain expressionless, stoic, and commissioner-like. "That kind of language is neither helpful to the commission nor appropriate. I want no more of that. Now, I will ask you again, Why should this commission break your existing contract?" I then added, "And, Mr. King, please refrain from any further outbursts. Continue, Mr. Tyson."

He leaned forward in his seat and made eye contact with me and the two other commissioners. Then he looked into my eyes again.

"Go ahead, Mr. Tyson," I said.

He continued. It was short but not sweet.

"The reason you should break my contract is because I was tricked into signing it. That's why I said I was getting fucked in the ass!"

With that, laughter rocked the room. Don King was, by far, the loudest.

"You tell them, Mike!" he roared, patting Tyson on a shoulder.

Once again, the stenographer took her hands off her keyboard and stared at me.

I didn't know whether to laugh or cry. Not wanting to do either, I exploded. I banged my brown, wooden gavel (yes, I actually had one of those) repeatedly on the block of wood made for, well, gavel-banging.

"Mr. Tyson!" I shouted. "What did I just tell you about using that kind of language? There are women present. I demand you respect them, along with everyone else in here. And Mr. King, one more outburst from you and I will demand you leave this room! Is that clear, Mr. King?"

"It certainly is, Mr. Commissioner," he said.

"Is that clear, Mr. Tyson?" I growled.

"It certainly is, Mr. Commissioner," said the heavyweight champion of the world.

I took a deep breath. I remember wanting to say, from so many movies I had seen, "If there is another remark or outburst like that again, I will hold you both in contempt." But being that this was my first hearing and all so new to me, and this was not a court of law, I thought better and refrained from saying it.

I looked at Tyson and said, "Please continue, and explain to us, as best you can, why you say this commission should break your contract. Explain it, Mr. Tyson." I was actually stifling a laugh.

"Well, it's like this," he began. "My original contract was signed by me and by Jim Jacobs. I understood that he was partners with Bill Cayton."

"Satan!" King said in a low but still-audible voice.

"Mr. King!" I shouted. "One more time and you are out of here!"

He smiled.

"Continue, Mr. Tyson," I said. "You were talking about Jim Jacobs being partners with Bill *Cayton*." I made sure I said the name loud and clear.

"Well, it's like this," said Tyson.

I always liked Jim Jacobs and Bill Cayton. But the relationships I had were with Cus and Jimmy. I understood that Cus didn't have the money to manage me. But, he didn't need to have the money. He was being supported by Jim and Bill. He used that money to keep up his house, the gym, to live and to feed us. I got that. But when Cus died, I lost my father figure. Jim Jacobs was like a real good big brother to me. I enjoyed being around him. We talked about lots of things. We talked about boxing. We talked about life. We talked about sports. We talked about girls. You know. Guy stuff. I don't have that kind of relationship with Bill. I never did.

He paused, then took a few breaths.

"Go on, Mike," I said.

"Well, shortly after my fight against Larry Holmes, Jim and Bill took me over to the diner near their office. Jose Torres met us there."

"To clarify, that's Jose Torres, who was then chairman of the New York State Athletic Commission, is that correct?" I asked.

"Yes, it is," said Tyson.

"Ok, sorry to interrupt you, Mr. Tyson," I said. "Please continue. You were at the diner with Mr. Jacobs, Mr. Cayton, and Commissioner Torres," I said, resetting the scene.

"Yes, I was at the diner," Tyson acknowledged. "We ordered lunch and I signed some autographs for customers at the diner who came over to me. We talked about my next fight, which would be in about a month in Tokyo. Then, Jimmy said something about how both of them are my managers. . . ."

"Both of them being Jacobs and Cayton?" I asked.

"Yes, Commissioner," replied Tyson.

"Continue," I said.

Well, Jimmy said that even though both he and Bill were my managers, the commission would only allow one manager's name on the contract. The name that was there was Jim Jacobs. Jim told me he would be going away for medical tests, because he wasn't feeling well. That's when Commissioner Torres told me that with my next fight very close, I'd need to redo my contract, just to make sure it was valid in Jimmy's absence. Then Bill jumped into it and started talking about my next fight, against Tony Tubbs. They told me everything except the truth. They didn't tell me Jimmy was dying. They wanted to get Bill's name on the contract because they knew, that without Jimmy in the picture, I never would have signed a contract which made just Bill Cayton my manager.

"Let me understand something," I said. "You claim you sat at that lunch with no idea Jimmy was dying?"

"That's correct," he said. "I had no idea. I signed that contract because Jacobs and Cayton asked me to sign it and because Commissioner Torres asked me to sign it. Three men I trusted were all over me to sign the contract. So, I signed it."

Next came Tyson's explosive finale.

"They tricked me into signing. If that's not getting fucked up the ass, then I don't know what is!"

Tyson's last sentence made the stenographer say, "That's it!" and slide back from the table. Don King erupted—roared—with laughter. The media laughed aloud. I, too, was close to laughing but knew I just couldn't. So, I did what I had to do. I began banging my gavel and yelling.

"Mr. Tyson!" I shouted, pointing at him. "I have now had enough of that!" I then pointed to King.

"And, Mr. King, I have warned you twice to refrain from your outbursts. You have refused to follow this commission's directives. I will now ask you to leave the room!"

With a smug grin on his face, King stood up. As he stood, he patted Tyson on a shoulder saying, "You tell 'em, Mike. You tell 'em." Then he headed toward the door and out to the hall.

I then called a 10-minute recess. I got up and walked to the end of the table and sat down next to the stenographer.

"I understand just how you're feeling," I said. "As a man with a wife and four daughters, I would not want them subjected to this kind of street talk; however, as a professional, you must do your job under any and all circumstances. Can you ride the rest of this hearing out?"

She nodded. Then she added, "He's disgusting. Both of them are!" She was referring to Mike Tyson and Don King.

From there, I walked down the hall and into my office. Passing Michele's desk, my secretary looked up at me.

"Having fun, Commissioner?" she asked.

I rolled my eyes.

The best was yet to come.

I sat down at my desk and took a few deep breaths. Rich Hering walked in a few moments later.

"They are each a piece of work," he said, referring to Tyson and King.

I just shook my head slowly.

"Don't let them get to you, you're doing fine. You just ask a few questions and let Tyson give you the answers. And, by the way, you handled the situation with his remarks beautifully. Keep doing what you've been doing," related Hering.

I returned to the hearing room a few minutes later. I allowed Don King to return but told him he was to remain absolutely silent. I told Tyson he was to refrain from using crude and obscene language. If he failed to comply, I told him I would end these hearings. Both King and Tyson complied with my wishes.

When the hearing resumed, Tyson took us back once more through his early days as a pro, through his being mentored by Cus D'Amato, suffering from D'Amato's death one year before becoming champion, being trained by Kevin Rooney, and his relationship with Jim Jacobs and Bill Cayton.

His closeness with Jacobs seemed real, although his claim that he disliked and sought distance from Cayton seemed manufactured, born from his friendship and business relationship with King. On a few occasions, Tyson mentioned the re-signed contract and Jacobs's death soon thereafter. On each occasion, he swore it was a death he never saw coming, a death he was never told about, a death he had no idea about.

As Tyson continually denied any knowledge of Jacob's illness and impending death, my thoughts carried me back to Atlantic City in January 1988. It was the week before Tyson's fight against Larry Holmes. I thought of the TV interview Bruce Beck and I taped with Tyson, the photo I took with him following the interview, and his words to me after the photo was taken.

"Did you hear about Jimmy? Jimmy is sick, very sick. He's not gonna make it. He's gonna die!" (See chapter 9.)

Tyson was sitting there, telling us he had no idea, no clue, Jacobs was dying. *He's lying*, I thought. *Tyson is lying to this commission. He wants us to believe he was tricked into signing the new contract, having no knowledge of the seriousness of Jacobs's health. He is out-and-out lying. He wants us to break the contract, thinking he was tricked—fooled—into signing a new one.*

Tyson's words were not the truth. I knew the truth.

"Mr. Tyson, let's make this 100 percent clear," I said. "Is it your contention, are you stating that you had no idea Jim Jacobs was deathly ill? Are you stating that, up until Jim passed away on March 3, 1988, you had no idea of his impending death?"

Tyson nodded his head, then spoke in a low, somber voice.

"That is correct, Commissioner. I had no idea he was so sick."

I held both hands in front of me.

"Okay, hold it right there," I said. "I am going to call a two-minute break. I want to show you something."

The other commissioners looked at me. So did the complainants.

"I'll be right back," I said.

I arose from the table and headed to the door. I walked down the hall and into my private office.

"What's going on?" asked Michele.

"I'm getting a photo from my wall," I replied. "I just caught Tyson in a huge lie."

I removed a framed photo from the wall. Then I turned and headed back to the hearing room. All eyes were on me when I returned and sat back down at the commission table, placing the photo facedown.

"Mr. Tyson, I am going to show you a photo," I said. "Tell me if you remember it being taken."

I first showed the photo to my two other commissioners, then handed the photo to Rich Hering. He then gave it to Tyson.

"Do you recall taking that photo with me?" I inquired.

"Yes, I do," he said softly.

"Would you please tell this commission where and when that photo was taken," I said.

"It was taken in Atlantic City, a few days before my fight against Larry Holmes," he replied.

"And do you remember what you said to me, what you told me right after the photo was taken?" I asked.

Tyson looked at me nervously. "I, I don't recall what I said, Commissioner," he replied in a voice that was barely audible. If ever there was an example of silence being deafening, that was the moment. In a packed room, all you could hear was some breathing.

"Think, Mr. Tyson, think," I said.

He was thinking, all right.

"I don't remember," Tyson said to me and the commission.

"Do you remember three of us being together, Mr. Tyson?" I asked. "It was you, me, and my broadcast partner, Bruce Beck. Do you remember that?"

He shook his head.

"Is that a 'yes,' Mr. Tyson?" I asked.

"Yes," he said clearly.

I continued.

"You told me something right after the photo was taken. Look at the photo. You told me something that was heard by Bruce Beck. Do I have to get Bruce Beck on the phone? I'm sure he remembers what you said."

Tyson took a deep breath.

"I think I told you that Jimmy was sick," said Tyson.

"You did, Mr. Tyson," I replied. "In fact, you did more than tell me Jimmy was sick. You told me he was dying. I found out that Jim Jacobs was dying from *you*." I put a heavy emphasis on *you*.

Before anything else was said, one of Tyson's attorneys stood up.

"That's a wonderful story, Commissioner," he said. "But you just became a witness. This hearing is over!"

"*What?*" I exclaimed. I turned to the commission's legal counsel, Carl DeSantis.

"Is he joking? What's going on?" I questioned.

"He's right, Commissioner," said DeSantis. "By saying what you said, you just became a witness. You removed yourself from being a hearing officer."

"Why didn't you stop me? Why?" I yelled.

In the greatest fit of rage I have ever had, I exploded. I flipped the table in front of me over.

"Son of a bitch!" I growled. I stormed out of the room and into the men's room across the hall. I punched the paper towel dispenser. I kicked the large garbage can over. I then picked it up and threw it across the room.

The door to the men's room opened. In walked one of King's attorneys.

"Calm down, Commissioner," he urged, motioning with his hands. "Cool off. Why are you taking this so personal?"

"Personal?" I said.

Tyson signed that contract of his own free will but now wants to get out of it, to turn his career over to Don King. He lied about knowing the facts about Jim Jacobs, but the worst that would have happened is that he would have been forced to stay in the contract, something he didn't want. But, at least with Cayton, he wasn't gonna get screwed. Now, by me becoming a witness, I can't make the obvious ruling, which is that the contract is valid. Now, you can continue this battle in a court of law to have the contract broke. It's bullshit!

"Stop getting upset, Commissioner," said King's attorney. "It's not *your* money!"

"It's not yours either!" I fired.

And it's not Don King's. Tyson wants to put his career and his money in the hands of Don King. He has no idea what he is doing. His dislike of Bill Cayton comes from Don King. That contract is valid and you, King, and Tyson know it. Mike will regret having trusted Don the way he does.

I stormed out of the bathroom, past an army of reporters, past Tyson, King, and members of my staff, and retreated to my office. I realized what I had done. I was a hearing officer. I was a judge. Hearing officers and judges listen. They analyze. They ask pertinent questions. My inexperience led me to take it too far. I became a witness, and the hearing came to a crashing end.

The next morning, I received a call from Governor Mario Cuomo. He could not have been nicer. He said he was in Manhattan that day and asked me to come to his office at the World Trade Center, where he had appointed me chairman of the commission a little more than one year earlier.

This time, when the elevator doors opened and I saw the uniformed state trooper, I knew exactly whose office it was and why I was there.

"Good afternoon, Commissioner," said the trooper. "Have a seat for a few moments while I let the governor know you're here."

My arrival this time was quite different than my first visit to Governor Cuomo's office.

A few moments later, I made my trip through the bulletproof airlock, down the long hallway, and toward another state trooper and the governor's office.

After a knock on his door and a firm, "Come on in," the state trooper opened the door and I entered. Governor Cuomo was sitting at his desk, wearing reading glasses and thoughtfully studying a pack of papers, which he held out to me as I walked toward him.

"The minutes of your hearing with Mike Tyson," he said.

I rolled my eyes.

"Oh, come on," said the governor. "You did a fine job."

The governor had coffee brought in for us, then we sat down for my law lessons.

"As long as you learned something here, that's what's important," said one of the most brilliant, dynamic—and *honest*—politicians who has ever lived. He gave me a few hours' worth of instruction, which felt as if I had just finished four years of law school.

In addition to the legal lesson Governor Cuomo gave me, he also asked, "Do you trust your commissioners and your legal counsel?"

When I told him I didn't, he said, "Then let's change them."

A few days later, I fired the legal counsel. Governor Cuomo followed by removing one of the other two commissioners and bringing aboard a businessman from Rochester, New York, Herb Washington.

The meeting with Governor Cuomo made me a better commissioner with an even greater respect for the job he had bestowed upon me one year earlier.

As for Tyson, I returned to the office knowing his relationship with Don King would come to the same inglorious end as our hearing.

In 2013, I sat in a theater in New York City with my wife to watch Tyson's one-man play, *Undisputed Truth*. During the play, he pointed to a picture of Don King, which was on a large screen behind him, and said, "I thought he was one of my two closest friends, but he screwed me."

Then a picture of Robin Givens appeared on the screen.

"I thought she was my other best friend," he told the audience, "but she screwed me, too!" Then he added, "And in more ways than Don King did!"

In the ring and at his best, Mike Tyson was a fierce, ferocious fighting machine. Every tick of the clock during one of his bouts was thrilling. He was in-your-face action. In the ring, he was as real as real could be. Nothing about him was fake. He was the truth.

Outside the ring, he searched for the same kind of truth that he found in the ring. The truth eluded him, when no gloved opponent ever could.

During those years, all he found was trickeration.

15

THE GOOD
GUY AWARD

Each year, the Boxing Writers Association of America holds their annual banquet where they present their annual awards. Included among them are the Sugar Ray Robinson Award (fighter of the year), Ali–Frazier Award (fight of the year), Eddie Futch Award (trainer of the year), Nat Fleischer Award (excellence in boxing journalism), John F. X. Condon Award (long and meritorious service), A. J. Leibling Award (outstanding boxing writing), and Bill Crawford Award (courage in overcoming adversity).

There is also the Marvin Kohn Good Guy Award. Quite possibly, I had a lot to do with the creation of the award, which was first handed out in 1996. Artist LeRoy Neiman was the first recipient of the award. Other notable recipients have been Hall of Famers George Foreman, Don Dunphy, and Alexis Arguello. My SiriusXM sidekick, Gerry Cooney, won it in 2005. Hall of Fame boxing analyst Al Bernstein won it in 2011. So did Hall of Famers Steve Farhood (2012), Jimmy Lennon Jr. (2013), and Don Chargin (2015).

The Good Guy Award. Prior to 1996, it had been given out just once before, to former featherweight champ Jackie Fields in 1966. I guess the BWAA ran out of "Good Guys" after that, because the award was trashed, not to resurface for 30 years. When it did, it was resurrected as the Marvin Kohn Good Guy Award.

Marvin Kohn was a member of my staff when I was appointed chairman of the New York State Athletic Commission in 1988. He was not a commissioner, as he had told many members of the boxing media and boxing fraternity. But he liked the way "Commissioner Kohn" sounded and for years had been addressed as such. In truth, he was an athletic assistant who was overpaid and underworked. A former publicist for Mamie Van Doren, he had been a member of the NYSAC for a few decades before I took over at the top in 1988.

The four chairmen before me, going back to James J. Farley in the mid-1970s, had tried to fire/terminate/remove Kohn from the commission, but none had any luck. He was too cunning and clever.

Kohn had been the liaison between the commission and the media when I arrived, but that was more or less a self-appointed position, as was the title he even had put on business cards—"director, media relations." At the NYSAC, Marvin Kohn came and went as he pleased. He did what he wanted to do. He collected an annual salary of close to $60,000 but did nothing to earn that money or contribute to the growth of the commission I had taken over from former light heavyweight champ Jose Torres.

Marvin, almost bald, overweight, and in his early 60s, walked with a cane and a limp, the result of a club foot. He always wore black shoes with red socks. Always. Looking at him, you couldn't tell he was as dangerous in his job as young Mike Tyson was in his.

Boxing writers, especially ones from New York City and its surrounding areas, loved Marvin, however. For years, he was their go-to man. He was their eyes and ears inside the commission. Nothing was safe or sacred inside the offices of the NYSAC at 270 Broadway, where we shared the fifth floor with the office of Department of Cemeteries and the Speaker of the House. If something was going on with a fighter, manager, trainer, cornerman, or promoter, writers and columnists knew immediately. Rarely did the chairman ever get to truly break news to them. That's because Marvin Kohn broke it first.

I had known Marvin from my days with Stanley Weston and then from being at *Ring Magazine*. I'd see him at press conferences and hand him the newest edition and tell him, "Enjoy it." He'd thank me and reply, "I'll keep you posted to what's going on at 270 Broadway."

When Jose Torres left his post as chairman in the summer of 1988, to finish writing his book on Mike Tyson, *Fire and Fear*, Governor Cuomo's hunt for his replacement was on. Rumors circulated as to who would be getting the job. As the color analyst for the boxing-busy Madison Square Garden Network, I was right in the thick of everything boxing in New York. At 39, I was the prime candidate for the job. Naturally, my name was included in the rumors as to who would be replacing "Chegui" Torres.

After my initial June 1988 meeting with Governor Cuomo, at which time he decided to appoint me chairman of the commission, the rumor spotlight turned to me. The governor had asked me to "keep it quiet for a few days," so I did.

A day or two after the meeting, I was at ringside in what was then called the Felt Forum, announcing a boxing card on the MSG Network with Sam Rosen. A few minutes before the show started, Marvin Kohn approached me.

"Hi, Randy, do you have a few minutes to spare?" he began. I told him I would be going on the air in about four minutes and would be happy to speak with him after the show.

"I just want to know, have you been appointed as chairman of the commission?" he asked.

I smiled at him. Hearing Governor Cuomo say "keep it quiet for a few days," I denied the appointment. Actually, I wasn't lying to Marvin. I hadn't been *appointed*. I had been *nominated* by Governor Cuomo. The Senate confirms the nomination with their approval of the governor's nomination. Betcha' didn't know that!

"I've heard that rumor, too, Marvin," I said. "I've heard lots of names."

He shook his head.

"It's not a rumor. I've heard it's you. I heard you met with the governor and he liked you and appointed you as chairman."

Appointed. There's that word again.

"Nope. Wasn't appointed," I said. Then, pressing my hand to my earpiece, which is called an IFB, I made like the producer was talking to me.

"Gotta run, Marvin. The producer wants us in place."

Marvin wasn't leaving.

"I'll wait for you after the show," he said.

Lucky me!

After the final bout and after Sam said, "For Randy Gordon, Producer John Gallagher, Director Warren Pick, and our great MSG Network crew, until next time, I'm Sam Rosen. Good night everybody," we then heard, "That's a wrap, nice job everyone" from John Gallagher and removed our headsets. Rosen and I high-fived it. Then, I saw Rosen's eyes cut to someone behind me. I turned to see who it was. It was Marvin Kohn, virtually breathing down my neck.

"Do you have a minute to talk now?" he asked.

"Sure, Marvin," I replied. "What's on your mind?"

"I know you can't say anything," he began. "But I know you are about to be named as chairman of the commission. I just want to be the first, outside of your family, of course, to wish you the very best, and to tell you I will be there to give you any assistance you need. I will be your right-hand man if you afford me that honor."

I looked at him and smiled.

"All that sounds very nice, Marvin," I said, "but I haven't been . . ."

"Stop!" he said. "I know you have to play the good soldier. You can't say anything. I respect that. I admire that. But I *know* for certain you are the new chairman, or are about to be named chairman very soon."

I just looked at Marvin. What could I say? I didn't want to confirm his words, nor did I want to deny them. So, I looked at him and extended my right hand. He extended his.

"Let's just give this whole scenario a few days to play out," I said. "Then we'll know more."

He nodded his head. But he knew. He already knew.

"When you come aboard, have you thought about changes you are going to make in policy and within the staff?" he inquired.

"Marvin, *stop!*" I insisted. "I am not the commissioner."

He wasn't buying it.

"Well, let's just say you are. Would you keep the staff the way it is?"

I looked at him incredulously. He wasn't giving up.

"Marvin, I haven't even thought about that," I said, almost gasping at his unending questioning.

"Well, think about it a second. Would you keep me? Would you keep me as part of your staff?"

In an attempt to stop him, I made like I didn't hear his question and gathered my papers.

"I've got to catch a train," I told him. "Don't wanna miss it."

He wasn't giving up.

"Will I still have a job after you've come on and make whatever changes you intend on making? Will I still be employed by the New York State Athletic Commission?"

I had never seen such persistence in my life. In the ring, not even Joe Frazier put on so much pressure. I laughed.

"Okay, Marvin, for what it's worth, if I was the chairman—and that's *if*—you would not be going anywhere. You would still be a full-time employee of the New York State Athletic Commission."

"And would you at least consider me to be your right-hand man?" he further pressured.

"Of course, Marvin," I replied. "But that's if I become chairman of the commission."

He then left me speechless when he pulled out a typewritten letter and handed it to me.

"If what you say is true, that I am safe in my job and you will consider me to be your executive director, will you sign the paper?"

I couldn't believe my eyes. It was a contract. He actually was thrusting a contract at me. It was a contract that guaranteed him employment with the NYSAC until he, and he alone, decided it was time to leave. In no circumstances, said this ridiculous contract, could his job be terminated.

I read it quickly, then politely handed it back to him.

"Marvin, I cannot sign it," I said. "I am not the commissioner."

Then I closed my attaché case and walked away.

As I left him, I said, "Not for a few more hours, anyway!"

The look on his face was priceless.

As chairman, I had a choice: have a driver or have a car. I took the car. It was a brand-new 1988 Pontiac Bonneville. White. The most impressive thing about it was the New York State Department of State placard on my dashboard. It allowed me to basically park where I wanted to park and zoom past bumper-to-bumper traffic in the HOV lanes, saving me hours of travel time. Still, I hated traffic, so I left my home on Long Island at 5:30 a.m. and got to my office on Chambers Street and Broadway, across from City Hall, between 6:00 and 6:15. I'd then go to the corner coffee truck, pick up my black coffee, and head up to my office.

My secretary, Michele, was like clockwork. She'd be in by 8:00, despite the fact she didn't have to be in until 9:00. Marvin Kohn was right behind her.

From day one, Michele gave me the lowdown on every employee within the NYSAC. She told me their good qualities and bad qualities, their strong points and weaknesses. She included herself in her rundown. I appreciated her honesty.

I also knew she would play a big role in my new position. The same can be said for the man I selected to be my executive director and right-hand man. It wasn't Marvin Kohn. It was Richard Hering, a court judge from the town of Liberty, New York, some 100 miles from the NYSAC office in New York City. Hering, while not a boxing guy, was a meat and potatoes, cross-every-t-and-dot-every-i kind of worker. He was also as loyal as a puppy dog. Marvin's loyalty was to himself. Michele told me that. And so did his coworkers. And so did many boxing insiders I spoke to in the days leading up to my starting the job.

The most damning assessments of Marvin came from the men who knew him well—Jose Torres, John Branca, and Jack Prenderville—my three predecessors. All three called the first week I was in office to both congratulate me and also warn me to be cautious around Marvin.

My first day in the office was Monday, August 1, 1988. It was one of the rare times I ever walked in as late as 9:00 a.m. Michele took me around and introduced me to my staff. I met Petey, Joe, Jackie, Ruby, Emma, Maribel (she was dating Mike Tyson at the time), Eva, Jose, and Rich. And, of course, there was Marvin.

Remember that ridiculous job-for-life contract Marvin pushed at me at the Felt Forum? On his very first visit into my office, he pulled out the contract again.

"Last week, you said you couldn't sign this because you weren't commissioner. Well, now you are. Here."

He handed me the contract. I hadn't gotten angry the first time. I did on this occasion, however.

"Marvin, what are you doing?" I asked him. I didn't expect an answer, nor did I wait for one.

"I can't sign this, and I won't sign this," I said, handing the contract back to him. "Nobody gets a lifetime guarantee on a job, unless your name is Fidel Castro or Jose Sulaiman." He didn't laugh.

I ripped the contract into tiny pieces, then handed it all back to Marvin. He looked stunned.

"Don't play games with me, Marvin!" I admonished. "Don't play me for a fool! Ever! This topic is done! Finished!"

Then I asked, "Is there anything else?"

"I just want assurance that my job . . ." he continued.

I cut him off.

"Marvin, stop!" I said, raising my voice. "I said this topic is finished. Now, please excuse me. I have tons of paperwork to fill out for the Governor's Appointment Office."

Incredibly, he wasn't through.

"I just want to know if my job is safe," he said.

I glared at him and pointed to the door.

"Out!" I demanded. "Out!"

Just then, Michele walked in. Her office was right outside mine, and she heard me raising my voice and knew Marvin well. She knew what was going on.

Marvin and I looked toward the door when we heard it open.

"Let's go, Marvin," said Michele. "The commissioner has a lot to do today. Let's go."

As he turned to leave, he looked at me and, one last time, pleaded, incredulously, "Could you just think about what I've asked you?"

I didn't reply. Michele did, however.

"Let's go, Marvin. Now!" she demanded.

And that's how my first moments as commissioner began!

From the first day I walked in the office, Marvin made a stop in my office even before he could put his briefcase down in his. Many times, Michele would stop him, as he had to walk through her office to get into mine. Quite often, she even locked my door so no one could get in if she had her back turned or was on the phone and not watching.

During the first couple of weeks, however, I allowed Marvin to come into my office whenever he wanted. I noticed, immediately, how he quickly went from talking to me to interviewing and questioning me.

"How long have you been married?"

"I'll bet you have a million girls on the side."

"C'mon, all the other chairmen had somebody on the side, that pad you could go to for the night. You *must* have someone."

His line of questioning was straight out of interrogation. He wanted to know where I had been and where I was going. What was my next move? What was in my head and who was in my bed? Because I knew where he was coming from, I'd answer him with something like, "Know what I think I'm gonna do, Marvin? It's been eating at me all day." He'd lean forward and say, "What are you gonna do? I promise to keep it to myself."

"Marvin, there's nothing secret about what's been on my mind. I have been agonizing whether to take myself to lunch in Little Italy or Chinatown. I have decided on Chinatown." That's the kind of information I gave Marvin Kohn.

You should have seen him when our commission attorney, Jeff, came in from Albany. Marvin would pace back and forth outside Michele's office when Jeff disappeared inside my office with Rich Hering and me. She never allowed him in until I buzzed her. Then, when he came in, he'd do his best to find out what was going on.

From 1988 until early 1994, lots of commission business went on that should have stayed commission business until I, as chairman, decided it was time to tell the media; however, "Good Guy Marvin Kohn" was always there to beat me to it.

When an eye surgeon came to the office to discuss former middleweight champ Iran Barkley's surgically repaired eye, the media found out before Barkley could even blink twice.

When Don King's attorneys came up to discuss a Mike Tyson contract, the media was on the phone with me as soon as they left.

When I was about to cancel an Aaron Pryor bout because of a failed eye examination, boxing journalists lit up the NYSAC's phone lines, wanting to know where, when, and how I planned on breaking the news to Pryor.

Like Clark Kent running into an alley and becoming Superman, Marvin would see what he had to see, hear what he had to hear, and find out what information he could before hurrying into his office, closing the door, and becoming "Good Guy Marvin Kohn." Of course the media loved him. He was truly a good guy to them.

By the start of 1994, I had taken all I could stand from the unfaithful chirper. I decided to set him up. I wanted to make sure Marvin was 1,000 percent guilty.

My scheme would be to tell Marvin I was having lunch with Don King, when, in fact, I wasn't. I would wait to see how long it took the news of my "meeting" to get around.

I told only one person of my plan. It wasn't Michele. Nor was it Rich. Or Jeff. The person I told about my plan was my boss—Governor Mario Cuomo. He listened intently. When I was finished, he said,

> You are doing the right thing. You are testing his loyalty. You are finding out, once and for all, where his loyalty lies. If he is the canary you think he is, the media will know about your "meeting with King" before you get home. Having somebody as untrustworthy and devious as that working for you, and doing what you say he does, is totally unacceptable. Keep me posted.

As for Michele, all I told her on the day of "The Setup" was, "Let Marvin come into my office when he gets in. I have something to tell him." Michele just looked at me. She knew I was up to something. She didn't know what, but she didn't ask. But she knew something was going on.

It was just after 8:30 when Marvin stepped off the elevator. When Michele saw him outside her office, she said, "Marvin, the boss wants to see you."

I can imagine the nervousness, sweats, and palpitations he had right then.

"Is everything all right?" he asked Michele.

"I have no idea," she replied.

"Was he angry? Did he seem like anything was wrong?" he asked her.

"No," she said. "As a matter of fact, he seemed to be in a really great mood."

The truth is, I was in a great mood. I was getting rid of Marvin.

When he walked in my office, I was going over the proposed matchups for an upcoming boxing show. I put the papers down when Marvin walked in.

"Good morning, Commissioner," he began. "Is everything okay?"

"Yes, Marvin, it is," I said. "But I wanted to tell you about something I am doing today at 1:00. It's very important and very sensitive and classified."

His eyes lit up.

"What are you doing?" he asked excitedly.

I looked over his shoulder at the door to my office, as if to make sure no one was walking in to hear what I had to say. Then I motioned Marvin to come closer. When he leaned in, I spoke in a low voice.

"I'm meeting Don King for lunch."

Then I held an index finger to my lips and held my other hand up, motioning Marvin not to even repeat what I said.

"What are you meeting him about?" asked Marvin.

"It's about Mike Tyson," I said. "He's going to be fighting in a massive fight this summer at Yankee Stadium. Don and I are going to be meeting at [former New York Met] Art Shamsky's place to discuss the details. Art is giving us the corner table in the back. I am very excited about this."

"Does anybody know about this?" Marvin asked.

"Nobody," I said. "You are the only one I've told."

"You haven't told Rich?" Marvin asked. "He's your right-hand man."

"I haven't told Rich," I said. "I'm not sure he'd understand."

"And Michele? She knows everything you are doing," he said.

I shook my head.

"Almost everything," I answered. "Almost everything. But not this."

"Why are you telling me, then?" he inquired.

I expected that question and was ready for it.

"Because someone may see King and me in there," I said.

They may contact the media. I just wanted you to be prepared in case you get some calls from the media on it. You can tell them I did indeed have lunch with King. Tell them I have lunch with lots of boxing people. Tell them it was lunch and that's all you know. If they have any questions, they can call me. I won't tell them anything other than we had lunch.

I then added, "But let's keep this totally under wraps. Even after I come back I am not telling Michele, Rich, or anybody. So, that's it. Not a word to anybody, okay? This is so exciting!"

"I understand," said Marvin. "I won't say a thing."

Then he asked, "Who's Tyson gonna fight that night?"

I looked at him and said, in a near-whisper, "George Foreman."

"Really! That is amazing!" Marvin exclaimed.

"It sure is," I said.

"Just one question," said Marvin, looking at me puzzled.

"What's that?" I asked.

"Why does King want to meet with you?" was his question.

"Because there are some issues with Tyson's contract, and King would like to have them resolved long before announcing this fight," I told him.

"What kind of issues?" he asked.

I shrugged.

"That's why he's meeting with me," I said. "And you said one question. That was two!" I laughed. He didn't.

"Will it just be the two of you?" asked Marvin.

"Just us," I replied. "Just Don and Randy. Just King and the Commish."

I stood up and walked around my desk. I walked to Marvin.

I extended my hand. He extended his.

"Thank you for confiding in me," he said. "It means a lot."

I'm sure it did. I'm sure the top boxing writers gave him plenty for being an informant. Boy, would he have a story for them in a little while.

When I left my office, first and foremost on my mind was, "How long will it take Marvin to begin making calls?" As I found out, it wasn't long.

The truth of the matter is, I really did have lunch at 1:00 that day at (former New York Met) Art Shamsky's restaurant. It was a restaurant I frequented quite often; however, I met my longtime friend from high school, Ira, there, not Don King. I had let the young lady at the front desk at Shamsky's know that there would probably be someone calling and inquiring if I was there. That someone could only be Marvin Kohn. I asked that, if such a call came in, to say I was indeed having lunch there. I asked her to do me a favor and say I was with boxing promoter Don King if the caller asked who I was with. Yes, it was dirty pool, but this was the game Marvin had played for years.

It came as no surprise when the young lady came to my table at about 1:30 and handed me a note. It said, "We just received a call with someone looking for you. It was a male caller." She asked if I wanted to speak outside. I said, "No, this is one of my best friends. I explained to him what was going on. You can talk to me here."

She went on to say that the male caller wanted to know if I was there and if they could please be told who I was with.

"Normally," she said, "we wouldn't divulge any information, but you said to tell them it was boxing promoter Don King, you were with, so I did. They said thank you and hung up."

"You did well," I said. I went to give her a tip. She refused, saying, "Thank you very much."

Then she paused and added, "The last two times Marvin Kohn was in here, he was rude and nasty. It was a pleasure to do this." Believe me, I understand.

Following the lunch, I went to Gleason's Gym in Brooklyn and watched a handful of fighters—including bantamweight champion Junior Jones and budding superstar Arturo Gatti—work out. Then I headed to a boxing gym in Queens and two more on Long Island before heading home.

Early that evening, I received phone calls from several sportswriters, including Michael Katz from the *New York Daily News* and Wallace Matthews from the *New York Post*. Basically, it was the same phone call from two different writers. They went something like this:

"Hello, Commissioner," began Katz, who, in 2012, was inducted into the International Boxing Hall of Fame in the observer category.

RG: Hi, Mike. What's going on?

MK: You tell me.

RG: Same ol' stuff. Couple of club shows coming up, that's about it.

MK: Anything this summer?

RG: This summer? We're talking five or six months away. Nothing this summer that I know of yet.

MK: What about this summer at Yankee Stadium?

RG: Huh? What are you talking about?

MK: You know what I'm talking about.

RG: There's nothing that I know about at Yankee Stadium this summer except some Yankee games.

MK: Okay, give it up. Mike Tyson has leaked what you'd like to keep secret. Plus, you were seen at Art Shamsky's restaurant today.

RG: I was? Was I alone?

MK: Yeh . . . alone with Don King.

RG: With who?

MK: Come on. Don't play games. You were seen with him.

RG: By who?

MK: By a friend of mine a few tables away. My friend is a huge boxing fan. He knows you, and he certainly knows King. He wanted to come up and get autographs, but he said you guys were totally engrossed in conversation.

RG: Nice try, Mike.

MK: What do you mean?

RG: Nice try making up a story about who saw me and King. The fact is, however, I wasn't with King. I was with Ira.

MK: What are you talking about? Who's Ira?

RG: Ira is a high school pal of mine. That's who I was there with. I was with Ira, not Don King!

MK: What are you talking about? You were seen with King.

RG: Okay, it's time to stop. You're continuing because you think I am trying to deny being with King. The thing is, I know you heard from Marvin Kohn. I set him up this morning. I told him I was going to lunch with King because of a big fight involving Mike Tyson at Yankee Stadium. I wanted to catch Marvin making calls to the media. I wanted to catch him breaking my trust. I wanted to catch him being the big-mouth canary he really is. Guess what? I caught him.

MK: It, uh, it wasn't Marvin who called me.

RG: Nice attempted save, Mike. But nothing is gonna save Marvin now. I'm sure we'll speak tomorrow. Good night, Mike.

That same scenario was played out minutes later, when the *Post*'s Matthews called me. Afterward, I sat back in the chair in my home office and stared at a picture on my wall of Governor Cuomo and me. His words were ringing in my head.

"If you catch him red-handed informing the media of sensitive information, if you can prove he is the leak in your agency, he is a cancer to the agency and must be removed."

The next morning, I arrived at my customary 6:30. When Michele arrived to work at about 8:00, I called her into my office. She walked up to my desk and looked at me. She knew my facial expressions. She knew my body language. She knew my eyes.

"What is it?" she asked. "Is anything wrong?"

"Actually, things are great," I told her. "In a few minutes, I will be firing Marvin Kohn."

Her mouth dropped open in disbelief.

"What!" she gasped.

I explained the entire story to her.

"Do you know that every chairman out of the last . . ."

She began thinking.

". . . five or six have tried to fire him. He has survived every one. Do you think he'll bring up . . ."

"Roni?" I said, completing her sentence.

"Yes, Roni," she replied. "I know Marvin. He will stop at nothing in order to save his job."

Roni was my girlfriend. She had been my high school sweetheart. We broke up right after high school and got back together almost 20 years later. There were two problems, however. Her husband was one of them. My wife was the other.

"It doesn't matter, Michele," I said. "My situation is different than the others."

"I know that," she said. "But do you want Roni's name thrown out there? Do you want Marvin telling everyone that you are having an extramarital affair?"

"I am totally prepared for anything Marvin can come up with," I told her. "He doesn't know the whole story. He will find out. Marvin Kohn will be gone in just a little while."

"Wow!" Michele exclaimed. "Are you sure you want to go through with this?"

"Tell me, Michele, just what does Marvin do around here? Other than sit in my office and try to find out what newsy item is happening next so he can call his friends in the media, just what does he do around here? Yes, I'm sure I want him out. I have Governor Cuomo's support on this. Marvin Kohn is gone! Gone!"

As I said that, there was a knock on my door.

"Come in!" I said loudly.

The door pushed open. It was Marvin.

"Come on in," I told him.

Michele turned and walked quickly out of my office.

She never made eye contact with Marvin as she blew past him and out of the blue door with the sign, "Chairman, Randy Gordon."

"Good morning, Commissioner," he began.

"Good morning, Marvin," I replied. It indeed was a good morning. It was about to become a great morning.

"How did it go yesterday?" Marvin asked.

"How did what go?" I asked him.

Marvin looked quizzically at me.

"The lunch with Don King," he said.

"You mean my lunch with Ira," I said, correcting him.

The look of puzzlement on his face was priceless.

"Who is Ira?" asked Marvin.

"My longtime friend from high school," I told him. "Ira came to meet me for lunch yesterday."

"But you were with Don King," said Marvin. "You were at Art Shamsky's place. I called over there looking for you. They said you were with Don King."

"Why did you call over there?" I asked him, banging my fist on my desk.

The question caught him completely off guard. In fact, the entire incident had him totally shaken up. He took a deep breath but was speechless.

I asked him again.

"One more time. Why did you call over there?"

"What are you doing?" he asked, sounding totally out of breath.

"Final time, Marvin." My voice grew louder. "Why did you call over there?"

Beads of sweat glistened atop his bald head.

"I had to ask you what time you were going to be back. I didn't know if you wanted me to wait for you," he said, reaching for the lie. The sweat was now rolling down his forehead.

I added to his sweat.

"So you called to find out what time I was coming back, huh?" I grilled him. "Actually, you then asked who I was with and where I was sitting. You did that so guys like Mike Katz and Wallace Matthews and who knows who else would know what to ask me when they called me up last night at home."

"And you think I called them?" he asked.

"I know you called them!" I shouted. "I have been onto you for years. You have been the massive leak in this commission for years. Now, I caught you red-handed. I had lunch with Ira, not Don King. Nobody here knew except you. You're finished! Done!"

He tried fighting back. "I'll make you a deal," he offered.

"A deal?" I asked incredulously.

"I know you've been having an affair," he stated, as sweat poured down his face. "I am prepared to let everyone know about you and Roni and your affair. Your wife will find out. I will say nothing if you drop this whole thing!"

"You son of a bitch!" I screamed at him. He actually smiled. He was certain he had me. Then I composed myself and realized he was using a pea-shooter against a battleship.

"Marvin. I am not having an affair. I am legally separated. I have been separated for several years. So has Roni. Roni and I will be getting married when my divorce is finalized." I glared at him for a moment. Then I pointed to the door.

"Get out!" I snarled loudly. "Pack your office and get out! Quickly!"

Marvin stood up. When he did, he grabbed his chest.

"I think I'm having a heart attack," he moaned.

I wasn't in the mood for any more of his games.

"Go have the heart attack in your ex-office," I told him. "Have the heart attack, then get out! Go!"

As he left my office, Marvin moaned, groaned, and whimpered. Seconds after he left, Michele pushed open the door to my office. We looked at one another. She rolled her eyes.

"He looked numb when he walked out," Michele said. "Numb and very pale."

"He brought it on himself," I said. "He had this coming for a long time. A very long time."

The following day, Marvin called and asked Michele if he could send up a man who would take the belongings out of his desk, pack them in boxes, and carry them out. Michele said he could.

The next time I heard about Marvin was less than a month later. Michele received word he had suffered a massive stroke. It killed him immediately. The *Post*'s Matthews followed with a story about Kohn, about his long years of service with the NYSAC and dedication to boxing and its wonderful athletes. Matthews wrote about how Marvin was nothing but a help to writers and how they admired him.

Matthews also made it quite clear that I was responsible for his death. I never believed that. Not for a second. I still don't. I fired Marvin Kohn because he deserved to be fired. He should have been fired years before I sent him packing. Writers liked him, but they liked him for the wrong reason. He opened doors for them that should never have been opened. He was as disloyal as an employee can be. He lasted longer at the NYSAC than he ever should have. My conscience is clear about what happened to "good guy" Marvin Kohn.

When I was a journalist, I enjoyed Marvin Kohn. I enjoyed his quick wit, humor, and storytelling. But to the state agency I ran—the New York State Athletic Commission—Marvin Kohn was disruptive.

I recently did a writer a favor and got a Hall of Fame inductee who I am friendly with to do an interview with the writer. Afterward, the writer said, "Thanks, Randy. I really appreciate the help. I am a member of the Boxing Writers Association's Awards Committee. Would you mind if I put you in for the Marvin Kohn Good Guy Award?" I almost choked. Obviously, he didn't know the story. Few people do.

But can you imagine *me* winning the Marvin Kohn Good Guy Award? Now, wouldn't that be something!

16

GENTLEMAN GERRY

The fury, speed, and power that were being unleashed on the head of the former heavyweight champion were frightening.

"Stop it!" yelled veteran sportswriter Red Smith of the *New York Times*.

"Stop it!" shouted veteran sportswriter Bob Waters of *Newsday*.

"Stop it!" shouted *Ring Magazine*'s publisher, Bert Randolph Sugar. "Stop it, Tony! Stop it!"

"Stop it!"

Those two words reverberated throughout the ringside as referee Tony Perez hesitated to stop the fight. This was no fight to hesitate on. Punches can kill. Punches *have* killed. By the time Perez did stop the fight, the beaten former champion looked more dead than alive.

Gerry Cooney had just done to Ken Norton in 54 seconds what Muhammad Ali could not do in 39 rounds and what Larry Holmes could not do in 15 rounds against the powerfully built former heavyweight king.

At the postfight press conference, where a still-glassy-eyed Norton surprised the media by showing up, Norton fielded questions.

"How hard does Cooney hit?" came one dumb question. Norton looked at the reporter, ignored him, and took another question.

"With what punch did he first hurt you?" Norton was asked.

He shrugged his shoulders.

"I don't remember," he said. "You saw it. I didn't. You tell me what punch it was."

"Does Cooney hit harder than George Foreman [who had stopped Norton in the second round six years earlier]?"

"If I remembered getting hit, maybe I could tell you," said the man, who, just two years earlier, had battled Larry Holmes 15 rounds in an all-time heavyweight classic. The media chuckled at his expense.

"Do you think Cooney can beat Larry Holmes?" was another question.

"If he lands like that on Larry, or anyone else, he's going to win," Norton told the crowd. Then, the man who had broken Muhammad Ali's jaw and beaten him in 1973, and gave him hell in two subsequent fights, the man who had savaged Jerry Quarry in 1975 and fought that classic 15-rounder against Larry Holmes, announced his retirement.

"There's nowhere else to go," he said. "I achieved all I set out to do. This was my last fight."

He stuck to his words.

As the boxing career of Ken Norton was ending, Cooney's was in full swing. The victory against Norton had taken his record to 24–0. Included were 20 knockouts. A pro just three years, Cooney now was being talked about as standing in a very short line to face heavyweight champion Larry Holmes.

It was May 9, 2009. Producer Ricky "Bones" Bonnet stood at the control panel in Studio 4 at SiriusXM Radio in New York City.

"One minute until air, guys," he said, looking at me and my cohost, who sat on my right. I reached across the console and fist-bumped Bones. Then I turned to my cohost—Gerry Cooney—and extended my average-sized right fist. He reached over and did the same with his oversized right fist. Then he gave me a playful tap on my arm with his left, the same left he used to deliver one of history's most devastating left hooks. "Gentleman" Gerry Cooney, the ex-heavyweight contender, was about to become "Gentleman" Gerry Cooney, talk-show host.

At the Fights was on the air for the first time. *At the Fights* is still going strong. We call ourselves "Cooney & the Commish" and joke about being identical twins, when, physically, nothing could be more opposite. Yet, working alongside Gerry is so much fun, not only because of his knowledge and passion for the sport, but also because of his easygoing demeanor and personable, outgoing, almost-boyish nature with his colleagues and boxing fans.

As we are moments away from another show, it's always the same for me: My adrenaline glands seemingly burst, my heart rate accelerates, and I get a bit nervous. But then, I look over at Gerry and see how relaxed he is, how at ease he seems to be. His aura of calm is soothing. A smile came to my face as I looked at him on our very first show together. That smile has reappeared at the start of every show for almost a decade. Gerry Cooney is at complete and total peace with his life. It wasn't always that way for him.

Cooney was raised in a modest Cape Cod home in the blue-collar town of Huntington, New York, which is nestled on the North Shore of Long Island. He is one of four sons and two daughters of Eileen and Tony Cooney.

Tony was an iron worker who ruled the Cooney household with a hand as hard as the metal he worked with every day. He gave love the way he learned it himself as a kid.

"My dad was really tough on all of us," recalls the soft-spoken, hard-hitting giant. "He regularly told us, 'You're nothing, you'll never amount to anything. You're a failure. You're a loser. Don't trust anybody.' When you're told that enough, you begin to believe it. We heard it from him all the time."

Tony was a drinker. A big drinker. He was also a hitter. When Tony asked a question, a wrong glance, a hesitation, a wrong answer—just about anything—drew his wrath.

"He'd hit us with anything he might be holding," Gerry recalled. "If he wasn't holding anything, he'd hit us with his hands."

The beatings led to the Cooney boys learning to fight. While older brother Tom may have been the best fighter of the Cooney bunch, his lack of discipline kept him out of the ring. It was Gerry's desire to please his father that kept him in it.

When Gerry was 16, he stood 6-foot-4 and weighed in at 160 pounds. That year, he won the New York Golden Gloves novice 160-pound title. While Gerry thought that winning a Golden Gloves title would make Tony proud, the elder Cooney had a tough time showing it.

"Is that the best you could do?" Gerry recalled his father saying. "'You could have finished him earlier, but you didn't.' No matter what I did, it wasn't good enough for my dad."

His Golden Gloves championship had made Gerry somewhat of a celebrity throughout Huntington, and thoughts entered his mind to continue with his boxing and try to make the 1976 U.S. Olympic team.

However, when Tony fell ill with lung cancer, which eventually took his life in 1977, Gerry abandoned his thoughts of competing on and traveling with the U.S. National Team. Gone were his plans to represent the United States in the Montreal Olympics. His thoughts went from gold to green. He decided to turn pro.

Cooney was 20 when he signed with real estate executives Mike Jones and Dennis Rappaport in 1976. He had impressed the duo with a couple of one-punch knockout victories in the amateurs. One of them came in a U.S.A. vs

U.S.S.R. meet at Madison Square Garden. Cooney's Russian opponent had been singled out to face Cooney by Russian officials because he loved to fight tall opponents and had tremendous success against them. What Russian officials didn't realize was how hard the 6-foot-6 Cooney punched, especially with the left hook. A single one put the Russian "giant killer" to sleep midway through the first round. Soon thereeafter, Cooney met with Jones and Rappaport. They promised to guide him to the heavyweight title. They talked of a fight against Muhammad Ali in just a few years. They spoke of him becoming a great and popular heavyweight champion. A small, weekly salary also helped Cooney make up his mind. Rappaport and Jones brought in Victor Valle—a lightweight contender 40 years earlier—to be his trainer.

On February 15, 1977, at the half-century-old but soon-to-face-the-wrecking-ball Sunnyside Arena in Queens, New York, Cooney turned professional. His opponent was, well, exactly that.

"While Cooney could have come right out of the gate and beaten just about anybody put in front of him, his managers wanted somebody they were certain would give him a big victory in his pro debut," matchmaker Johnny Bos told me.

"'Get us a guy who will make Cooney look great,' Mike Jones said to me," recalled Bos.

> I told him, "Your guy can fight. Your guy can punch. He's one of the hardest hitters I have ever seen. Let's put him against somebody who will test him a little." Do you know what he said to me? He said, "We're not testing him! At least not now, anyway. Get him a guy who will come to New York and leave with a loss."

Bos picked up the phone and called "Big Bill" Jackson, who fought out of the notorious group of professional opponents (losers) from Columbus, Ohio, called the "Columbus Cooler Gang." Jackson gladly accepted the fight. He came into the fight with a record of 0–7. In all seven fights, he had been knocked out. Cooney handed him loss number eight, ending it with a wicked left hook to the body and a follow-up hook to the head in 1:32 of the first round.

Cooney's next two opponents were not much better. Each was 0–1, with their lone loss being by knockout—first-round knockout. Cooney treated them a little bit better than they were used to. He stopped each man in round two.

In his sixth pro fight, Cooney was put in with an opponent from Baltimore named Quinnie Locklear. Locklear claimed to have Native American blood and was billed as "Chief Quinnie." He looked more like a professional wrestler than a fighter. In the first round, during an exchange in mid-ring, Cooney hit Locklear with a double left hook. The first was to the body, the second was to the chin. The body hook broke two of Locklear's ribs. The hook to the jaw broke it in two places and knocked him out.

By the end of 1977, Cooney had pounded his way to a 7–0 record. Included were six knockout victories. Cooney was just 21. His managers drooled at the thought of their prospect being matched against Muhammad Ali for the heavyweight title the next year. The fight would not come to fruition, however.

In February 1978, Leon Spinks, who had won a gold medal as a light heavyweight in the 1976 Olympic Games in Montreal, pulled off one of boxing's greatest upsets, beating Ali on a split decision in 15 rounds for the heavyweight championship. Prior to Spinks shocking the boxing world and with the new movie *Rocky* setting records at the box office, Ali versus Cooney was the fight on everyone's lips. Spinks's victory made everyone forget their talk of Ali–Cooney. The only fight that mattered now was Spinks–Ali II—and this wouldn't happen until September 1978.

In the meantime, Cooney's progression and growth continued. Included was a bout against S. T. Gordon in Las Vegas, which Cooney won on disqualification on St. Paddy's Day in 1978. Shown on CBS, the bout didn't do much to enhance Cooney's reputation as a bona-fide heavyweight contender. Gordon, who would go on to become the cruiserweight champion of the world, weighed 187 pounds. Cooney weighed in at 219. With the strict standards currently being exercised by state athletic commissions, it would be highly unlikely that bout would be shown on television today, or even sanctioned.

CBS's color analyst, Gil Clancy, who trained Cooney for his final fight, would often shake his head when he talked about Cooney's managers and their choosing of opponents for their rising heavyweight contender.

Because of the headaches Jones and Rappaport gave promoters and matchmakers, and because of their attitude (they wanted to be known as the "Gold Dust Twins"), the duo became known instead as the "Wacko Twins."

"They two of them really had no idea how good Cooney was," said Clancy.

But they knew how much he could earn if he continued to win. So, instead of putting him in against quality opposition, they overanalyzed and overscrutinized every single name put before them. In reality, they had nothing to worry about. Gerry was too big, talented and hard-hitting for any heavyweight who stepped in the ring against him.

Throughout the remainder of 1978, Cooney stayed active. He stopped trial horses and opponents in G. G. Maldonado, Charlie Polite, and Grady Daniels, and pounded tough Sam McGill to a decision in eight rounds.

The local media, which entailed New York, New Jersey, Pennsylvania, and Connecticut, loved covering Cooney's fights, just the way they loved covering young Mike Tyson less than a decade later. The fights were fun, fast, and exciting. The media, however, were less-than-enthralled with Cooney's managers, who loved to take the spotlight at postfight interviews. While Cooney was always soft-spoken, the "Wackos" never held back. It was obvious they even tried to "outquote" the other.

"Gerry is going to be the man who ends the career of Muhammad Ali," Rappaport loved saying after Ali regained the title from Spinks in their September 1978 rematch.

"Cooney is going to be the first billion-dollar athlete," Jones bellowed.

Even the normally quiet and reserved Victor Valle couldn't hold back after another Cooney victory.

"Gerry is a work in progress," Valle would say. "He's a diamond in the rough, and I am the diamond-cutter. When I am through, Gerry will be a fully cut and polished gem."

As the three spoke at these postfight press conferences, feeding the media endless quotes and stopping short of calling Cooney the greatest heavyweight of all time, the only one in the room who looked uncomfortable with all the hoopla was the man himself: Gerry Cooney.

"It was embarrassing," Cooney says now. "If I looked uncomfortable, it's because I *was* uncomfortable."

In his 16th fight, in January 1979, Cooney won a unanimous eight-round decision against Eddie "The Animal" Lopez, whose only loss in 13 previous fights had been a close decision to future heavyweight titleholder Big John Tate 16 months earlier. The Cooney–Lopez fight is notable because it was the last decision Cooney would win in his career. He would fight just 15 more times in the next 11 years.

By the end of 1979, Cooney had begun to make his move upward. So had I. While Cooney entered the world ratings, I compiled them as Bert Sugar's right-hand man and the next in line for Nat Fleischer's old office at *Ring Magazine*.

As 1980 approached, Cooney was 22–0. The "Wacko Twins" were now in full gear in their talk of Gerry fighting for a world title; however, it was no longer Muhammad Ali they were focused on. Ali retired after beating Spinks in their September 1978 rematch. The man the "Wackos" were now after was the reigning World Boxing Council heavyweight champion, Larry Holmes, who was under promotional contract with Don King.

King offered the "Wackos" some lucrative and meaningful fights for Cooney, but only if he signed a promotional deal with him. The "Wackos" wanted no part of that and kept Cooney a free agent.

"We will stay active and force Holmes to fight us," said Rappaport. "We will leave him no choice but to face us."

In 1980, Cooney faced perennial contender Jimmy Young in May and slugger Ron Lyle in October. The victory against Young was impressive. The victory against Lyle was breathtaking.

Just three years earlier, Young had outboxed, outfoxed, and outclassed George Foreman—even knocking down the former heavyweight champion in the final round—beating him on a 12-round decision and sending him into a 10-year retirement. Against Cooney, he looked overmatched from the start before one of Cooney's ramrod jabs crashed through his guard and sliced open his right eyebrow late in the third round. The fight was stopped at the end of the fourth.

At the postfight press conference, the "Wacko Twins" began beating the drums for Cooney's expected future coronation to the heavyweight throne.

"You haven't seen more than a fraction of the best Gerry Cooney," Rappaport crowed to the press.

"He's a few fights away from the title," said Jones.

Five months later came the breathtaking performance against Ron Lyle. At 39, Lyle's best days were in his rearview mirror. In 1976, he had engaged in a slugfest with George Foreman that fans talk about and watch on YouTube to this day. Against Cooney, Lyle was a punching bag with arms and legs. Cooney's left hook never was so on target or so hard, especially to Lyle's body. The shots made Lyle bend, wince, and gasp.

After being hurt by a left hook to the body, Lyle sagged against the ropes. As he did, another Cooney hook slammed into his rib cage. Remember Rocky Balboa hitting the slab of beef in the original *Rocky*? That was Cooney's hook to Lyle's right side. The punch broke two of his ribs and knocked him out of the ring and onto the press table.

"He hit me harder than Foreman hit me," Lyle said of Cooney. "It felt like a cannonball hit me!"

Watch the YouTube video of the knockout. You'll see hands coming up from the members of the media seated at the ringside press table. Those hands were mine. Cooney actually knocked Lyle out of the ring and almost into my lap. Cooney was 24 and reaching for the stars, which seemed to be within his grasp. The fight against Lyle was a prelude and a tune-up to Cooney's next fight, which was seven months away.

His opponent: Ken Norton.

The winner of the fight would be given a title shot against Larry Holmes. That winner, in 54 brutal seconds, was Gerry Cooney. At a press conference one week before the fight, former heavyweight contender Jerry Quarry pulled Cooney aside and asked a favor of Cooney.

Six years earlier, Norton had savaged Quarry in Madison Square Garden, stopping him on cuts in the fifth round. Following the fight, Norton had seen Quarry's wife, the blonde and beautiful Arlene Charles, known to everyone as "Charlie." He let Charlie know that he was the better fighter in the ring and asked her for the chance to let him prove he was the better all-around man. Years later, Sylvester Stallone, in *Rocky III*, perhaps with Norton in mind, had Mr. T's character, "Clubber Lang," say to Adrian, "Come on over to my place and I'll show you what a real man is."

Of course, Charlie, who always played with Jerry's emotions, just had to mention that to her husband, who was being stitched up in the dressing room. He flew off the table in a rage, hell-bent on getting to Norton. In a street fight, Norton was not going to beat an enraged Jerry Quarry, who was restrained by Madison Square Garden security and members of his team. So, when it was fellow Irishman Gerry Cooney's turn to face Norton, Quarry needed to, wanted to—*had* to!—ask a favor of Cooney.

He told Cooney of the incident six years earlier. Cooney listened intently. When Quarry finished his story, Cooney shook his head sadly and slowly.

"What's the favor you want to ask of me?" Cooney said, placing his hands on Quarry's shoulders.

"I want you to beat Norton up. I want you to beat him worse than George Foreman did [KO 2, '73] and faster than Earnie Shavers did [KO 1, '73]. I really want you to hurt him. Do that for me, please? Do that for me, will you, Gerry?"

Cooney smiled and said, "You know I'm gonna take care of business, Jerry, you know it!"

Quarry walked away feeling as if the beating that was coming to Norton was redemption. For him, it absolutely was. But Cooney never intended to hurt Norton for any reason other than this was boxing. This was the life they had chosen. It was hurt or be hurt.

"I did to Norton what I tried to do to every opponent," Cooney told me. "I wasn't thinking of anything except to punch, punch hard, and keep punching. It wasn't until after the fight, when Quarry walked up to me and said, 'Thank you,' that I realized what Quarry thought I did was for him."

Ironically, the fight took place on the same date when, four years earlier, previously unbeaten heavyweight contender Duane Bobick was stopped in 58 seconds of the opening round by the same Ken Norton who was about to face another unbeaten heavyweight contender. Again, there was another knockout in less than a minute; however, this time it was Norton on the receiving end of the knockout blows.

The devastating knockout by Cooney made it back-to-back first-round knockouts. He was on top of not only the boxing world, but also the sports world. With his boyish charm and sense of humor, and affable nature toward the media and fans, the words of his comanager, Mike Jones, about Gerry becoming the first billion-dollar athlete no longer seemed like a fight manager's pipe dream.

But instead of this victory propelling Cooney to the status of world heavyweight champion, it was the start of nine years of self-doubt, alcoholism, and drug abuse.

"The Ken Norton fight should have been the start of some great things for me," Cooney later reflectd. "But it had the opposite effect. The win changed my life for the worse. I kept hearing my father say, 'You'll never amount to anything' and 'You're a loser!' It's amazing how things like that can come back to haunt you."

He and his brothers opened a bar in Huntington called, fittingly enough, "Cooney's East Side."

"I was in there more than I was in the gym," Cooney admitted.

So was I. It was Long Island's "in" place to be. I went in there with my wife and my friends. I don't recall a night where I didn't see Gerry holding a drink in one hand and his other arm wrapped around a pretty girl—or 10.

In a one-on-one conversation I had with him in the spring of 2017, I asked him, "Did your problems start because of your bar?" He shook his head.

"Every bar was my bar," he said.

I used to joke with my friends as we walked down a street. It could have been anywhere. Long Island . . . New York City . . . anywhere. When we'd see a bar, I'd say, "Follow me." We'd walk into the bar and everyone knew me. The patrons knew me. The waiters knew me. The bartenders knew me. The owners knew me. In a second, they'd buy us all drinks. And another one. And another one. I'd walk to the tables and talk to patrons. Many times, *they* bought me drinks. I didn't know when to quit. I began stopping in bars after the gym and then even *before* the gym.

"Did you ever train while you were drunk?" I asked him.

"Ever?" he replied in a "you've-got-to-be-kidding!" voice. "Ever?"

I nodded.

"I walked into the gym drunk on many occasions," he told me.

"Why didn't Victor Valle say something to you?" I inquired.

"Oh, he did," Gerry replied. "He yelled at me many times."

"But you'd do it again," I said. "Why?"

"I heard every word Victor said," Gerry explained. "But I had become a drunk. I couldn't stop. So, the easiest thing to do was tell Victor, 'I'm sorry, I won't do it again.' But, of course, I just said that to get him off my back."

Soon after the opening of his bar, I noticed Cooney wasn't particularly nice to me.

"When are you getting back in the ring, Gerry?" I'd ask, when I saw him in his bar.

"Whenever my managers tell me," he'd say, barely looking at me.

This kind of exchange and its "warmth" went on for months. On one occasion I asked him, "Are you mad at me for something?" He didn't reply. He merely walked away. I didn't press the issue, but I was hurt. And angry. I was editor of *The Ring*, and this top heavyweight contender kept ignoring me or walking away from me. I began to dislike him. I wanted him to lose to Holmes— who I had become friends with—or whoever he fought next.

Following the destruction of Norton, the "Wackos" went to work, trying to get Cooney a title fight against Holmes; however, they were continually put off by Holmes's shrewd promoter, Don King, who continued to demand promotional rights to Cooney.

While Cooney had only the 54 seconds of action against Norton in 1981, King kept Holmes busy. At about the same time Cooney was ending Norton's career, Holmes won a comfortable unanimous decision against Trevor Berbick. Only a few months later, Holmes was back in the ring, stopping Leon Spinks in the third round. But when Holmes climbed off the canvas in November, King figured it was time to make Holmes–Cooney happen.

In late 1981, I received a call from Larry Holmes.

He knew that I, as editor of *The Ring*, had access to lots of fighters. He had a question for me.

"Would you know of any tall heavyweights I can work with?" asked Holmes.

"Tall, as in Gerry Cooney tall?" I inquired.

"Yes, the fight is going to be made," Holmes told me, "but please don't say anything. Don King will be making a big announcement in New York City next week. I'm looking for sparring partners who are tall like Cooney and have good jabs. I'll be paying $500 per week. Do you know of anybody?"

I didn't have to think.

"Mitch Green is who you want, Larry," I told him. "He's a 5–0 heavyweight from around here. He goes by the nickname of 'Blood.' Let me call his manager, Shelly Finkel. I'll call you right back."

Finkel, who would go on to become one of the greatest managers in boxing history, was excited to have Green spend time as Holmes's sparring partner.

"When does he start?" Finkel asked me. I told him I'd put him in touch with Larry Holmes so they could work out the details.

"You're really excited for Mitch to make $500 a week, huh, Shelly?" I said with a smile.

"It's much more than that," he replied. "When Don King sees how good Mitch is, he'll probably try to steal him from me."

"That won't matter. You have a contract with Green, right?" I said.

"Yes, I do," replied Finkel. "But Mitch is such a headache, I won't even fight it. I'll release him from his contract. He'll then be King's headache, not mine."

Finkel was bull's-eye correct with his prediction. It didn't take a week before King made a move to sign Green to a promotional contract and move someone from Don King Productions to be his manager. Finkel released Green with a smile. He then became more than King's headache. He became King's migraine! But one thing Green did, is prepare Holmes for Cooney.

Today, Cooney and I laugh about me arranging for Green to become Holmes's chief sparring partner.

"I can't believe you did that to me," says Gerry. "I can't believe you were with the Holmes camp for that fight!"

The fight was originally going to take place in February, in Las Vegas.

"The February date had to be scrapped," Cooney explained, "when I injured my right rotator cuff. It didn't need surgery. It just needed rest."

The fight was rescheduled for June 11, at Caesars Palace in Las Vegas.

Both King and the "Wackos" used the time to promote the fight; however, they did it in an ugly way: they turned the fight into a racial battle.

"Larry is proud to be an African American," bellowed King. "African Americans all over the world look up to him and idolize him. He is their inspiration." To further emphasize the theme of the fight, Evangelist minister Reverend Jesse Jackson often stood at Holmes's side during the many nationwide press conferences for the fight.

The "Wackos" got just as ugly.

"Gerry is more than a 'Great White Hope,'" Dennis Rappaport said. "He is the 'People's Champion.' He is popular with all races. He is Joe Louis and Rocky Marciano rolled into one. When he beats Holmes, he will be idolized and adored by all races, creeds, and colors. Larry's time is up."

"The pressure is going to be humongous on Holmes," said Mike Jones. "He will not be just fighting Gerry Cooney. He will be fighting America."

For months, the craziness, bitterness, and ugliness continued. Holmes and Cooney could not even be near one another without the threat of a fight between them starting. It continued to the point that both men received death threats: Holmes got them from white supremacist groups, Cooney from black militant groups.

Federal and state authorities took the threats so seriously that FBI sharpshooters were positioned on the roof at Caesars Palace and on platforms located throughout the makeshift parking lot arena on the day of the fight.

If tension was high leading up to the fight, it was off-the-charts high in the moments before the fight. Incredibly, Holmes—the champ—entered the ring first. Historically, the champion never enters first, never is left standing there, never kept waiting. Moments later, Cooney made his entrance.

As referee Mills Lane brought both fighters to the center of the ring and quickly went over the rules (which he had gone over at length in each fighter's dressing room a short while earlier), he asked each if they had any questions. Each man shook his head.

Then came Lane's signature call: "Let's get it on!"

As the fighters reached out to touch gloves, Holmes said to Cooney, "Let's have a good fight."

"I remember that more than anything," Cooney says whenever he is asked to discuss the fight.

There was all this bad blood between us in the months leading up to the fight. Now, here we were, where seemingly everyone wanted us to be—standing in a ring seconds away from fighting—and Holmes is telling me, "Let's have a good fight." For a moment, I thought it was a ploy. I thought he was trying to get me to relax, to drop my guard, to make me not want to hit him. But when I looked him in the eyes, I could see he meant it. He was the heavyweight champion of the world, one of the best ever, and all he wanted was a good, clean fight. I knew that's what I was going to give him. Those words he spoke let me know that's exactly what he was going to give me. His words were actually very calming. They are what I remember and think about most . . . more than being knocked down by a Holmes right in the second round . . . more than the low blow in round nine . . . and more than the fight's ending. His words as the fight was starting is what I think about most.

The second-round knockdown was a perfectly timed right hand that caught Cooney on the chin. He wobbled, then dropped. As he did, the crowd exploded.

Cooney recalls thinking, "Good shot, Larry! Keep your left up, Gerry. Get your ass up now and fight him!"

The ninth-round low blow was a left uppercut to Holmes's groin. The punch was so hard it was heard throughout the many rows of the press section surrounding the ring and several rows back into the ringside seats.

In unison, the crowd let out a loud, "Ohhhh!" as if they felt the shot. Holmes was the one who really felt it. He doubled over at the waist, clutching his crotch with both hands. Cooney immediately turned away from Holmes and walked to a neutral corner.

"I thought I would be disqualified," said Cooney, "but I hoped I wouldn't be. The punch wasn't intentionally low. I was looking to land a shot on Larry's body. At the same time, he threw a jab which went past the right side of my head. As the punch passed me, Larry pulled my head down. As he did, the punch strayed low."

"I knew it was an accidental shot," said Holmes. "But it really hurt. It caught me under the cup and drove it right up into my package. For a few moments, I thought I had just had a sex change!"

The incident occurred at 2:38 of the round. Referee Lane gave Holmes five minutes to catch his breath, but Holmes only used about two of them. The two touched gloves to show there were no bad feelings as action resumed. The round concluded with no further drama.

Cooney began to take over in the next few rounds. But his lack of actual time in the ring coming into the fight against Holmes (less than four minutes in 25 months) was working against him and for the polished heavyweight champion. As the 13th round started, Cooney's heart was willing. The rest of him wasn't.

After taking a right hand to the head with about one minute gone in the round, Cooney wobbled, barely able to stand. He crashed against the ropes, draping his right arm over the top rope to keep himself upright. As he did and as Holmes moved in for the finish, Victor Valle bolted into the ring and waved an end to the fight. Technically, the bout should have been declared a disqualification defeat for Cooney. It was ruled a TKO win for Larry Holmes at 2:52 of the 13th round.

At the postfight press conference, Cooney—wearing sunglasses to hide his bruises and tear-filled eyes—apologized to his legion of fans who he felt he had let down. His late father's words about being a loser and never amounting to anything slapped Cooney across the face harder than any punch Holmes landed during their fight. Quickly, Cooney sunk deep into a world of drugs, alcohol, and depression.

He remained out of the public eye for the next two years, always apologizing when he was seen on rare occasions throughout Long Island.

In the summer of 1984, it was announced he was coming back. His comeback would take place against undefeated Phillip Brown in Anchorage, Alaska, of all places.

At the summer press conference to announce the fight, I walked up to Cooney and said, "Welcome back." He just nodded. This time, I couldn't hold it in.

"Why are you mad at me?" I asked. "What did I ever do to you?"

His answer shocked me.

"You write bad about me all the time," he said.

"What!" I blurted. "I write bad about you? You've got to be kidding! Where did you read a story I wrote which says anything bad about you?"

"I didn't," he said. "My managers told me you are constantly writing negative stories about me."

I couldn't believe what I was hearing.

"Gerry, I swear to you I have *never* written anything bad about you. *Never!*" I insisted.

"Well, this is what I was told," he replied.

"Tell you what," I said. "How about you meet me in Roosevelt Field [one of Long Island's largest shopping malls] tomorrow. We can have lunch. I will bring lots of *Ring Magazines* with me and show you stories I have written about you."

The next day, we met in a restaurant in the mall. I brought about a dozen different issues of *The Ring* with me. In each one, I had articles about Cooney. What he saw were such lines as, "Cooney has one of the hardest left hooks in heavyweight history" and "With any luck of the Irish, Gerry Cooney will one day wear a heavyweight title belt" and "The left jab owned by Gerry Cooney can already be rated with the jabs owned by Joe Louis, Muhammad Ali, and Larry Holmes."

"Show me the bad stuff, Gerry, show me!" I demanded. "You can take the magazines home. Read them from cover to cover. You will not find one negative line I wrote about you. Nor have I ever said anything bad about you on ESPN or on the USA Network. You have been angry at me for no reason."

He extended his hand.

"My apology," he said. "Friends?"

"Friends," I said. We shook hands.

My friend, Gerry Cooney, paid for the lunch.

He didn't have a drink during our lunch. It was one of the few moments in his life at that point where he went without having alcohol.

In September, undefeated Philipp Brown fell in four. Three months later, George Chaplin, who had ended the career of Duane Bobick five years earlier, went out in two against Cooney; however, Cooney was battling nonstop with the "Wacko Twins" and drinking excessively. He took off all of 1985 and almost half of 1986, spending short periods in the gym but longer periods in a bar—any bar.

He returned to the gym in the spring of 1987, when he was offered a fight against International Boxing Federation heavyweight champion Michael Spinks. In September 1985, Spinks had ended the unbeaten run of Larry Holmes with a hotly disputed 15-round decision, then took an even-closer split decision against Holmes in May 1986. After stopping outgunned Danish fighter Steffan Tangstad in September of that year, the boxing media came down hard on Spinks to defend his title against a worthwhile opponent. That worthwhile opponent was Gerry Cooney.

But the 30-year-old Cooney was worthwhile only in name value, his three knockout wins in a row since losing to Holmes, and his 28–1 record. That was all surface stuff. Inside, Cooney was a full-blown alcoholic.

"For Spinks, I trained on a quart of scotch a day," Cooney told me while we were at breakfast in Las Vegas the morning of the Floyd Mayweather Jr.–Manny Pacquiao super event but super dud-of-a-fight in May 2015.

"If May 11, 1981, was the high point—the very top—of my career," Cooney told me, "June 15, 1987, was the absolute lowest point. I was still with Rappaport and Jones, wanting nothing to do with either of them. I was unhappy with every aspect of my life. My drinking was out of control. I belonged in rehab or counseling or AA, not in a gym and in a boxing ring."

In the Atlantic City Convention Center on that lowest point in his career, Cooney was knocked down twice in the fifth round and being battered when referee Frank Cappuccino waved an end to the bout at 2:51 of the round.

"Michael Spinks was a great light heavyweight champion, but he was no heavyweight," says Gerry, still angry at that part of his life.

He was given two gifts over Larry Holmes, then a gift in a Danish fighter [Steffan Tangstad], and another gift against a drunk named Cooney before he faced Mike Tyson. If I had been the fighter I was against Ron Lyle, Ken Norton, or Larry Holmes, I would have wrecked Spinks, that I know. That is the one loss I will never truly be able to accept. But I have only myself to blame.

Following the fight, for which he was paid $2.5 million, Gerry retired. He was 30; however, although he was able to walk away from the "Wacko Twins" and boxing, he couldn't walk away from the alcohol. He fought it, not only on a daily basis, but also hour by hour.

In November 1987, Cooney and I were paired on TV in Port-of-Spain, in Trinidad & Tobago, when Donny Lalonde faced Gerry's stablemate, Eddie Davis, for the vacant WBC light heavyweight title. In the two days we were there, I never saw Gerry without a drink in his hands.

While Davis didn't win his fight, Gerry won his. Five months later, Cooney won the biggest fight of his life. He beat alcoholism. Cooney remembers the date without thought.

"It was April 21, 1988. That was the last day I had a drink!" he says proudly.

"I had enough. I took a deep breath and said to myself, 'Gerry, enough!' I made up my mind, then and there, that it was over. I began going to AA meetings. I went to counseling. I go to AA meetings every week. I never, never miss one, no matter where I am."

In mid-1989, and free from drink and drugs, Cooney began to work out again. First slowly, then harder. Then, he decided to have one more fight. He felt a change needed to be made, however. As much as he loved Victor Valle, Cooney wanted a new voice in his corner. He called fellow Irishman, fellow Long Islander, the great trainer and announcer Gil Clancy.

Clancy, known as "The Giller" in boxing circles, always believed Cooney had the tools to be champion. He accepted Cooney's request to train him. But he did so with one condition: that Cooney tell Valle the news face-to-face, rather than on the phone.

"He deserves that," Clancy told Cooney, who was then 33. "Be a man and sit down with him. After all the time you spent together, you owe him more than a phone call."

Cooney listened, then met with Valle. The old veteran was hurt but understood. He only wanted the best for Cooney, said he wished things could have been different, then shook Cooney's hand. With the dismissal of Valle, all ties to Cooney's boxing past were severed.

In late fall of 1989, Cooney got the fight he so badly wanted. He'd be facing Big George Foreman in Atlantic City. The fight was billed as the "War on the Shore." Foreman was 41. Cooney was pushing 34. Cynical boxing writers dubbed the fight "Two Geezers at Caesars."

The fight against Foreman was Cooney's first since his ill-fated fight against Michael Spinks. Prior to that was his first-round stoppage of Eddie Gregg in

1986. In reality, this would be Cooney's first booze-free fight since the Ken Norton bout, 10 years earlier.

I was hired by Showtime's Jay Larkin to call the fight, alongside Steve Albert. At the time, I was New York State's boxing commissioner. The state frowned upon its appointed officials doing outside work. So, I donated my rather substantial paycheck to the Burn Unit of the Nassau County Medical Center. It was actually a great feeling to be able to give back to the NCMC, as that is where I spent four months when I suffered my severe leg burns in 1959.

After a first round that saw both men land heavy shots, and with Foreman even being rocked, Foreman stepped up the pace in the second round. A right uppercut dropped Cooney for the count in the second.

"I needed a tune-up fight or two," Cooney believes.

"I'm glad you didn't have tune-up fights," jokes Foreman. "I didn't need you being any better or punching any harder than you did that night. You hit me harder than anyone in my career."

Cooney handled the loss well. He didn't go into hiding. He didn't resume drinking or using drugs. He dealt with it and moved on. Today, he counts both Foreman and Larry Holmes as two of his closest friends. Both have been on our show countless times.

In 1996, he married Jennifer. Together, they have a son, Jack, and a daughter, Sarah. He also has a son, Christopher, from a previous relationship. He is a doting, caring, supportive father. He ends every phone call, not only to Jennifer, but also to his kids, with "I love you."

In the spring of 2009, while sitting at a computer at SiriusXM, putting my next MMA show—*Fight Club*—together, a show I had been doing for two years, company president Scott Greenstein walked past me. He seemed to be in a hurry.

Seeing him, I said, "Good afternoon, Scott."

"Good afternoon, Randy," he said as he whizzed past me.

Suddenly, he stopped. He did a 180 and faced me.

"Randy, why are you working here and doing an MMA show instead of a boxing show? You are one of the leading authorities on boxing, and we're not doing a boxing show? Why is that?"

I explained to him that, two years earlier, when I heard Sirius Radio (they weren't SiriusXM yet) wanted to do an MMA show, I applied for the job. After an audition, I was hired.

"How'd you like to do a boxing show?" Greenstein inquired.

My mouth fell open but no words came out.

"Well?" asked Greenstein. "Would you like to do a boxing show?"

"I absolutely would, Scott," I replied. "I absolutely would."

"Tell you what," he said, looking deep in thought. "Do you know Gerry Cooney?"

"Yes, I do," I replied. "I haven't spoken to him in several years, but I do know him." I gave Scott a puzzled look.

"I want you to call him. I have always wanted to meet him. Where does he live?" Greenstein inquired.

"I believe he's somewhere in New Jersey now," I answered.

"Okay," continued Greenstein. "I will be here all next week. I've got no travel plans. I want you to get Cooney up here. We'll send a car for him. We'll pick him up and take him home. I'll expense it. See if he can come up next Wednesday."

"What should I tell him, Scott, when he asks why is he coming up?"

"Tell him the president of SiriusXM wants to meet him."

I put aside my show prep and called the number I had for Cooney.

Gerry answered in his typical, playful fashion.

"Louie's Luncheonette," said Gerry. I recognized his voice right away.

"Gerry, hi. It's Randy Gordon." There was a pause. It had been several years since we had spoken.

He was shocked to hear from me but sounded genuinely glad.

"Randy! How are you?" asked Gerry. "What are you doing these days?"

I told him I was at SiriusXM Radio and that the president of the company was a longtime fan and wanted to meet him and take him to lunch. I told him a car would pick him up and take him home. He accepted the invitation.

The following Wednesday, Cooney came to the Midtown Manhattan studios of SiriusXM. As Scott walked Cooney around, giving him a "tour" of the impressive studios, Scott was just as impressed by how many show hosts, producers, engineers, security, and staff recognized the former heavyweight contender, calling out to him, shaking his hand, and even taking pictures with their cell phones. After the tour, the two went into Scott's corner office on the 36th floor. After a few minutes of small talk, Scott cut to the chase.

"How'd you like to host a show here, Gerry? I want you to work here."

To say Cooney looked surprised is an understatement.

"You mean, like me and Larry Holmes, something like that?" asked Gerry.

"Not Larry Holmes," replied SiriusXM's president. "You and Randy Gordon."

Cooney's expression was priceless. He looked like a wide-eyed kid opening presents at Christmas.

"I'd love to, Scott," he replied.

"Done!" said the man whose credits include being executive producer of the Academy Award–winning movie *English Patient*.

Greenstein stood up and shook Cooney's hand. Then he shook my hand.

"Congratulations, guys. You are now the cohosts of SiriusXM's new boxing show."

I was dizzy with excitement. My dream of talking about the sport I love so much on a national platform had just become reality.

"What happens next, Scott?" I inquired.

"I will call Steve Cohen [the president of SiriusXM Sports] and tell him to set this up. He'll take care of everything."

And everything he did. Cohen gave us a starting date, time, hours, and a producer. He gave us a salary. I once got paid to write about boxing. Then I was paid to announce boxing matches. Then came a salary to regulate boxing. And then, to promote fights. Now, I would be paid to talk about boxing. Steve Cohen even thought of a name for the show: *At the Fights*.

Now, nearly ten years later, Cooney and I are going stronger than ever. The show has become part of who we are and a positive part of the fabric of boxing. We are not just *At the Fights*. We are "Cooney & the Commish." We are the real-life version of Arnold Schwarzenegger and Danny DeVito's *Twins*.

Life has been Gerry Cooney's boxing ring. He has had his brilliant moments, and he has had his rough, uphill moments. He has been on the cover of many magazines, and he has had to push himself off the canvas.

In the years we've been doing *At the Fights*, Cooney has talked openly, freely, and honestly about his battle with alcoholism. He has even counseled listeners who have found the courage to call into the show to ask Gerry for help in beating their drinking problem.

He's quick to let them know that, before he can help them, they have to be willing to help themselves. They hear him. They listen. Many of them constantly call in to give Gerry updates. They talk of their progress and tell Gerry it's because of him they are on the road to recovery. He thanks them but is always sure to let them know that all the credit goes to them.

To watch him in the studio with me and listen to the passion he brings to the show makes me smile. I know, I truly know, that the man called "Gentleman" Gerry is, in every sense of that word, both gentle and a man.

He came close to winning the heavyweight championship of the world inside a boxing ring. Tony Cooney was wrong. Gerry *did* amount to something. He is *not* a loser. Not by a long shot.

Outside of the ring, he's one of the greatest champions ever.

EPILOGUE

Have you ever wondered, *What if?* Many people have. Many do. It's very common. I hear it asked all the time. I'm in the minority, however.

What if I did this? or *What if I did that? What if I took that job?*

Although I ask it now, I never wonder what would have happened to my life-long career in boxing had I not left Stanley Weston's *Boxing International* and *World Boxing* magazines for Bert Sugar's *Ring Magazine*. Weston's publications were small but well run. They were making money. Sugar purchased a name in *Ring Magazine*, not a gold mine. In boxing terms, *Ring Magazine*, the oldest sports magazine in the United States, was on the ropes. It was about to fall.

On the day he hired me in the summer of 1979, Sugar reminded me that there was a chance the once-great *Ring Magazine* might not survive the batter-ing—from the poor artwork, awful covers, and a major scandal—the magazine had endured throughout much of the 1970s.

"If we don't make it," Sugar said, "the chances of you returning to work at Weston's publications are slim."

I knew they were less than that. Much less.

Some friends advised me to stay with Weston. With Weston, they reasoned, "At least you have a secure job."

I wanted something more than secure, however. I wanted to be in the core of the boxing world. I didn't want to cover fights off of television, as Weston had us do. I wanted to cover them from ringside.

Life is choices. We make good choices, and we make bad choices. We make right choices, and we make wrong choices. Hopefully, our good choices and right choices outweigh the bad and wrong ones by far.

That's because, in many cases, a bad choice or a wrong one can be a life-changer. Just ask the former teenager who has been sitting in prison for the last 50 years because of a dreadfully wrong decision he made all those years ago.

Choices.

I made my choice years ago. Part of me wanted to follow my dad into the airline business. Part of me wanted to be a pilot. The other part of me, that 11-year-old, wheelchair-bound kid, the one sent to the principal's office many times for reading *Ring Magazine* in class, wanted to live in the world of boxing.

What if?

What if I had become an airline pilot? I know I would have loved that career. I believe I would have been terrific at it. But I also know I would have longed to be at ringside. Oh, I could have flown to any fight I wanted to attend and I would have sat in a ringside seat. But, I would have wanted more.

I wanted a headset on. I wanted a microphone in my hands. I wanted more than a ringside ticket. I wanted a ticket that read "working press" or "media."

I needed to be close to my love, closer than a ringside seat would bring me. I needed more than covering the major fights on television. I needed to cover them and watch them from as close as I could get. I needed to be as close to the center of the boxing universe as I could get, not on the distant outskirts.

So, years ago, I made a choice: The "Sweet Science" over air science. Fisticuffs over flying.

I became Commissioner Gordon instead of Captain Gordon.

It was my choice, and I never dwell on, "What if?"

My big, beautiful family—which includes my wife and best friend, Roni, along with five children and 12 grandchildren—fulfill me.

Throw in my lifetime of boxing in the "eye" of the sport, and that completes me.

I have no self-doubts. I don't dwell on, "What if?" I had choices, and I made the correct ones.

To think those choices even got me inducted into the New Jersey Boxing Hall of Fame and the New York State Boxing Hall of Fame is still astounding for me to think about.

I am, without question, the luckiest boxing aficionado the good Lord ever created.

To every man and woman who has ever laced on a pair of boxing gloves, to every manager, trainer, cornerman, commissioner, referee, judge, inspector, boxing journalist, and fan, thank you for being a part of my "glove affair."

INDEX

ABOUT THE AUTHOR

Randy Gordon has been involved in the boxing business since graduating high school in 1967. He has been a fighter, a trainer, a cornerman, a judge, a referee, a ring announcer, a TV analyst, a manager, editor in chief of *Ring Magazine*, New York State boxing commissioner, a promoter, and a boxing talk show host. Since 2009, Gordon has cohosted with former heavyweight contender Gerry Cooney the boxing show *At the Fights* on SiriusXM Radio. Commissioner Gordon was inducted into the New Jersey Boxing Hall of Fame in 2004, and the New York State Boxing Hall of Fame in 2016. He lives with his wife Roni in Melville, New York. They have 5 children, 12 grandchildren, and 2 granddogs. They have become professional babysitters.